WITHDRAWN

THE
IRAQI
PERSPECTIVES
REPORT

THE

IRAQI

PERSPECTIVES
REPORT

*Saddam's Senior Leadership on
Operation Iraqi Freedom from the
Official U.S. Joint Forces Command Report*

KEVIN M. WOODS
with Michael R. Pease, Mark E. Stout,
Williamson Murray, and James G. Lacey

NAVAL INSTITUTE PRESS
Annapolis, Maryland

First Naval Institute Press edition 2006

No part of this book may be reproduced or utilized in any form or by any means, electronic or mechanical, including photocopying and recording, or by any information storage and retrieval system, without permission in writing from the publisher. This work was originally published in March 2006 as *Iraqi Perspectives Project: A View of Operation Iraqi Freedom from Saddam's Senior Leadership* by the U.S. Joint Forces Command.

Library of Congress Cataloging-in-Publication Data

Woods, Kevin M.
The Iraqi perspectives report : Saddam's senior leadership on Operation Iraqi Freedom from the official U.S. Joint Forces Command report/Kevin M. Woods; with Michael R. Pease . . . [et al.].
    p. cm.
  Includes bibliographical references.
  ISBN 1-59114-457-4 (alk. paper)
  1. Iraq War, 2003- 2. Iraq War, 2003—Sources. 3. Iraq—History—1991-2003—Sources. I. Pease, Michael R. II. Title.
  DS79.76.W655 2006
  956.7044'3--dc22
                                        2006010772

Printed in the United States of America on acid-free paper ∞

12 11 10 09 08 07 06   9 8 7 6 5 4 3 2

CONTENTS

FOREWORD

Operation Iraqi Freedom (OIF) overthrew Saddam's regime and opened up one of the world's most secretive governments to outside analysis, presenting a once-in-a-generation opportunity for military leaders and historians to delve deep into the decision-making processes of a former adversary. For the first time since a similar project at the end of World War II, we have an opportunity to evaluate military events from not only our own vantage point but also from the perspective of the opposing political and military leadership.

Admiral Edmund P. Giambastiani originated this vital and interesting work when he was Commander, United States Joint Forces Command (USJFCOM). As part of a major effort to ensure we fully understood the lessons of OIF, he commissioned a comprehensive analysis of US strengths and weaknesses. This first-of-its-kind venture was led by Brigadier General Robert W. Cone, the then-Director of USJFCOM's Joint Center for Operational Analysis and Lessons Learned (JCOA). Almost as soon as this effort got underway in the spring of 2003, Admiral Giambastiani realized that the study would not be complete unless information about what drove the Iraqis to make the decisions they did was fully integrated into the analysis.

To accomplish this, project leader Kevin Woods led a small team of professionals in a systematic two-year study of the former Iraqi regime and military. This book is the first major product of that effort. It presents a comprehensive historical analysis of the forces and motivations that drove our opponent's decisions through dozens of interviews with senior Iraqi military and political leaders and by making extensive use of thousands of official Iraqi documents. Kevin and his team have crafted a substantive examination of Saddam Hussein's leadership and its effect on the Iraqi military decision-making process. Moreover, it goes a long way towards revealing the inner workings of a closed regime from the insiders' point of view. Presented herein is crucial information currently missing from still ongoing analyses of OIF, and much of its content will counter currently accepted wisdom.

While the practice of self-critique and gathering lessons learned are distinguishing features of the US military, in almost every past instance our understanding of events remained incomplete because any assessment was limited to a "blue" only view of the situation. While we often had a relatively complete picture of what our adversary did, we remained in the dark as to what motivated his actions. At the conclusion of past conflicts, we were left to speculate which of our actions were causing specific enemy responses and why. Expert analysts and "red team" assessments attempt to make this speculation as informed as possible, but because of the impenetrability of closed regimes, even their usefulness is somewhat limited. In this case, however, by adding the actual "red team's view" to the compilation of multiple, differing viewpoints, this study hopes to contribute to a more fully developed history of the war, and allow all concerned to get closer to "ground truth."

General Lance Smith, the current USJFCOM Commander, and the JCOA team remain committed to this and similar projects as part of an ongoing process of learning and improving through the sharing of "ground truth." Though this project is an important initial step, we acknowledge the history of OIF is far from complete. Researchers continue to locate, translate, and analyze information that will shed new light on our former adversary's perspective of the conflict. It is in the interest of getting as much accurate information as possible into the hands of those already studying Operation Iraqi Freedom that we release this book.

Anthony A. Cucolo III
Brigadier General, United States Army
Director, Joint Center for Operational
Analysis and Lessons Learned
U.S. Joint Forces Command

ACKNOWLEDGMENTS

The direct involvement and support from the task sponsor has been a critical component of this project. This project benefited from the support, feedback, and encouragement of the senior leadership at US Joint Forces Command. In particular, Admiral Edmund Giambastiani (US Navy), Brigadier General Robert Cone (US Army), and Colonel William Hix (US Army) were essential in framing the study design and crafting the initial insights presentation for senior decision-makers. Additionally, a significant portion of the initial research conducted in Baghdad was made possible through the skill, insight, and patience of Colonel Bernie Harvey, Mr. Quinn, and the entire team from the Joint Center for Operational Analysis and Lessons Learned—Baghdad Detachment.

In addition to the principal authors noted on the cover, the project is indebted to the review comments, research skill, and patience of many members of the research staff at the Institute for Defense Analyses, especially Ms. Christine Shoemaker, Ms. Adrienne Janetti, Ms. Elizabeth Nathan, Ms. Lucy Williams, Ms. Kate Price, Major Jenns Robinson (US Air Force), Mr. Jim Kurtz, and Major General Waldo Freeman (US Army, ret.). Finally, the direct feedback, informal reviews, and professional exchanges with many analysts across the intelligence and operational communities have been and continue to be of immeasurable value.

A NOTE ON CITATIONS

As described in the Annex, this study derived its Iraqi perspectives from the most relevant material available. Wherever possible a full citation to the original material is used. In some cases, footnotes refer to a "Classified Intelligence Report" and a date. These "reports" are, for the most part, interviews of senior personnel from the former regime of Saddam Hussein conducted by personnel not directly associated with the Iraqi Perspectives Project. The record copy of some of this material remains classified for reasons unrelated to the specific topics contained in this study. All materials derived from these classified reports and contained in this study were cleared for public release by the appropriate US Government agency.

INTRODUCTION

Statue of Saddam being torn down, April 9, 2005[1]

They want the Regime to be overthrown and they want to bring it down. Even if they fight for one thousand years the Regime won't be overthrown and for one thousand years they won't be able to bring it down.

—Saddam Hussein[2]

INTRODUCTION

> Professional historians...tend, perhaps naively, to underrate the degree of unwisdom prevalent in the world of action, and too often expect political leaders to behave rationally—as men of goodwill with the advantage of hindsight define rationality. Mussolini's outwardly erratic course and irresponsible decisions, and above all his failure, have therefore aroused widespread contempt, which in turn has inhibited analysis of his intentions and actions on their own terms.[3]
>
> — MacGregor Knox

Iraq's response to the Coalition's military threat was dictated by the nature of the regime and of Saddam Hussein himself. While to Western eyes the choices Iraq made may appear dysfunctional or even absurd, the regime's responses to the threat and then the invasion were logical within the Iraqi political framework, even if later proven to be counterproductive. Saddam may have been, to a large extent, ignorant of the external world; he was, however, a student of his own nation's history and culture. Thus, the Iraqi response to threats and the invasion of Coalition forces was a function of how Saddam and his minions understood their own world, a world that looked nothing like the assessments of Western analysts.

As the massive buildup of coalition forces proceeded in 2002 and early 2003, two major assumptions governed Saddam's preparations. The first assumption was that the greatest danger the regime faced was an internal coup. In fact, Iraq's national history is littered with military coup attempts with one following another in dreary progression. Even Saddam's Ba'ath Party saw its first try at seizing power in the early 1960's collapse under the hammer blow of a military coup that overthrew the first efforts of the Ba'ath party to mold Iraq in accordance with its ideology. In response to the catastrophic defeat of Arab armies by Israel in the Six Day War, another military coup ushered the Ba'ath return to power on July 17, 1968, with Saddam as one of its leading players.

Saddam and his colleagues were determined that this time the military would not overthrow their new Ba'ath regime, and created a multitude of secret police organizations to ensure the unswerving loyalty of the population. These secret agencies immediately proceeded to infiltrate the military in order to ensure its loyalty. Once he had established himself in absolute power, Saddam set about creating a number of military organizations in addition to the regular army. In the desperate days of his war with Iran, Saddam created the Republican Guards to have a military organization closely tied to the regime and its ideology rather than to the country. With the best military equipment that Iraq's oil money could purchase, the Republican Guard, unlike most other private armies, established a regional reputation for military competence.

However, the fundamental purpose of the Republican Guard was to protect the regime from not only the Iraqi Army but also the Iraqi people. In the 1991 Gulf War, its units died in large numbers while accomplishing little against Coalition forces. However, when the Shi'a and others rebelled in March 1991 in reaction to the regime's military defeat at the hands of the Coalition, the Republican Guard proved its worth, putting down the rebellion with devastating effect. Yet even among the elite Republican Guard, connections to Saddam's family or to his tribe counted for more than military competence.

For the remainder of the 1990s, Saddam confronted increasing discontent among his population as United Nations sanctions significantly impacted the life of Iraq's people. The discontent spilled over into several failed coup attempts, including at least one by members of the Republican Guard. Hence the need to establish the Special Republican Guard, and then the Saddam Fedayeen, the Al Quds, and the martyrs brigades, as means to ensure that Iraq's military forces would be too splintered to organize a coup. The regime's security was the priority in military affairs, not preparations to fight against an external enemy.

Because Saddam was unwilling to trust anyone except for his sons and a few close relatives, he forbade the military to train in anything resembling a rigorous fashion. Fearing that any training maneuvers might well turn into another coup attempt, Saddam severely restricted unit movements and even social contacts between senior officers. For commanders, Saddam only picked the most loyal, those tied to him by blood. Most of the competent fell by the wayside, retired if they were lucky, dead if Saddam had any reason to distrust them. Military effectiveness, at least in Western terms, ceased to exist.

The second assumption that Saddam made had to do with the nature of his opponents. Through the distortions of his ideological perceptions, Saddam simply could not take the Americans seriously. After all, had they not run away from Vietnam after suffering what to him was a "mere" 58,000 dead? Iraq had suffered 51,000 dead in just one battle on the Fao Peninsula against the Iranians. In the 1991 Gulf War, the Americans had appeared on the brink of destroying much of Iraq's military, including the Republican Guard, but then inexplicably stopped—for fear of casualties, in Saddam's view. Somalia, Bosnia, and Kosovo all added to Saddam's belief that the Americans could not possibly launch a ground invasion that would seriously threaten his regime. At best they might be willing to launch an air campaign similar to OPERATION DESERT FOX[4] in 1998 with a few small ground attacks around Iraq's periphery. But from Saddam's point of view, the idea that the Americans would attack all the way to Baghdad appeared ludicrous.

A few senior military officers believed that the coalition might launch a ground campaign, especially given the enormous buildup that was taking place in Kuwait. But even they believed that as in OPERATION DESERT STORM, the Americans would wage a sustained air campaign before they launched their ground forces on an invasion of Iraq. Therefore, the entire Iraqi leadership—military and civilian—was surprised by Coalition ground forces beginning their offensive into Iraq at the same time the air campaign was starting. Adding to their incomprehension were the speed and power of the American offensive, which were simply beyond their understanding of military operations and logistical capabilities.

Undergirding Saddam's assumption about the Americans was a profound misunderstanding of things military. Like the First World War generals, Saddam's conception of military effectiveness revolved around the number of casualties that an army suffered. To Saddam war was about warriors willing to die for their country, not about killing the enemy. In effect, he turned General George S. Patton's famous aphorism ("No bastard ever won a war by dying for his country. He won it by making the other poor dumb bastard die for his country") on its head. Thus, the lack of training in Iraq's military organizations never crossed Saddam's mind as carrying with it dangers in a war against a foreign opponent. Ignorant of military history, logistics, technological changes, and any conception of modern military operations, Saddam was incapable of addressing the looming threat in any sensible fashion.

Exacerbating all these difficulties was the atmosphere of fear that Saddam had instilled throughout his civil and military bureaucracies. Iraqis at all levels understood that in this regime the bearer of bad news was in almost every case punished severely. When Saddam developed a new plan for the defense of Iraq that made no military sense, his generals with few exceptions applauded the wisdom of their great leader.

Once combat operations began, Iraqi commanders at the rapidly moving front reported one success after another against the invading Coalition forces. On 31 March 2003, the Minister of Information, Mohammed Saeed al-Sahaf ("Baghdad Bob"), reported to the international press:

> Those mercenaries of the international gang of villains sent their failing louts, but the snake is trapped in the quagmire now. The lines of communications now extend over 500 kilometers. Our people from all sectors, fighters, courageous tribesmen, as well as the fighters of the valiant Arab Socialist Ba'ath Party fought battles and pushed the enemy back into the desert...Now hundreds of thousands of the fighters of the valiant Iraqi people are distributed in all places. Saddam's Fedayeen and some small units of the Iraqi Armed Forces began to engage the louts of the villains of the US and British colonialism day and night. We have decided not to let them sleep...[W]e destroyed 13 tanks, 8 tracked personnel carriers, and 6 half-tracked vehicles.[5]

In the West such comments appeared as palpable nonsense. But from the point of view of Iraq's leaders, Baghdad Bob was largely reporting what they were hearing from the front. In such an atmosphere Iraq's leaders could not make coherent decisions on what they were actually confronting.

The conduct of Coalition operations also helped to contribute to Iraqi misperceptions as to what was going on. The Ba'ath Party bureaucrats in the cities along the Euphrates reported that the fanatical Saddam Fedayeen attacks, in which the Iraqis died by the thousands, were having an enormous success. What made these reports even more believable was the fact that the US Army's 3rd Infantry Division had screened off these cities, rarely entering them. "Baghdad Bob" was able to claim that the Americans had been driven back into the deserts with which few urban Iraqis had any experience. But those at the top appeared convinced that their strategy was working. When the US Marines pulled back from ad-Diwaniyah during the Coalition "pause" at the end of March to avoid giving away their next move, the Ba'ath regime was able to claim another success for Iraqi arms.

But the largest contributing factor to the complete defeat of Iraq's military forces was the continued interference by Saddam. Just as soldiers of the 3rd Infantry Division were about to push through the Karbala Gap, Saddam decided that all of that fighting was a mere feint, with the real threat coming from American forces moving from Jordan. His attempted reorientation of Iraqi forces added to the list of targets destroyed by Coalition aircraft. More important was the fact that those defending the Karbala Gap were robbed of any chance to establish defensive positions that could hold the Americans for anything more than a couple of hours. Once the Americans were through the gap, the Iraqi regime was finished.

The arrival of American forces at Saddam International Airport must have brought some sense that things were not going well. The desperate claims of Baghdad Bob were becoming even shriller. Now the regime's military forces were literally falling apart at the seams, no longer possessing the ability to put together anything resembling an effective defense. Most of the Iraqi army were voting with their feet. Those who still desired to fight had to do so in small groups with no coordination and little leadership.

There were Iraqis who had suggested alternative courses of action. General Raad Hamdani, the commander of the Republican Guard II Corps, suggested a defensive approach in which Iraq's military forces would use urban landscapes to defuse the advantages that Coalition forces enjoyed with their superior technology. Such an approach would not likely have changed the outcome—the disparity between Coalition forces and those of the Iraqis was just too great—but it would have probably added considerably to the casualties the Iraqis could inflict on Coalition forces. However, Saddam and his advisors lived in a world determined by personal ideology and the narrow perspectives of people who grew up in small Iraqi villages. It is this insular mindset, and its subsequent manifestations, that this book describes.

Notes

[1] Reprinted with permission from Laurent Refours, AP/World Wide Photo.

[2] Captured media file (approximately 1997) "Saddam meeting with Iraq Aziz."

[3] MacGregor Knox, Mussolini Unleashed, 1939–1941: Politics and Strategy in Fascist Italy's Last War (Cambridge University Press, 1982) p.1.

[4] December 16–19, 1998.

[5] FBIS, (31 March 2003) "Iraq's Al-Sahhaf Holds News Conference on Military Situation," Doha Al-Jazirah Satellite Channel Television.

THE
IRAQI
PERSPECTIVES
REPORT

I. THE NATURE OF THE REGIME

The Leader[1]

We are here to serve our nation, not to kill them, yet, we are not that easy and whoever needs slaughtering, we will slaughter him! Furthermore, we will even ...we will even cut heads off, in order to serve fifteen million, if it is necessary. – Saddam Hussein[2]

The measure of a regime of terror is the victims of its peace, not the casualties of its wars. – Kanan Makiya[3]

I. THE NATURE OF THE REGIME

"You could not be sure in your own house that you are safe."

— Chief of Iraq's Military Industrialization Committee[4]

The Setting

Saddam Hussein did not spring upon the world from the ether. Both he and his Ba`ath Party were products of a region whose modern history had been shaped by violence. Being a product of a violent political culture does not absolve Saddam for his role over the past three decades. He was, in fact, not just a product of a violent era, he was the master of it. In an environment of violence, Saddam rose to the pinnacle of power because he was the most ruthless and determined of the lot. His atrocities differ from those of Hitler and Stalin only in scale, not intent. However, it is only by appreciating the historical and social milieus that formed the modern Iraqi state and Saddam's world view that we can understand the choices Saddam and his military made during the course of his final war.[5]

Iraq, as part of the Cradle of Civilization, possesses a long, complex, and often tormented history. The valley formed by the Tigris and Euphrates Rivers gave rise to man's earliest civilizations and also the birth of the first empires, armies, and interstate warfare. Its geography may have made ancient Mesopotamia rich, but it also made it vulnerable to invasion. Since the rise of the first rich city-state at Sumer, envious neighbors have launched themselves in a succession of invasions over the region. The new rulers subsequently formed their own empires, only to be toppled in turn, leaving remnants of their cultures and echoes of their people in their wake. At one time or another, Chaldeans, Assyrians, Medes, Persians, Greeks, Parthians, Romans, Arabs, Mongols, Ottoman Turks, and the British conquered the lands that currently form modern Iraq. But the strongest persisting influences are from the Ottoman Turks who ruled Iraq with a combination of political guile and authoritarianism for almost half a millennium. The Ottoman influence could be seen in Iraqi politics long after the Ottoman Empire's expiration and the formation of modern Iraq.

The British formed modern Iraq somewhat haphazardly in the aftermath of the Ottoman Empire's collapse in 1918. At first the British government was set on making Iraq a colony within the Empire. However, a massive uprising, mainly among the Shi'a, challenged this attempt in 1920. The rebellion caused significant British casualties and was only put down after a difficult counterinsurgency campaign.[6] The political and material costs of this rebellion added to a growing Iraqi restiveness and nationalism, which, in turn resulted in a 1932 British decision to confer independence on Iraq.

At independence Iraq was a state in name only. Its king received a crown that rested on the promises the British had made during World War I to the Hashemite sheiks and a Sunni minority who were installed as a ruling class by the British. The new state remained ethnically divided between the Arabs, Kurds, and other smaller groups left behind by three thousand years of history. Iraq also had to find a way to meet the challenge of the religious division between Sunni and Shi'a. The Sunni, as was the case in the Ottoman Empire, held power, but the Shi`a were more numerous. The only semblance of political loyalty in the new country was that which Iraqis felt towards their local tribes and leaders. Tribal loyalty was an uncertain base for a nation where tribal blood feuds made confrontation more common than cooperation.

Threatened by early rebellions, one of the new Iraq's first acts was to launch its British-trained army to crush a minor uprising in Kurdish Mosul in the far north. This 1933 attack began a long tradition of using the army to brutally suppress various elements of Iraq's own population. It also led to the Iraqi Army's involving itself closely in political affairs. Military involvement in politics became commonplace. Between 1936 and 1941, Army officers launched six temporarily successful coups and a number of unsuccessful efforts, the last of which in 1941 aimed to bring the Nazis into the region. The British, who had maintained bases in Iraq after its independence, rapidly crushed the attempted pro-Nazi coup of May 1941 and, for the remainder of the war, ruled Iraq in near-Ottoman fashion. The British success in 1941 so humiliated the Iraqi Army that it remained aloof from politics until 1958, when a small group of officers overthrew the monarchy and established what became the Iraqi version of a "republic," that is, dictatorial rule by a small group of ambitious officers. Saddam would refine this concept of a "republic" by centering power on a single person—himself.[7]

As the nascent Iraqi state and army struggled to find their moorings, the Ba'ath ideology that was to have a major effect on Iraq was hatching elsewhere. In the early 1930s, two young, French-educated Syrian intellectuals, Michel Aflaq and Salah al-Din al-Bitar, developed a peculiar creed that mixed elements of Marxism with a solid dose of Adolf Hitler's National Socialism. While neither possessed Hitler's political acumen nor "will to power," their ideas proved seductive to many Syrians and Iraqis, with its mixture of an emphasis on the strong "leader" with Arab nationalism, a rejection of Communism, and a ferocious anti-Semitism.[8] Dubbed *Ba'athism*, this new ideology stressed Arab nationalism but paid only lip service to Islam. At its heart, Ba'athism was a secular, fanatical belief that the Arab world should be restored to its former greatness as the world's leading civilization.

The 1958 military coup, which overthrew the Hashemite monarchy ushered in renewed political instability. An evolving Ba'ath Party took advantage of the political chaos and seized power in 1963. At the time the Party possessed neither the infrastructure nor the discipline to maintain its grip on power. A counter-coup quickly overthrew the Ba'athists and restored control of the state to the army. The Ba'athists went off to lick their wounds, learn the lessons failure teaches the survivors, and bide their time.

One of those survivors was a street-tough youth named Saddam Hussein. Possessed with cunning and ruthlessness, Saddam contributed his talents as a hit man to the underground movement. A short period of exile in Egypt provided a veneer of education and a bit of social acceptability as he paid his dues on his way up the Ba'ath ranks.

Seizing Power

Anger and humiliation over Israel's overwhelming victory in the Six Day War in 1967 destabilized Arab governments. Sensing opportunity, the Ba'athists struck. Proving they had learned from past mistakes, the party leadership selected Saddam, now a senior leader, to organize its secret police and conduct a reign of terror that eventually touched all aspects of Iraqi society and life. The party faithful soon ensured no one would dare question the Ba'athists' right to govern.

However, it was not just the Party that absorbed the lessons of the past: Saddam also proved himself a very attentive pupil. For him, the fundamental lesson of past failures was that, in the grim roulette of Iraqi politics, gaining power was the easy part. Staying in power, however, required the neutralization of the military through a harsh regimen of purges and spying on those displaying any independence of mind. For Saddam, slavish political obedience should be the foremost military attribute, with competence coming in a distant second.[9] This approach worked well in controlling Iraq, but it had devastating consequences in foreign wars.

By making liberal use of methods developed and refined by the Soviet Union and Nazi Germany to quash internal dissent, Saddam rapidly consolidated the Ba'ath party's grip on power. Spies and informers became omnipresent and Iraq truly became what Kanan Makiya called a "Republic of Fear."[10]

Normal societal intercourse broke down as neighbor no longer trusted neighbor, and citizens feared denunciation even by their families. Children denounced their parents:

> A woman whose father had forbidden her to marry a Lebanese businessman denounced both her father and her brother for spreading rumors and insulting the Ba'ath regime. After an extended stay in care of Saddam's Security Service, during which the son attempted suicide, both received six months in prison.[11]

And brother turned upon brother:

> In a meeting of Ba'ath Party officials one of Saddam's thugs singled out for special praise to Saddam a man who had

executed his own brother for blaspheming the regime.[12]

Such individual cases only hint at the extent of Saddam's and the Ba'athists' ruthlessness. Stalin once said, "One death is a tragedy, a million is a statistic." In Saddam's Iraq there would be many individual tragedies and many more "statistics": whole tribes, ethnic groups, and non-Sunni religious factions were to become "statistics" under his rule. Saddam's soldiers killed Kurds by the tens of thousands, and used chemical weapons on Iraqi citizens. In 1991, the military was unleashed to slaughter hundreds of thousands of Shi'ites as punishment for their revolt against Saddam's tyranny.[13]

Had the United States failed to expel him during the 1991 Gulf War, Saddam's plans for Kuwait suggest the degree to which he was willing to use violence against civilians:

Saddam:	We will divide the [Iraqi] tribes into groups. Each group will be assigned to liberate a certain area of Kuwait and allowed to take any spoils they find there.
Minister:	What kind of spoils?
Saddam:	Spoils like buildings and stores. Also the chief of the tribe will take full control of the area his tribe has liberated-though the chief and tribe must obey my orders without arguing. I ask the security services to kill any rebellious individuals they find, their children as well.
Minister:	Your Excellency, what if we find that some of the rebellious ones have little brothers and sisters that may one day avenge them?
Saddam:	Kill them all.[14]

The power to speculate about actually exercising such savagery was yet to come however. But first Saddam had to secure absolute authority within the Ba'ath Party and then within Iraq. By July 1979, he felt strong enough to make his bid for power. In a meeting of the senior Ba'ath leaders, Saddam purged those colleagues who might one day stand against him.[15] Throughout the meeting Saddam watched silently, smoking Cuban cigars, as his henchmen announced the discovery of "a painful and atrocious plot" to overthrow the party's rule.[16] One by one they identified 66 senior party members as betrayers of the party. They were then led out of the conference hall. All 66 were executed. According to one source, their replacements provided the firing squads.[17] In one stroke Saddam had wiped out the potential political opposition, put blood on the hands of his new ministers, and focused the minds of the surviving Ba'athists on the fate of any who dared oppose Saddam. Tariq Aziz, Iraq's Foreign Minister, recalled this purge as, "The cruelest thing Saddam did that I know of... He executed them all. That could have been taken care of differently. It was not necessary."[18]

For the next quarter century Saddam kept his grip on power through merciless repression of all dissent, which he viewed as the only way to deal with enemies, real and imagined. Externally, Iraq's enemies were generally of his own making. Iran became an implacable foe when Saddam launched his Army against it only eight months after seizing power. He greatly exacerbated the internal threats by the eight years of bloody and fruitless war that followed. In the north, the Kurds remained restless and eager for independence. When they received outside support, which on occasion the Iranians happily provided, they became particularly troublesome. Additionally, the Shi'ites, who predominated in Southern Iraq, were always under suspicion of supporting their Iranian co-religionists.

Saddam's atrocities, such as the 1987 gas attacks on the Kurds, created an undying hatred for the regime within large segments of Iraq's population. So while Saddam's aggressive foreign policies added to the list of the nation's external enemies, his regime also had reason to feel besieged by internal threats as well. The resulting personal and organizational paranoia profoundly affected how Iraq addressed its strategic and military problems.[19]

Always high on Saddam's list of worrying conspiracies was that of international Zionism. In the early 1990s, Saddam explained that Iraq's difficulties with the United Nations were exacerbated by the fact that Butros-Butros Ghali had a mother who was Jewish and, even more damningly, had married a Jewess.[20] Among Saddam's other apparently strongly held beliefs was that the Zionists were responsible for diverting the Mongols away from the Christian West and towards Baghdad, which they had then sacked, leaving a vast pyramid of skulls in their wake. As Saddam explained to his entourage, "The Jews and their supporters played a remarkably malicious role against Baghdad in the past, and this conspiratorial, aggressive, and wicked role is again today evident..."[21]

Saddam and his security services could at times become absurd in their attempts to uncover Zionist plots. In one particular example, in 2001 the General Security Directorate provided Saddam a memorandum reporting that the cartoon character "Pokemon" really represented a subterfuge by international Zionism to undermine Iraq's security. Supposedly, "Pokemon" meant "I am Jewish" in Hebrew. They found the fact that the Pokemon character was "widely beloved by Iraqi youth" particularly alarming.[22]

Once secure in power Saddam Hussein saw himself as an Arab leader to rival Nebuchadnezzar and Saladin.[23] His growing sense of destiny not only allowed him to justify many horrendous acts, but it also led to the destruction of much Iraq's historical heritage. For instance, Saddam ordered the reconstruction of Nebuchadnezzar's ancient Babylon, in which the builders were to inscribe every brick with Saddam's own initials.[24] He had this new Babylon built directly over the remains of the ancient ruins, resulting in irrecoverable damage to one of the world's greatest archeological treasures.

Almost from his first days in power Saddam sought ways to create an empire commensurate with his vision of himself as the new Saladin. It is ironic that Saladin was born in Tikrit (like Saddam Hussein), and was ethnically a Kurd. Saddam became convinced that he too was charged with leading the Arab world in liberating Jerusalem. Once that task was completed he would be positioned to establish a new pan-Arab caliphate with himself as Caliph (leader of all Muslims everywhere). In a 1990 meeting with the leader of the Palestinian Islamic Jihad, he was even encouraged to declare himself Caliph, to which he responded "It is too early for that."[25]

For the new Saladin nothing was impossible, even driving the United States out of the Middle East. In April 1990, shortly before Iraq's invasion of Kuwait, in a bizarre but revealing conversation with Yasser Arafat, the leader of the Palestinian Liberation Organization, Saddam made it clear that he was seeking a direct confrontation with the United States in the near future. He announced to a thoroughly attentive Arafat:

> We are ready for it, we will fight America, and, with God's will, we will defeat it and kick it out of the whole region. Because it is not about the fight itself; we know America has a larger air force than us...America has more rockets than us, but I think that when the Arab people see real action of war, when it is real and not only talk, they will fight America everywhere. So we have to get ready to fight America; we are ready to fight when they do; when they strike, we strike...[26]

The conversation then meandered until Arafat brought up how America recently destroyed Manuel Noriega's Panamanian regime in a single evening. Saddam exploded,

> "Panama—Panama is nothing while comparing to us! I swear we are something to defeat, we will roast them and eat them."[27]

Just as Louis XIV believed it when he uttered "*l'état, c'est moi*" ("I am the state"), Saddam identified Iraq with his own persona. In a speech in the summer of 2000, Saddam articulated his position at the "center" of Iraq:

> The one talking to you is Saddam Hussein, a son of a poor peasant father who died just months before my birth, and if it weren't for my Iraqi nationality and the Ba'ath Party I would have been lost... Many people lived through better circumstances than I, yet they didn't benefit from them. None of them left their finger prints on the course of history. There were many elites that weren't recognized in their time, and weren't tested under pressure; they came and left without any recognition. If one isn't

given a chance, he must create it in such a way that he becomes the center of rotation for the lives benefiting from him.[28]

Once Saddam identified himself as the center of the Iraqi state, from which all things great and good flowed, it was a small leap to the conviction that his own survival was of paramount importance.[29] He became wary of competent subordinates, and soon undertook a policy first described by Herodotus 2,500 years ago of "cutting the ears of grain that stuck out above the rest."[30] Warning his supporters about the futility of attempting a coup became a constant refrain within the regime. An example from a 1999 gathering of Ba'ath Party officials depicts the typical warning:

> People coming from here and there could create one of these days a coup. But it won't work against us. No one will make a coup against us. The one who would do it, we will smash him and use iron chains to stop him immediately.[31]

After OPERATION IRAQI FREEDOM, Tariq Aziz commented on how dangerous it became to raise one's head above the others, "If a military leader disappeared one did not ask to know what happened, since it was known that the security services had dealt with the unfortunate individual."[32] Ali Hassan al-Majid, better known as "Chemical Ali," and a consummate regime insider, observed that Saddam was always wary of intelligent people, especially those who made frequent appearances on television.[33]

A commander in the Republican Guard commented after the war, "By his decisions [Saddam] throws out the clever men, or the clever men learn not to involve themselves in any decision making."[34] Reminiscent of earlier despots, fear stalked the corridors of power. Saddam's subordinates knew that torture and death were always imminent possibilities. Stories circulated widely in the military about generals imprisoned or shot by Saddam personally for transgressions, which included excessive competence or an argumentative nature. Innocence was not a defense: Saddam would announce that he knew when someone was going to betray him, even before that person himself knew it.[35] In the absence of real grounds for punishment, Saddam did not shy away from fabricating charges against those he wished to destroy.[36]

A 1982 incident gives a small taste of what the next two decades of Saddam's tyranny would entail. At one low point in the Iran-Iraq war, Saddam asked his ministers for candid advice on what to do. With some temerity the Minister of Health suggested that Saddam temporarily step down but resume the presidency after the establishment of peace. Saddam had him carted away immediately. The next day chopped-up pieces of the minister's body were delivered to his wife. According to the head of the Military Industrialization Committee, a relative of the murdered minister, "This powerfully concentrated the attention of the other ministers who were unanimous in their insistence that

Saddam remain in power."[37]

Flawed Decisions

As time passed, Saddam developed a reputation of punishing the bearers of bad news. Not surprisingly, lying became endemic throughout the Iraqi government and the military. In time, rumors began circulating among senior officials that summary execution awaited anyone contradicting the dictator.[38] Officers were aware of the story of the brigadier general who spent over a year in prison for daring to suggest that American tanks might be superior to those of the Iraqi army.[39] Unable or unwilling to risk speaking the truth, most of those around Saddam fed him a regular diet of lies and half-truths. As one military adviser put it, "Telling the truth was not to your own benefit."[40] Iraqi officers who tried indirect routes for getting truthful information to Saddam soon learned that Saddam was not alone in his distaste for bad news. According to the Director General of the Republican Guard General Staff, Saddam's son Qusay found the truth similarly distasteful: "Any commander who spoke the truth to Qusay would lose his head."[41]

By the mid-1990s, most of those near the regime inner circle recognized that everyone was lying to everyone else. All of this lying soon had a crippling effect on military readiness and planning. The effect of this environment is clearly demonstrated by this recounting of a 1995 meeting between Saddam and his senior military commanders:

> On 23 December 1995, there was a big military science lecture and conference. Saddam attended along with most of the military leadership. Three of us were scheduled to make presentations. The central idea of my presentation was simple. I realized in 1993 that the gap between us and the Americans was growing. Our capabilities were weakening. The Americans' technological capabilities were growing. The American dependence on air was growing. They own the big space.[42] They know everything because they own this space. Even if you build a new brigade America can see it and destroy it. So why try to build it? If you build up a large army the Americans will just destroy it again. By 1995 we knew we were moving to conflict and lacked the capability. I said we should immediately change the whole picture of the Iraqi military. We need to change from a heavy mechanized force to a light infantry force. We should make simple light infantry formations and start fighting right away in a guerilla war. Like in Vietnam—fight and withdraw. In war there is fight and there is maneuver. Maneuver cannot happen without air cover. So all we had left is the fixed fight—we cannot win with that.

I was the first presenter and Saddam became very angry at my thesis. I was singled out as being a mental hostage of American thinking. Saddam said, "If Hamdani's presentation is right then all these officers (Saddam pointed at the assembled officers) would be dead. But since they are here he is wrong and we were victorious [referring to the 1991 Gulf War]." Even an infant could see his logic was flawed.

At the same conference (23 December 1995), Saddam was so mad at my presentation that the other presenters who were going to say something similar became too scared and changed their reports. About two days later the Air Force was going to deliver a major report to Saddam. The report said that by the end of 1996 the Iraqi Air Force was finished (lack of parts, training, etc). They changed the study so Saddam would not get mad. They reported that, instead of being finished, the Air Force would increase its capability by the end of 1996.

It was around this time, 1996 and 1997, that everyone started lying. Everyone started lying a lot. They lied about things like "we won the 1991 war" and such as that. Since that time all military planning was directed by Saddam and a selected few. It was much like Hitler and his generals after 1944. Saddam took interest with military plans in great detail.[43]

By 2003, Saddam's personal secretary reported that Saddam was substantially unaware of the weaknesses of the Iraqi military. The secretary stated that earlier in his time in office, Saddam would visit units and talk with individual troops. However, as time went on, he relied more and more on written reports of doubtful veracity.[44] Not surprisingly, others blamed the secretary as being complicit in Saddam's deception.[45] In December 2002, only months before the American invasion, some senior Republican Guard commanders had steeled themselves to tell the truth about Iraqi military readiness. However, shortly before their meeting with Saddam, the personal secretary came to them and instructed, "If you talk with Saddam you must do so with high morale. You must make him happy."[46] So warned, they went in and lied once more.

Saddam's ignorance of contemporary military affairs encouraged an interest in various wonder weapons, including many programs that his technical experts knew to be infeasible. In late 2002, for example, he ordered the Military Industrialization Commission to provide a young hacker nicknamed "Usama" with anything he required to support his claim he could hack into and infect US reconnaissance satellites with a computer virus.[47] More generally, entrepreneurs who were not part of the Military Industrialization Commission continually sought opportunities to attract Saddam's attention to their pet projects. Saddam would often latch onto such projects on only the flimsiest evidence that they were practicable. He would then reward their proponents with money, new cars, and an order to the Military Industrialization Commission to fund their work. As the Military Industrialization Commission chief recounted it, "This created a perverse incentive for poorly paid university professors to exaggerate their results in an effort to gain further favor with the President."[48]

Given this incentive structure, anything became possible, even easy, at least when it was reported to Saddam and Qusay. Military units always reported their morale, training, and equipment as "good" or "very good"; scientists always reported the next wonder weapon was right around the corner; and everyone constantly told Saddam how beloved he was by the Iraqi people."[49]

This unwillingness to present unpleasant news or contradictory opinions worked its way downward through the power structure. A general officer in the air defense forces noted, "One lied to the other from the first lieutenant up, until it reached Saddam."[50] As a result, faulty information permeated the military and security structures. So difficult did it become to know what to believe that many actually believed the Minister of Information, Mohammed Saeed al-Sahaf ("Baghdad Bob"), when he denied US forces had entered Baghdad on April 7, 2003. A Ba'ath party militia commander who had a close encounter with an M-1 tank in central Baghdad, later recalled, "I was absolutely astonished...I had no idea there were American tanks anywhere near the city."[51]

Constant spying on officers and other officials coupled with demands that all underlings act only when given direct orders created a stultifying atmosphere throughout the Iraqi bureaucracy and military chain of command. The result was a climate of "pervasive inaction." As one senior Iraq general noted after the war:

> Based on...my contacts with officials involved in strategic planning, I found in most of them in a pattern of behavior that always put a positive spin on the fate of Iraq, because political behavior imposed itself on all the levels of officialdom. They ensured their hold on their current positions, even though the Iraqi ship was about to sink.[52]

Saddam could not avoid entrapment in this world of his own making. Because he had concentrated all important and often trivial decision-making in his own person, the fact that much of what his subordinates told him were lies or otherwise corrupted ensured that major decisions had little relationship to international realities. Tariq Aziz asserted that Saddam, despite all of his achievements over the years, had "lost touch with reality during the 1990s" and had taken on an "unrealistic outlook." Aziz added that he believed that Saddam was in denial about his loss in the 1991 Gulf War, and that this denial resulted in the demise of his regime.[53]

War Planning

As Iraq began its run-up to a final confrontation with America, Iraq's information and decision processes became even more dysfunctional. By the late 1990s, the regime had generally succeeded in cutting most Iraqis off from outside influences. While this helped to keep a lid on internal dissent, it had a pernicious effect on the governmental instruments concerned with national security. Nowhere was this isolation more destructive than within the armed forces, which remained "officially" isolated from nearly all military thought and analysis outside the borders. For the military, no secure method was available to use the information they could access as it might counter Saddam's self-styled military genius.[54]

It is still unclear as to what the Iraqi Intelligence Services were able to collect or what parts of their collection efforts actually went forward to Saddam. We do know they collected voluminous open-source materials from the West, ranging from articles written by American analysts such as Kenneth Pollack and Richard Betts to military and technical journals.[55] On the other hand, Iraq's intelligence services were just as likely to gather information from obscure political and social organizations, which they then treated as respectfully as if they had a key source of strategic insight.[56] It appears that volume counted for more than substance and that the security services had no adequate method of sifting the important from the trivial.

For most of the developed world, this information vacuum is hard to understand. After all this is the information age where the biggest problem is avoiding the constant bombardment of unwanted information. In Saddam's Iraq, the situation was the exact opposite. Among government officials, only a select few had access to the Internet. Ironically, most of those with access refused to use it because the secret police monitored their activities and could charge them with disloyalty for visiting the wrong site even inadvertently. Even for those who did access the Internet, attempting to gather information was often an exercise in frustration. A captured document dated late 1999 from the Directorate of General Security notes that "reliance on the Internet is very limited because the National Center for Internet Service has put in place restrictions against all information on the Internet that is hostile to the country...these restrictions hinder our examination of the Internet." In Saddam's Iraq, it appears that even his secret police often remained in the dark. Another fascinating document from the same file notes that there were not enough secret police to watch over the other secret police who were tasked with spying on Iraqis using the Internet. The secret police, in particular, were vexed on how to establish an organization that could effectively spy on their own use of e-mail.[57]

In short, quality information was not available to the only decision-maker who counted. Instead of accurate reports of the realities around him, Saddam received increasing amounts of flawed assessments and lies that only served to strengthen his preconceptions. Real knowledge was not a prized commodity in Iraq, and its final worth was established by the dictator himself when, in front of a group of senior officers, he singled out a future Republican Guard Corps commander, known to read widely in military history and theory, and publicly ridiculed him for "thinking like an American."[58]

Saddam's Leadership Style

Based on accounts of Saddam's personal style of leadership, even if he had received wholly accurate information, it is not clear this would have prevented an eventual disaster. In the computer world, "garbage in, garbage out" is a well-known aphorism. In Saddam's world, even the input of quality information could easily lead to the output of disastrous decisions. This resulted from Saddam's reliance on a decision-making process that according to some senior aides verged on the mystical.[59]

A close associate once described Saddam as a deep thinker who would remain awake at night, pondering problems at length before inspiration came in dreams.[60] These dreams became dictates the next morning, and invariably all those around him would praise Saddam's great intuition. Questioning these dictates was only done at great personal risk. Often, the dictator would make a show of consulting small groups of family members and long-time advisers, though his record even here is erratic.[61] All of the evidence demonstrates that he made his most fateful decisions in isolation. The decision to invade Iran, for example, occurred while he was visiting a vacation resort and was made without any consultation with his advisers. He made the equally fateful decision to invade Kuwait in consultation with only his son-in-law.[62]

In a wide-ranging discussion with his closest advisors in the fall of 1990, Saddam provided an insight into his "unique" abilities:

> America is a complicated country. Understanding it requires a politician's alertness that is beyond the intelligence community. Actually I forbade the intelligence outfits from deducing from press and political analysis anything about America. I told them that [this] was not their specialty, because these organizations, when they are unable to find hard facts, start deducing from newspapers, which is what I already know. I said I don't want either intelligence organization [IIS or GMID] to give me analysis—that is my specialty...we agree to continue on that basis...which is what I used with the Iranians, some of it out of deduction and some of it through invention and connecting the dots, *all without having hard evidence.*[63]

Saddam's supreme, even mystical, confidence in his own abilities and wisdom allowed him to ignore or discount the practical considerations raised by others. All things were possible. For instance, in October 1994, he called his senior Republican Guard officers to a meeting. Qusay, speaking for his father, announced that Saddam had decided on a second invasion of Kuwait. The commander of the Republican Guard immediately jumped on the bandwagon and said that his forces could easily conquer Kuwait. However, some of the division commanders summoned up sufficient courage to gently warn Saddam that their forces were not yet capable of fighting the U.S. forces. Saddam told them their thinking was faulty since they saw war in terms of numbers of losses, whereas he saw it as a "spiritual battle."[64] He reportedly considered imprisoning the chief naysayer, but in the end only warned him, not for the first time, not to read so much.[65] In the event, war was averted when the Iraqi build-up was detected and tens of thousands of American soldiers poured into Kuwait.

The voice of caution by Republican Guard division commanders in the 1994 case was unusual. Normally, once Saddam had made a decision, his subordinates were loathe to question his judgment. An Iraqi Brigadier General recalled that before the American assault in the 1991 Gulf War, no senior officer had the courage to suggest to Saddam the possibility of a withdrawal before President Bush's 15 January deadline. Such a suggestion might have implied Saddam's original move into Kuwait had been a mistake, and the dictator's response to such impertinence was likely to be fatal.[66]

Occasionally, courageous individuals did offer dissenting opinions or pessimistic analyses. Such negative commentaries rarely made it past the surrounding gatekeepers. Not only did Saddam's secretary manage to cut off a realistic assessment of Iraq's military power, but so did Qusay, Saddam's youngest son. The Republican Guard II Corps commander, alone among his peers, objected to Qusay that Saddam's plan for the defense of Baghdad as being unworkable. Qusay immediately brushed aside the objection with the argument that Saddam had already approved the plan and "it is you who will now make it work."[67] No appeal to Saddam himself was possible after Qusay had invoked his father's name.

The rare dissenting opinions that did mange to reach Saddam seldom changed his mind; more often than not, the opinion rebounded against the dissenter. Typical was the experience in 1990 of Army Chief of Staff Nizar al-Khazraji, who had not been a party to the decision to invade Kuwait. Not long after the invasion, he submitted his analysis of the situation to Saddam:

> I explained that war with America was now inevitable...there were clear indications. I explained the potential dangers for Iraq. I also explained the status of the balance of powers, saying that Iraq would lose the war. A meeting was held at the general command on 18 September to discuss my two reports in Saddam Hussein's presence. I began by reviewing the strategic and field situation and explaining the balance of powers and the huge technological gap between the Coalition forces and the Iraqi

forces, which were exhausted after the eight-year war with Iran. The commander in chief expressed his anger and ended the meeting before I finished my report.[68]

Khazraji was fired from his post prior to the American assault because he alone had the impudence to warn Saddam that an American victory was certain.[69]

Saddam's Distorted Worldview

For all the reasons outlined above, Saddam's conception of the world beyond his country's borders was particularly distorted. What is apparent from listening to Saddam discuss his opponents is that his understanding of them was based on the belief that none possessed the ruthlessness, competence, or ability to thwart his aims over the long run. His actions seem to indicate that he believed he could intimidate or buy off foreign opponents off as easily as potential foes in Iraq.[70]

It is not clear that his opponents in the West understood the full implications of Saddam's perceptions of reality. For instance, in October 1994 when he ordered two Republican Guard divisions to deploy to the Kuwaiti border, the reaction from the United States and world community was swift and sure. American military forces rapidly deployed to the region, and the United Nations Security Council issued Resolution 949 condemning Iraq's moves. When Iraq pulled back from the brink, the world community was certain that its show of common resolve had forced Saddam to back down. Saddam's impression could not have been more different or wrong:

> It is really something, four nations, among them two of the greatest nations of the world: Russia and America. I mean, they have nuclear bombs, missiles and so on...and England and France. They came to me and handed me a memo. They gave me a warning and timing. In case we would not abide by it, we would endanger our existence.[71]

In other words, Saddam found the world's response contemptible. He was prepared to launch a war and all the world could do was send him a "memo." After his speech commenting on the weakness of America's response, Saddam left the room, trailed by a loud chorus from the assembled Ba'athist sycophants: "You know that the Iraqi army is the strongest army in the region!" and "It is the strongest, the strongest army..."[72]

The 1994 near-confrontation was just one more example of interactions that seemed to strengthen Saddam's world view and increase his contempt of world opinion and resolve. Scornful of others and supremely confident in his own abilities it seems that Saddam was, by the end of 2000, incapable of listening to advice. In his recorded conversations with senior staff, he constantly reminded them of the source for his confidence. Had he not by force of his own extraordinary will led Iraq to its great victory in the Iran-Iraq War? Was he not responsible for designing the successful invasion of Kuwait? Had he not stood up to the Americans and won the "Mother of All Battles"?[73] Had he not suppressed the Shiite and Kurdish rebellions during the "Page of Treason and Treachery" of 1991? And had he not successfully defied the United Nations and the United States for over a decade? Saddam's political and strategic logic had recast all of his greatest setbacks as victories. Consequently, by the end of the century Saddam viewed himself as enormously competent in every field of policy—not only in Iraqi internal affairs but in diplomatic and military matters as well.

A growing conviction of his own infallibility coupled with the desire to become the new Saladin and lead the Arab world against the "New Crusader" state of Israel was a prescription for another war. Despite his 1991 military defeat and the continuing sanctions, Saddam became ever more disdainful of the remnants of the Gulf War Coalition in general and the United States in particular. In an address in 2000 to senior members of Iraq's air defense forces, Saddam described his (and Iraq's) superior position *vis-à-vis* America:

> There may be some people who say they are like the Iraqis. But so far, we do not have any evidence to say that any of them fight as well as the Iraqis. You are brave men, and your bravery is exceptional. Iraq is qualified to carry a heavy burden because God Almighty has given it a strong back, a great degree of perseverance, and an extraordinary ability to endure. You have broken the morale of America, and this is much more important than warplanes and missiles. We have lost some material things, true, but who remained firm in the field at the end? Your faith, which is supported by great morale, remained firm. You broke America's confidence and made people make fun of them. Despite their allegations that they are a superpower, they shamelessly say that their planes flew, bombed, and returned safely to base, as if they consider their safe return to base a gain for the superpower that considers itself the leader in technology and so forth.[74]

From Saddam's point of view the possibility of an American invasion verged on nonsense: After all, America ran away from Vietnam in complete disarray after suffering only slightly more than 58,000 killed in action. Iraq had suffered as many dead in a single battle on the Fao Peninsula during the war with Iran.[75] More recent events only confirmed Saddam's conviction that lack of will made America a "paper tiger." The United States was simply not the long-term threat. He began learning this lesson with his first direct encounter with American military power, when Iraqi aircraft accidentally attacked the USS Stark. The American response, which he had been awaiting with some trepidation, was a diplomatic note.

Even OPERATION DESERT STORM (1991) failed to impress Saddam. A summary of Saddam's opinion derived from hours of taped discussions is that America had spent an inordinately long time bombarding Iraq from one end of the country to the other before they were finally willing to commit ground forces.[76] Once American ground troops were committed, American irresolution allowed the bulk of the elite Republican Guard forces to escape; left the oil exporting city of Basra unoccupied; and, most critically, failed to do anything that threatened the regime's survival.

Immediately after the war ended, America did encourage the Shi'a revolt, but then left them in the lurch as Republican Guard forces and Ba'ath secret police slaughtered the rebels by the tens of thousands.[77] Saddam thought that the Americans almost unceasingly displayed a complete unwillingness to engage in what he regarded as real war: straight up, direct slugging it out, mano-a-mano. Saddam offered this diagnosis of American timidity: "America is not in the prime of youth. America is in the last stage of elderliness and the beginning of the first stage of old age."[78]

Nothing that occurred in the decade after DESERT STORM did anything to change Saddam's view that the United States remained irresolute and could ultimately be deterred. The American exit from Mogadishu in Somalia after suffering what to Saddam were a mere 19 killed in action further fueled his contempt.[79] The ongoing spectacle of American and European policy in the Balkans as the Serbs ethnically cleansed their neighbors and generally ignored Western military might hardly alarmed the dictator. The eventual air war against Serbia over Kosovo also failed to impress, particularly since Iraq was proving daily that it could endure constant air attacks throughout the northern and southern "no-fly zones."[80]

Finally, while the method of the American success in Afghanistan caused concern, it failed to make a deep impression. Saddam seemed incapable of appreciating that September 11th, 2001, had changed everything. From his perspective, he had seen America topple an enemy on the cheap, with airpower and a few Special Forces operators, and with most of the hard fighting being done by the Northern Alliance. It must have been apparent to Saddam that when America did have a chance to destroy its enemy at Tora Bora, it shrunk away from committing enough conventional military forces to ensure the job was done properly.

Given his impressions of previous military engagements with the United States, Saddam likely found it inconceivable that America would engage in a major land campaign to overthrow his regime.

Notes

1   Captured document, (1 January 1998) "The Leader and the Masses: A Book About Saddam."

2   Captured audio tape, (27 May 1987) "Saddam and Inner Circle Discuss USS Stark Incident."

3   Samir al-Khalil (AKA Kanan Makiya), Republic of Fear: The Politics of Modern Iraq (Berkeley: University of California Press, 1990).

4   Classified Intelligence Report, June 2004.

5   A biographer of Saddam described Saddam's use of violence to achieve his aims as "not strictly a personal characteristic, but rather an unattractive trait of the Iraqi people reinforced by their history." Said K. Aburish, Saddam Hussein: The Politics of Revenge (Bloomsbury USA; 1st US edition (January 15, 2000), p.1.

6   For a recounting of the 1920 rebellion, including descriptions of the nature and challenges of counterinsurgency operations in Iraq that might well have been written in 2004, see Sir Aylmer L. Haldane, The Insurrection in Mesopotamia, 1920 (Edinburgh and London: William Blackwood and Sons, 1922).

7   A concise description of this period of Iraqi history can be found in Phebe Marr's, The Modern History of Iraq (Second Edition, Boulder CO, 2004)

8   For the most thorough examination of Ba'ath ideology see the brilliant study by Samir al-Khalil (Kanan Makiya), Republic of Fear: The Politics of Modern Iraq (Berkeley, CA, 1990).

9   Dozens of captured media files containing conversations between Saddam and his generals over a 25 year time span demonstrated the impact of this characteristic. See also Chapters 3 and 4.

10 Samir Al-Khalil, aka. Kanan Makiya. Republic of Fear. (Berkeley: University of California Press, 1990).

11 Captured document, (1992) "Interrogation records of a father and son for insulting the Saddam Regime, the daughter informed the IIS." The investigation record of this seemingly trivial offense is over 200 pages. There are hundred like it in the captured document files.

12 Captured document, (8 July 1999) "Saddam Meeting with Ba'ath Party Comrades."

13 According to a U.S. Agency for International Development report over 250,000 Iraqi Shia were killed following the 1991 Persian Gulf War. Andrew S. Natsios, Iraq's Mass Graves, (USAID, 22 July 2004, http://www.state.gov/s/wci/rm/36198.htm)

14 Captured media file (Pre-August 1990) "Saddam Hussein and Officials discuss the case of Kuwait and the American Position."

15 This tactic may have been inspired by Stalin, whom Saddam appears to have admired deeply; he read extensively about the Soviet dictator. Said K Aburish, Saddam Hussein: The Politics of Revenge (London: Bloomsbury Publishing, 2000), p. 178. Saddam was reportedly only one of two foreigners to visit all of Stalin's dachas. The other person was reportedly Simon Sebag Montefiore, the author of Stalin: The Court of the Red Tsar.

16 Con Coughlin, Saddam: King of Terror (New York: Bloomsbury, 2002), p. 156.

17 Samir al-Khalil (Kanan Makiya), Republic of Fear: The Politics of Modern Iraq (Berkeley, CA, 1990), p.72.

18 Classified Intelligence Report, May 2003.

19 Perhaps the most glaring example of this effect is the regime's prioritization of internal threats over external threats even as Coalition forces crossed Iraq's borders in March 2003. See Chapter 3 and 4.

20 Captured media file, (15 April 1995) "Saddam Hussein, Council of Ministers, and Ba'ath Party Members Discussing UN sanctions against Iraq."

21 Saddam's Public Speeches, http://www.infoimagination.org/ps/iraq/iraq.saddam.html, 17 January 2003.

22 Captured document, (2001) "A Report on a Cartoon Character Called 'Pokemon' from Directorate of General Security." This Directorate of General Security report states that the name of the character is Jewish and means "I'm Jewish." The specific threat to Iraq was described as "pictures of this character have invaded the local Iraqi markets" and that the Iraqi kids "love it very much."

23 Nebuchadnezzar (reigned 605 BC - 562 BC) was perhaps the best known ruler of ancient Babylon. He is famous for his conquest of Jerusalem, in addition to his monumental buildings within his capital of Babylon. Saladin (1137-1193) was a 12th century Kurdish Muslim military general who founded the Ayyubid dynasty of Egypt and Syria. He was renowned in both the Christian and Muslim worlds for his leadership and military prowess, as well as for his chivalry in battles during the Christian Crusades.

24 Voice of America Report, 16 May 2003, www.globalsecurity.org/wmd/library/news / iraq/2003/05/iraq-030516-3e198477.htm. Downloaded 16 April 2004.

25 Captured document, (30 September 1990) "The Minutes of the Reception Held Between Saddam Hussein and As'ad Byud Al-Tamimi, Chief of the Islamic Jihad Movement (Bait Al-Maqis)." Also see captured document, (undated—believed to be pre-1990) "Discussion between Saddam and His Advisors about the Election in Iraq and Transportation after the War."

26 Captured media tape, (19 April, 1990) "Conference between Saddam and Yasser Arafat."

27 Captured media tape, (19 April, 1990) "Conference between Saddam and Yasser Arafat."

28 Captured document, (12 July 2000) "Saddam Speech to the Iraqi People Regarding Preparations for the Coming Battle."

29 Classified Intelligence Report, June 2004

30 Saddam here is in the role as a modern-day student of Thrasybulus, who demonstrated for the benefit of the novice ruler of Corinth his secret for remaining in power for more than thirty years. Herodotus, The Histories, trans. by G.C. Macaulay, revised by Donald Lateiner. (New York: Barnes and Noble Books, 2004), p 290.

31 Captured media tape, (1999) "Saddam Hussein's Meeting with a Group of Ba'ath Party Members to discuss Ba'ath Party Theories and Issues."

32 Classified Intelligence Report, April 2003.

33 Classified Intelligence Report, August 2003.

34 Iraqi Perspectives Report, "Perspectives on OIF from the Former Commander of the Iraqi II Republican Guard Corps," v3.3, 28 May 2004. [Hereafter noted as "Perspectives II Republican Guard Corps"]

35 Interview with Said K. Aburish. Frontline - The Survival of Saddam: Secrets of his Life and Leadership. Program aired November 2001. Transcript downloaded 15 March 2003. (HTTP:// WWW.Pbs.Org/Wgbh/Pages/Frontline/Shows/Saddam/Interviews/Arburish.Html)

36 Classified Intelligence Report, March 2004.

37 Classified Intelligence Report, June 2004.

38 Classified Intelligence Report, September 2003.

39 Jeffrey Fleishman, "Ex-Ba'athists Offer U.S. Advice, Await Call to Arms," Los Angeles Times, 27 April, 2004, p. 1.

40 Iraqi Perspectives Project Report, "Perspectives on OIF from the Former Commander of the Iraqi Navy and Assistant Senior Military Advisor to the Central Euphrates Region," v2.02, 17 March 2004. [Hereafter noted as "Perspectives Assistant Senior Military Advisor."]. Throughout this book the reader will note two distinct personalities in the Iraqi senior military. The first are those Iraqi Generals that, to the best of their ability, focused on the military tasks at hand and by their determination to work through the issues demonstrated a soldier's appreciation for the truth. The second, and more common variety, posses neither the soldiers appreciation for the truth nor the determination to work through the often Machiavellian world of Saddam's inner circle.

41 Project interview of Major General Hamid Isma'aeli Dawish Al R'baei, Director General of Republican Guard General Staff, 18 Nov 2003.

42 The Arabic translation includes the notion of air and space.

43 "Perspectives II Republican Guard Corps". Saddam's reaction to this suggestion appears to have been more theatrical than real. It appears that from Saddam's perspective there were two implications of an honest assessment of the 1991 war; first that Iraq actually lost in 1991 and second, that there was a better or alternative plan to the one taken. Both suggestions were clearly outside the political boundaries for Saddam. In fact, Saddam directed studies of other nation's wars, experiences against the Americans, in addition to a liberal dose of revised Arab history.

44 Classified Intelligence Report, April 2004.

45 Classified Intelligence Reports, June 2004.

46 "Perspectives II Republican Guard Corps."

47 Classified Intelligence Report, August 2004.

48 Classified Intelligence Report, June 2004.

49 Remy Gerstein, "Documents Show Urgent Iraqi Push to Recruit and Control Troops," New York Times, 18 April, 2003.

50 William Branigin, "A Brief, Bitter War for Iraq's Military Officers," Washington Post, 27 April, 2003, p. A25.

51 David Zucchino, "Iraq's Swift Defeat Blamed on Leaders," Los Angeles Times, 11 August, 2003, p. 1.

52 Unpublished memoirs of Raad Hamdani, (Former Commander of the II Republican Guard Corps). Original and translated copies held in project database, paragraph 26.

53 Classified Intelligence Report, May 2003.

54 See Michael Eisenstadt and Kenneth Pollack, "Armies of Snow, Armies of Sand: The Impact of Soviet Military Doctrine on Arab Militaries," Middle East Journal, vol. 55, no. 4, Autumn 2001.

55 Captured documents, (15 March 2002) "Report on the Study 'Next Stop Iraq' by American Kenneth Pollack" and (28 June 2002) "Report on Study by Richard Betts."

56 Captured documents, (12 May 2001) "Open Letter to the President of USA," (22 October 1999) "Correspondence from Ministry of Foreign Affairs to Iraqi Embassy in Tripoli Regarding Other Groups," (April 1998) "Um Al-Ma'arik Magazine Article," (26 April 2000) "SSO Study on Conspiracies Against Iraq," and (4 May 1998) "SSO Report on the Secrets Behind Their Hatred of Iraq."

[57] Captured document, (1999) "Presidential Order to Monitor All Internet News Concerning Iraq."

[58] "Perspectives II Republican Guard Corps."

[59] Classified Intelligence Report, Oct 2003.

[60] Project interview of Abid Hamid Mahmud Al-Khattab, Saddam's Personal Secretary, 15 Nov, 2003.

[61] International Crisis Group, "Iraq Backgrounder: What Lies Beneath," ICG Middle East Report, Number 6, Amman/Brussels, 1 October 2002, p. 9.

[62] "Saddam Hussein, the Ba'ath Regime, and the Iraqi Officer Corps," Armed Forces in the Middle East, ed by Barry Rubin and Thomas A. Keaney, (London: Frank Cass, 2002). http://iraqexpert.org/iraq_articles_2.htm and Classified Intelligence Report.

[63] Captured media tape, (Sept/Oct 1990) "Saddam and Members of the RCC Discuss American Reactions to Invasion of Kuwait."

[64] "Perspectives II Republican Guard Corps." Also Classified Intelligence Report, May 2003.

[65] "Perspectives II Republican Guard Corps."

[66] "Saddam Hussein, the Ba'ath Regime, and the Iraqi Officer Corps." Found online at http://iraqexpert.org/iraq_articles_2.htm

[67] "Perspectives II Republican Guard Corps."

[68] Ahmed Hashim, "Saddam Husayn and Civil-Military Relations in Iraq: The Quest for Legitimacy and Power," Middle East Journal, vol. 57, no. 1, Winter 2003.

[69] Hashim, "Saddam Husayn and Civil-Military Relations in Iraq."

[70] While Saddam had no problem resorting to assassination of internal opponents (even those who lived abroad) but with the possible spectacular exception of the plot against former President Bush in 1993, he seemed reticent to kill a foreign leader.

[71] Captured media tape, (late 1994) "Saddam Meeting with High Ranking Officials Regarding the New Clinton Administration and Its Attitudes about Iraq."

[72] Captured media tape, (late 1994) "Saddam Meeting with High Ranking Officials Regarding the New Clinton Administration and Its Attitudes about Iraq."

[73] That was certainly how Saddam viewed the war not only in political terms, but in military terms as well. And the further Desert Storm receded into the past, the more Saddam became convinced that his forces had thwarted an American victory in political terms.

[74] FBIS, "Saddam Addresses Air Defense Officers," Baghdad, Republic of Iraq Radio Main Service, 13 May 2000.

[75] Unpublished memoirs of Raad Hamdani. Lieutenant General Hamdani comments in his memoirs that in the 1986 battle against the Iranians on the Faw Peninsula that the Iraqi Army suffered no less than 51,000 martyrs by the end of the battle.

[76] Saddam often referred to the 1991 coalition as the 33 nations that attacked Iraq. But more often than not any discussion of the strategic decision making or related military issues the focus was on the United States and its political leaders.

[77] For the methods and the results of how Saddam suppressed the rebellion see Kanan Makiya, Cruelty and Silence, War, Tyranny, Uprising and the Arab World (New York, 1993).

[78] Captured media tape, (date unclear—late 1994) "Saddam meeting with high ranking officials regarding the New Clinton Administration and its Attitudes Towards Iraq."

[79] In a speech sometime after 1993, Saddam notes that "...a country's size and population has nothing to do with its strength." His examples were Somalia and Iraq who, although smaller in area and populations, "expelled" the aggression on their countries. Captured audio file, (Date unclear, but after June 1993) "Saddam Speaking about US, World, and Iraqi Politics to Republican Guard." In another audio tape Saddam opines that "if America doesn't condition [itself] to the new international situation and the new reality [that]...we now see in Somalia, they will see problems from it. Now those pagans [Somali's] didn't they shame the US Army? Didn't they ruin it...?" Captured audio tape, (Date Unclear- Late 1994) "Saddam Meeting with High Ranking Officials Regarding the New Clinton Administration and Its Attitudes Towards Iraq."

[80] In a meeting with the leader of Serbian Radical Party in 2001, Saddam discussed how he was not impressed with the "Imperialist tactics" of the U.S. because, in his opinion, Serbia was able to withstand them. Captured Iraqi document, (12 December 2001) "Meeting Minutes Between Saddam Hussein and Leader of Serbian Radical Party."

II. SKEWED STRATEGY

المؤتمر التنظيمي
لقيادة شعبة الاستخبارات العسكرية
للنصف الثاني لعام / ٢٠٠٣

The camel is crying and the Bedouin asks him why he cries.

The camel replies that he, the camel, carries the Bedouin, carries the things for him and when the Bedouin drinks the camel waits and maybe doesn't drink anything for himself. He knows the desert and how to get to the best places for water and forage, and when the Bedouin eats he has dates and tea while the camel has only rough thorn bushes, but all this is the life chosen for him by Allah.

The Bedouin then ask, so why are you crying?

Because you tie me behind a donkey who knows nothing of the desert and leads us all astray.

(Bedouin saying as related by the former commander of the II Republican Guard Corp's when describing Saddam's impact on Iraq.)[1]

Poster for the 2003 Iraqi Military Intelligence Conference[2]

II. SKEWED STRATEGY

Debriefer: "What did you think was going to happen with the Coalition invasion?"

Director of General Military Intelligence: "We were more interested in Turkey and Iran."[3]

In early 2003, mere weeks before the kick-off of OPERATION IRAQI FREEDOM, an invasion by Coalition ground forces remained low on Saddam's list of concerns. To understand why this was so, one must form an appreciation of the formative events during Saddam's rule. From an American perspective, Iraq's 1991 defeat in Kuwait should be foremost among them. However, for Saddam, OPERATION DESERT STORM paled in comparison to the Iran-Iraq War and the post-DESERT STORM Shi'a uprising. The hundreds of thousands of deaths suffered by Iraq in the war against Iran convinced Saddam that Iran was his foremost regional and enduring opponent—one that would shrink from nothing in efforts to topple him. Internally and not unrelated to the first concern, the revolt of millions of Shi'a throughout southern Iraq, which was only put down after a horrendous bloodletting, was the seminal event during Saddam's rule.

Saddam's Priorities

According to a senior Republican Guard officer, after the 1991 Shi'a and Kurd uprisings Saddam gave his armed forces three priorities: first, secure the regime; second, prepare to handle regional threats; and third, defend against another attack by an American-led Coalition.[4] Thereafter, only the air defense forces received significant resources in order to address the external (non-regional)[5] threat. The former Iraqi vice president recalled that Saddam considered only Israel and Iran as worthy conventional military threats. The dictator considered Iran the more formidable because it was the only power positioned to occupy Iraq physically.[6] Other senior Iraqi officials confirmed that Saddam always viewed Iran as the primary external threat, followed by Israel and then Turkey. However, some claimed Saddam was not so much alarmed by Iranian military power as by its political and theological threat, particularly given Iran's close ties to the rebellious Shi'ites.[7]

In fact, the link between the primary external threat (Iran) and the most significant internal one (Iraqi Shi'ites) was never far from the considerations of Saddam and his closest advisers. In this regard, Iran was not the only culprit. Saddam also knew the Americans had encouraged the Shi'ite uprising after Desert Storm and believed the United States had sponsored a series of coup attempts during the 1990s. With the imposition of no-fly zones after Operation Desert Storm, and throughout the 1990s, Saddam became increasingly incensed that the Western powers were enforcing two no-fly zones, which impeded his ability to bring the Kurds and, to a lesser extent, the Shi'ites, in line. This symbiosis between external and internal threats led Saddam to focus more on the immediacy of internal security even as the United States ratcheted up the external pressure.

One result of the no-fly zones was that the Kurds carved out a de facto independent state in northern Iraq under the protection of Coalition airpower. When the United States launched several days of intensive bombing in December 1998 (OPERATION DESERT FOX) as punishment for Iraq's non-compliance with United Nations resolutions, Saddam became concerned that the attacks would encourage a new round of rebellions. To forestall that possibility, he split the country into four administrative regions and placed trusted advisers in command of each region.[8] These politically loyal Ba'athists received full control of all military forces within their areas of responsibility. Perhaps this would have been an effective measure if revolts had been the primary threat, but it proved disastrous during the upcoming war. For instance, in the sector known as the Central Euphrates region, Saddam appointed a politically reliable former naval officer to the position of military advisor to Mizban Khidher Hadi, the regional commander and Revolutionary Command Council member. The new advisor, who possessed neither experience nor training in the coordination of large-scale ground forces, found himself tasked with coordinating the military response to the Coalition invasion soon after his appointment.

By 2002, Saddam was aware of various American efforts to induce Iraqi generals to cooperate in the event of US invasion. He was also becoming increasingly more concerned with the subversive activities of a Shi'a political group, the Supreme Council of the Islamic Revolution of Iraq (SCIRI), which was being sheltered by Iran. Tariq Aziz referred to this group and the Shi'a in general as the greatest internal threat to the Ba'ath regime.[9] These events fed into the regime's paranoia about internal enemies. Even as war with the United States loomed in the fall of 2002, Saddam met with his Revolutionary Command Council and senior officials of the Ba'ath Party, intelligence services, and other organizations to warn them that they must "keep the internal situation under control" while keeping the Iraqi people "satisfied." He further added that he did not wish to face internal unrest at the same time the United States was posing a direct threat.[10]

While in Coalition detention, one of Saddam's closest advisors, Ali Hassan al-Majid Takriti ("Chemical Ali"), made a similar point: "The key Iraqi weakness lay in the fact that the longer we were at war, the more difficult it would be to maintain control of the civilian population."[11] By mid-2002, even Saddam's oldest son Uday perceived a connection between internal and external threats. He noted the importance of meeting the "basic needs of the people in order to avoid discontent that could escalate into a repetition of the episodes of deceit and treason [the uprisings following DESERT STORM] on a wider scale."[12]

The security organizations of the regime, of course, had long experience with suppressing rebellions. The March 1991 reaction, "through killing, destruction, and eradication," to the Shi'ite rebellion represented only the most massive exercise of this type.[13] By 2003, Saddam was devoting enormous resources to internal security, creating a complex system to monitor and control not only the populace but also his various military and security organizations to preclude any possibility of a coup d'etat. This intricate collection of organizations was charged with spying on each other and specific individuals; as such, they proved quite suited for crushing dissent. It was not, however, well-suited for meeting and defeating a Coalition invasion.

Hobbling the Iraqi Military

On the eve of war, the primary intelligence and security services had developed their own military-like capabilities, often at the expense of both the Iraqi regular Army and the separate Republican Guard. On a day-to-day basis, the Iraqi Army was controlled by the Iraqi National Security Council, with Saddam ostensibly heading the Council, but in reality it was controlled by his younger son Qusay.[14] Saddam personally chaired a separate defense council that controlled the confusing welter of military forces (the regular Army, the Republican Guard, the Special Republic Guard, the Fedayeen Saddam, and the Al-Quds Army). As war approached, Saddam's decision to split the country into four military regions further centralized power under Saddam personally.[15] The four regional heads were charged with maintaining domestic order and reported directly to Saddam, bypassing the bureaucracies of the Ministry of Defense and the Iraqi intelligence chiefs.[16]

Fear of a military coup so dominated Saddam's thinking that he imposed a series of security restrictions on Iraq's assorted military organizations, which severely hobbled preparations to defend the country:

- Military forces were to be deployed in concentric rings, with the least trustworthy regular army on the outer ring and the more trustworthy Republican Guard closer to the center of the country. However, not even the trusted Republican Guard was permitted to enter Baghdad. Only the Special Republican Guard, which was carefully screened for loyalty and closely watched, was allowed.[17] At a time when Coalition military leaders were worried about Saddam using the Republican Guard to create a "Mesopotamian Stalingrad," he would not even allow his army to have maps of the city of Baghdad.

- Saddam forbade the Special Republican Guard (SRG) from coordinating with other forces. As the SRG Commander recalled after the war, "We never coordinated with the Republican Guard...I had no relation with any other units or fighting forces. No other units were ever allowed near our unit. No visits between officers [of the different military organizations] were ever allowed."[18]

- Saddam's security forces prevented military units from coordinating their defense plans and schemes with the units on their flanks. In Saddam's eye, the only possible reason general officers would ever want to talk to each other was to plan a coup.[19] Senior military leaders often stopped meeting each other even socially to be sure the security services did not misinterpret the nature of such meetings.

- In peacetime, any decision to initiate the movement of even minor military units required a complex and redundant approval process that often ran all the way up to Saddam.[20]

Strategic Calculus

Throughout the years of relative peace, Saddam continued to receive and give credence to optimistic assessments dished up by his top military officers. Tariq Aziz described the dictator as having been "very confident" the United States would not dare to attack; if it did so, it would be defeated.[21] In the draft of a speech to the Ba'ath Party leadership in 2002, Saddam asserted the United States would not attack Iraq because America had already achieved its strategic goals in the region. Tariq Aziz disagreed and carefully interceded and got Saddam to excise some of the language prior to the speech, but Saddam returned to the theme again in a public speech a month before the war, which suggests that he truly believed he would not have to confront an American invasion.[22]

What was the acute source of Saddam's confidence on the eve of OPERATION IRAQI FREEDOM? Judging from his private statements, the single most important element in his strategic calculus was his faith that France and Russia would prevent the United States from invading Iraq.[23] Tariq Aziz's revealed that this confidence was firmly rooted in the nexus between the economic interests of France and Russia and the strategic goals of Saddam:

> France and Russia each secured millions of dollars worth of trade and service contracts in Iraq, with the implied understanding that their political posture with regard to sanctions on Iraq would be pro-Iraqi. In addition, the French wanted sanctions lifted to safeguard their trade and service contracts in Iraq. Moreover, they wanted to prove their importance in the world as members of the Security Council; that they could use their veto to show they still had power. [24]

Undoubtedly, such confidence was likely perceived to be the fruit of Saddam's decade-long efforts to gain support in the United Nations Security Council through bribery and political influence buying. He had often received assurances and indications during this period that his strategy was paying off. For example, open sources have reported that the Iraqi Ambassador to Moscow sent a note to Baghdad on 4 October 2002 stating the following:

> Our friends [in Russian intelligence] have told us that President Putin has given very clear instructions to the Ministry of Foreign Affairs *vis-à-vis* Iraq. Our friends instruct us that Russia is very clear in its opposition to any attack on Iraq. It will not allow the new resolution to include any intention that would allow the use of force against Iraq.[25]

To help promote such efforts, Saddam avoided taking actions in the year after the September 11th terrorists attacks in the United States that would appear obstructionist or threatening. In late 2002, he told a group of officers that Iraq would provide UN inspectors with the access they needed, thus denying President George W. Bush and the Americans any excuse for starting a new conflict.[26] As the war approached, Saddam was bombarded by requests from Qusay and elements within the military to mine the Gulf, destroy the oil infrastructure, and conduct preemptive military operations in Kuwait. Saddam refused all of these requests to ensure that Iraq was not blamed for starting a war.[27]

Throughout fall 2002 and into 2003, Saddam's public and private comments reflected his belief that the United States and the United Kingdom lacked the stomach for war when confronting the "heroic resistance" of a united Iraqi people.[28] Indeed, this is the second major element of Saddam's strategic calculus. He remained absolutely convinced that Iraqis were intrinsically superior fighters to Americans. The Commander of the Republican Guard II Corps recalls Saddam speaking to his officers "in very spiritual terms about the fundamental difference between the character of the American and Iraqi troops." Saddam told them that Allah wanted to insult America by giving his strongest personal abilities to the materially weak Iraqis.[29] Saddam made a similar point in public in February 2003:

> Sometimes we see a champion boxer take vicious blows from a man who is not a champion boxer. What is his problem? The point is morale and faith. The latter believes in himself, and with belief he will surely win. The former does not believe in himself, and the shreds of his belief are undermined by blows from one who isn't a champion boxer. Thus, he is defeated even though he is a champion boxer...True, we do not have the means of the Americans and the British. But our superiority in other things, which we have already mentioned, is clear and decisive...[30]

A number of factors fed this delusion of American military incompetence. Foremost, was what Saddam saw with his own eyes. The fact that the United States had changed its policy on Somalia after sustaining what to him were incredibly minor losses amplified his contempt for American military might and the political will to use it.[31] Later, there were stories that he had copies of the movie *Black Hawk Down* issued to his lieutenants and ordered them to watch it, both to play up American strategic vacillation and to present it as a primer on how to defeat American forces in combat. Not surprisingly, given the nature of the regime, many of his ministers accepted Saddam's conception of America. Tapes of many of his meetings find ministers repeatedly parroting Saddam's own ideas. In a ministerial discussion of potential reactions to Iraqi brinkmanship with the United Nations in 1995, one of Saddam's senior ministers offered his "unique" opinion:

> I believe if any incident occurs, the Americans will utilize their air strike methods, which they prefer and used recently, instead of sending troops, based on their horrific experience in Somalia.[32]

It was not lost on Saddam that since DESERT STORM the American response to every Iraqi provocation was to launch air strikes. His conviction that America was hesitant to deploy ground forces was further reinforced by the US decision to bring Serbia to its knees through sustained air strikes. Even Iraq's attempt to assassinate former President George H. W. Bush in Kuwait was met with a relatively muted reaction by President Clinton.[33] Saddam likely believed that if this was the best America could offer in retaliation for trying to kill their former President was blowing up his intelligence headquarters long after everyone had gone home for the evening, then America surely was a paper tiger. In Saddam's calculus, the United States was unwilling to undertake any action that could result in even small numbers of Americans being sent home in body bags. It is clear from the totality of interviews that Saddam stubbornly maintained this belief even as Coalition forces massed in Kuwait.

If his international supporters failed him and America did summon the will to launch a ground invasion, there was a final element to Saddam's strategic calculus. If the invasion came, Saddam expected Iraq's "superior" forces to put up "a heroic resistance and to inflict such enormous losses on the Americans that they would stop their advance."[34] Moreover, the Army Chief of Staff claimed that Iraqi leadership believed American forces would rapidly bow to international pressure to halt any war, while simultaneously heavy casualties would prove politically unsustainable in the United States.[35] Saddam remained convinced that "Iraq will not, in any way, be like Afghanistan. We will not let the war become a picnic for the American or the British soldiers. No way!"[36]

In the final months, Saddam's confidence in ultimate victory grew. He told a group of senior officers that he hoped to avoid war, but if the United States im-posed it on him, Iraq would inflict great pain on the Coalition.[37] Several weeks later he explained to the Director General of the Republican Guard that the United States would not engage in ground combat and that "there is no way the Air Force would win a battle or a war as long as there is an Iraqi infantry soldier left."[38] Incredibly, Saddam held to his conviction of American moral weakness even after hostilities had begun. As he stated in a speech on 20 March shortly after the first bombs fell, "We will pursue them until they lose their nerve and until they lose hope."[39]

Sources suggest that Saddam and many senior Iraqi leaders believed the worst-case scenario for Iraq would be to survive air attacks and a Coalition occupation of southern Iraq, much as it had occupied northern Iraq after the previous war.[40] The commander of the Iraqi Air Force and Air Defense Forces noted, "We thought that this war would be like the last one in 1991. We figured that the United States would conduct some operations in the south and then go home."[41] Similarly, the Director General of the Republican Guard's General Staff commented, "We thought the Coalition would go to Basrah, maybe to Amarah, and then the war would end."[42] In fact, "Chemical Ali" joked during a post-war interview that America would quit the region after they had to deal with the troublesome Shi'a on a regular basis.[43]

Confident of Victory

When the Coalition assault did come, Saddam stubbornly held to the belief that the Americans would be satisfied with an outcome short of regime change.[44] Surprisingly, the overwhelming bulk of the evidence indicates that even with US tanks crossing the border, an internal revolt remained Saddam's biggest fear.[45] His belief in the regime's ultimate survival was also the primary reason his forces failed to torch Iraq's oilfields or open the dams to flood the south, options many analysts predicted would be his first moves in the event of war. In the words of Tariq Aziz, "He thought that this war would not lead to this ending."[46] If his strategic calculus was correct, Saddam realized he would need the oil to prop up the regime, the bridges to remain intact, and the fields to be open, i.e., not flooded) to rapidly move his forces to quell any revolt. According to the Chief of Staff, Armed Forces and Army Al-Sattar, "No Iraqi leaders had believed Coalition forces would ever reach Baghdad."[47] On this basis, Saddam planned his moves.

Some senior military officers did not share these assumptions, taking a more pessimistic view. The Director of Military Intelligence commented that except for Saddam and the inner circle, most knowledgeable Iraqis secretly believed that the war would continue all the way to an occupation.[48] The commander of the I Republican Guard Corps admitted, "There was nothing that could have been done to stop the Americans after they began."[49] The Minister of Defense later said,

> Iraqi military professionals were not surprised at US actions at all. We knew what preparations were required, and what would happen if those preparations were not done properly...Even if we had a real defense we wouldn't have stopped the Americans, but we would have made the price greater.[50]

So even as Saddam remained confident of victory, defeatism stalked his Army. As one Iraqi colonel put it, "We wanted the Americans to come on quickly and finish the war rapidly."[51]

As the war progressed, Saddam continued to receive optimistic reports from the civil and military bureaucracy, and from Ba'ath functionaries. These reports emphasized the effects of weather; Fedayeen Saddam attacks on Coalition forces; and, at least early in the fighting, the "failure" of the Coalition troops to enter most major cities. When gloomy reports did finally get to Saddam and Qusay, they either discarded them or considered the tidings to be exaggerated.[52] As late as the end of March 2003, Saddam apparently still believed his understanding of events to be correct. If not winning the war, neither was Iraq losing it—at least it seemed to the dictator. In the meantime, the Americans were amused by the seemingly obvious fabrications of the Information Minister (nicknamed "Baghdad Bob" by the media), wondering who could possibly believe such declarations. The evidence is now clear: Saddam and those around him believed virtually every word issued by their own propaganda machine.[53]

Last-Minute Diplomatic Maneuvering

During the first ten days of the war, Iraq asked Russia, France, and China not to support ceasefire initiatives because they believed such moves would legitimize the Coalition's presence in Iraq.[54] As late as 30 March, Saddam thought that his strategy was working and the Coalition offensive was grinding to a halt. On that day, Lieutenant General Abed Hamid Hamoud, Saddam's Principal Secretary, directed the Iraqi Foreign Minister to tell the French and Russian governments that Baghdad would accept only an "unconditional withdrawal" of American forces because "Iraq is now winning and...the United States has sunk in the mud of defeat."[55] At that moment, American tanks were a hundred miles south of Baghdad, refueling and rearming for the final push.

Notes

[1]   "Perspectives of the II Republication Guard Corp."

[2]   Captured document (2003) "Organizational Conference Poster."

[3]   Classified Intelligence Report, November 2003.

[4]   "Perspectives II Republican Guard Corps." According to interviews, interrogations, and debriefs, other senior officers shared this same observation, including Tariq Aziz, the Minister of Defense, Saddam's Personal Secretary, and "Chemical Ali."

[5]   "Perspectives II Republican Guard Corps."

[6]   Classified Intelligence Report, February 2004.

[7]   Classified Intelligence Report, April 2004. See also the section, "Strategic Intent," in Comprehensive Report of the Special Advisor to the DCI on Iraq's WMD, vol. 1 (Central Intelligence Agency, 30 September 2004), pp. 29–30. Also Classified Intelligence Report, April 2004; and Classified Intelligence Report, April 2004.

[8]   OPERATION DESERT FOX was a combined series of air attacks conducted against Iraq by the United States and United Kingdom, 16–19 December 1998. Primary targets were regime control and suspected sites of weapons of mass destruction. This operation was conducted after nearly two years of Iraqi interference and its ultimate expulsion of United Nation's monitors.

[9]   Classified Intelligence Report, May 2003.

[10]   Classified Intelligence Report, May 2003. While this report indicates some deception on the part of Prime Minister Muhammad Hamza Zubaydi because of his past personal involvement in war crimes, it clearly demonstrates the high level of concern for internal control within the inner circle.

[11]   Project interview of Ali Hasan Al-Majid ("Chemical Ali"), 10 November 2003.

[12]   MEMRI, "Iraq Wire Number 7," 12 August 2002. Found online at http://www.memri.org/bin/articles.cgi?Page=countries&Area=iraq&ID=INW702#I. Downloaded 17 October 2003.

[13]   For documents on the brutal suppression of the Shi'ite rebellion, see among others captured document, (22 March 1991) "Notes Between [field] Agents and General Military Intelligence Directorate (GMID) About the Riot Incidents in 1991."

[14]   Ibrahim Al-Marashi, "Iraq's Security and Intelligence Network: A Guide and Analysis," Middle East Review of International Affairs, September 2002, p. 2.

[15]   Anthony H. Cordesman, Iraqi Armed Forces on the Edge of War, Center for Strategic and International Studies, Washington, DC, 7 February, 2003, p. 2; and FBIS, (15 March 2003) "Iraq RCC Decree Forms Four 'Commands of Regions' in Case of War," announcement over Baghdad Iraqi Satellite Channel Television Arabic.

[16]   Project interview of Sultan Hashim Ahmed Al Hamed Al-Tai, Minister of Defense, 13 November 2003.

[17]   Project interview of Kamal Mustafa Abdullah Sultan Al-Tikriti, Secretary of the Republican Guard and Special Republican Guard, 14 November 2003. According to this interview and many debriefs of high-level Iraqi military officers, this restriction against Republican Guard or Regular Army forces operating inside Baghdad did not change until the first week of April 2003.

[18]   Project interview of Barzan Abd Al-Ghafur Sulayman Al-Tikriti, Commander, Special Republican Guard , 16 November 2003.

[19] IPP interview of Majid Hussein Ali Ibrahim Al Dulaymi, Commander, I Republican Guard Corps, and "Perspectives II Republican Guard Corps."

[20] Project interview of Salih Ibrahim Hammadi Al Salamani, Commander, Baghdad Republican Guard Division, 10 November 2003.

[21] Classified Intelligence Report, May 2003.

[22] Classified Intelligence Report, April 2004.

[23] Classified Intelligence Report, May 2003. Saddam's "faith" in his ability to influence the policies of these nations does not mean he was actually able to influence them. Like many things dealing with international relations, Saddam often overstated and acted on perceptions of success rather than the actual events. Numerous documents and interviews with senior regime officials support this contention. According to an August 2003 interview with Major General Keith W. Dayton, US Army (Iraqi Survey Group) after his extensive interaction with senior members of the former regime: "They thought that the French and Russians would protect them (they were told that would happen). They believed the French and Russians would prevent the war through UN action or would get it halted once it started. They thought the pause during the sandstorm was the end of it and were again surprised when we kept coming. Saddam was in denial for days and in that time Uday began issuing contradictory orders that had units scrambling if they acknowledged the direction." See also Steve Coll, "Hussein Was Sure of Own Survival," Washington Post, 3 November, 2003, p. A1.

[24] Classified Intelligence Report, May 2003.

[25] Richard Beeston, "Secret Files Show Saddam Deluded to the Very End," The Times (UK), 18 March 2004.

[26] "Perspectives II Republican Guard Corps."

[27] Classified Intelligence Report, May 2003; and project interview of Kamal Mustafa Abdullah Sultan Al-Tikriti, Secretary of the Republican Guard and Special Republican Guard, 14 November 2003

[28] In the right public context, Saddam seemed willing to take note of other "heroic" defenses in search of an optimal defensive strategy against the Americans. In 1995, Vietnam's Deputy Chief of the Army Staff made a secret visit to "exchange experiences between the two armies." Captured Document, (22 November 1995) Military Directorate Correspondence Regarding Secret Visit from Vietnam Army Chief of Staff." In 1999 Iraq hosted Major General (now Lieutenant General) Nguyen Van Than of the Vietnamese Air Defense and Air Forces to "discuss and study" American and British techniques and exchange "ideas and experts in operations and electronic [warfare]." More contemporary help with the Americans came in the form of a visit in early 2000 from a Yugoslavian delegation offering help with radars and "discussing the way of hitting an American F-117A [Stealth fighter]." Captured document, (3 February, 2000) "Correspondence Between Yugo Import and MOD Regarding Visiting Yugoslav Delegation."

[29] "Perspectives II Republican Guard Corps."

[30] Saddam speech printed in the Iraqi newspaper Al-Jumhouriyya, 4 February, 2003. Reported in MEMRI, Special Dispatch Series, No. 467, The Iraq Crisis (1): Iraq Prepares for War, 11 February, 2003 (http://memri.org/bin/articles). Also Classified Intelligence Report, April 2004.

[31] Captured document, (13 October 1993) "Iraqi Intelligence Service Memo to Iraqi Head of State Regarding American Position in Somalia." Saddam believed the Somalis took a lesson from Iraq's 1991 war with the United States. Iraq's refusal to surrender inspired the Somali people to refuse "in spite of their poverty and lack of weapons. The Americans couldn't find any significant targets to hit in that poor country." Captured document, (after 1999) Saddam Discusses Western Politics and America's Involvement in Somalia.

32 Captured media tape, (Approximately 1995) "Saddam and Senior Advisors Discuss international reaction to UN Inspection Report."

33 On June 26, 1993, US naval forces launched 23 Tomahawks on the principal command and control complex of the Iraqi Intelligence Service (IIS) in Baghdad. IIS had planned to assassinate the former president during his visit to Kuwait in April of that year. According to the White House, the strike took place at 2 a.m. Iraq time, which was "chosen carefully so as to minimize risks to innocent civilians." The White House, Office of the Press Secretary, White House Announcement of Tomahawk Strike (Text of a Letter from the President to the Speaker of the House of Representatives and the President Pro Tempore of the Senate), June 28, 1993.

34 Sama Abdul Majid, Saddam's personal interpreter cited in "Saddam May Be Using Vietnam Tactics," USA Today, 13 November, 2003, p. 10.

35 Classified Intelligence Report May 2003

36 MEMRI, "First Interview with Saddam Hussein in 12 Years," 5 November 200, www.memri. org.

37 "Perspectives II Republican Guard Corps."

38 Project interview of Major General Hamid Isma'aeli Dawish Al R'baei, Director General of Republican Guard General Staff, 18 November 2003.

39 "The Power and Peril of High-Speed Warfare," Brookings Iraq Series Briefing, Brookings Institution, 20 March, 2003. See also FBIS, "Saddam Addresses Iraqis on US Attack," 20 March 2003.

40 Project interview of Zuhayr Talib Abd al Satar Al Naquib, Director of Military Intelligence, 16 November 2003.

41 Project interview of Hamid Raja Shalah Al Hadithi Al Tikriti, Commander, Iraqi Air Force, 12 November 2003.

42 Project interview of Hamid Isma'aeli Dawish R'baei, Director, RG Staff, 18 November 2003.

43 Project interview of Ali Hasan al-Majid (Chemical Ali), 10 November 2003.

44 Project interview of Hamid Raja Shalah Al Hadithi Al Tikriti, Commander, Iraqi Air Force, 12 November 2003. Also interview of Zuhayr Talib Abd al Satar Al Naquib, Director of Military Intelligence, 16 November 2003.

45 Captured document, (15 March 2003) "Letter from Qusay Hussein Presidential Secretary Regarding Preparation of Fedayeen Forces to Strike Deep Within Kuwait if American Forces Converge on Baghdad." Also Classified Intelligence Report, July 2003.

46 Classified Intelligence Report, May 2003.

47 Project interview of Zuhayr Talib Abd al Satar Al Naquib, Director of Military Intelligence, 16 November 2003.

48 Project interview of Zuhayr Talib Abd al Satar Al Naquib, Director of Military Intelligence, 16 November 2003.

49 Project interview of Majid Hussein Ali Ibrahim Al Dulaymi, Commander, I Republican Guard Corps.

50 Project interview of Sultan Hashim Ahmed Al Hamed Al-Tai, Minister of Defense, 13 November 2003.

51 Joint Forces Command interview of COL Jamal Altaaey, Iraqi prisoner of war, Camp Bucca, 10 July 2003.

52   Project interview of Hamid Isma'aeli Dawish R'baei, Director, RG Staff, 18 November 2003.

53   Media transcripts of the Iraqi Minister of Information press conferences during OIF are amazingly consistent with reporting to Baghdad through the Ba'ath chain of command on the battlefield.

54   Classified Intelligence Report, April 2004.

55   Richard Beeston, "Saddam Stuck to His Fantasy of 'Victory' as Evil Regime Collapsed," New York Post Online Edition, 18 March, 2004. Found online at www.nypost.com/news/world-new/21186.htm. Downloaded 20 April 2004. This is a reprint of an article that first appeared in The Times (UK).

III. MILITARY EFFECTIVENESS

Cover of Undated Iraqi report titled "Lessons Learned from Past Trials"[1]

"We understand the theory of proper decision-making but are unable to do this in practice. Our academies teach the ideas of debate and discussion but for the last 10 years
or so our reality has been tribal. In a tribal situation you do not question things...I told
(Qusay) that I thought we were having a kind of cultural trouble that was limited our military effectiveness. I told him that most commanders understood the nature and theory of
modern warfare but in Iraq it was in conflict with the tribal nature."[2]

— Iraqi Corps Commander

III. MILITARY EFFECTIVENESS

> Yes, the guards play a very important role, and we thank Allah. In history when they write about Napoleon's guard, they will arrange them next to the Republican Guard of Iraq.[3]

> — Saddam Hussein

Any evaluation of Iraqi military effectiveness must first take cognizance of the often pathological behavior of most Iraqi generals and senior officers.[4] Saddam's Iraq, however, was a world apart from a Western conception of military professionalism. Iraqi officers rarely expected to give professional advice. Instead, they understood that their role was to ensure Saddam's dictates were followed to the letter, often no matter how infeasible or irrelevant to the military problem. They also expected and accepted intrusions into even the most mundane military affairs. For example, in a meeting in 1995 on the readiness state of the Republican Guards, a senior officer reported to Saddam:

> May God protect you sir. Despite all the moral considerations, there is another subject that should be brought up to you, sir, with complete honesty. We, the Republican Guard, feel prouder day after day. We are in better shape when it comes to training and accuracy in our job. The truth is we could not have achieved this without accurate follow up and the supervision of our honorable supervisor [Qusay Hussein]. He didn't leave any place of the Republican Guard without visiting it, whether at training or during normal daily activities. He visited the soldiers, their sleeping places, and the kitchens...All the guards are now talking about the visit of the honorable Qusay, and they declare it proudly in front of all people.[5]

In such an atmosphere, it is almost useless to judge Iraqi military effectiveness by the standard measures of equipment, organization, and doctrine. In Iraq, internal political concerns infused every aspect of the military and its employment. Simply put, the Iraqi military's main mission was to ensure the internal security of the Ba'ath dictatorship. Its second was to fight wars.

Assessing Iraqi Tactical Capabilities

Before the war, the US Central Command had developed a fairly accurate assessment of Iraq's tactical capabilities.[6] Nevertheless, the way the Iraqis employed those capabilities during the war often surprised US combat commanders. They found it a constant challenge to try and fathom future Iraqi military moves: so little of what they were witnessing on the battlefield made sense to soldiers trained in the Western tradition. However, within the context of Saddam's regime, even apparently logic-defying moves made perfect sense. None of this should suggest that reasonable courses of action were actually open to the Iraqis that could have changed the war's outcome. Coalition forces had prepared to meet an Army that would fight tenaciously but in a style more familiar to their own outlook on the employment of military forces. That the Coalition fought a force focused on internal affairs and bedeviled by political interference was so much the better. However, to develop an understanding of Iraqi decision-making and actions on the battlefield, it is vital to understand all of the factors within their political-military system that limited military effectiveness.

By 2003, the Iraqi military was reeling from 13 years of almost continuous engagement with Coalition air forces, the accumulating effects of sanctions, and the insidious impact of dysfunctional regime policies. These pressures had all helped to propel the Iraqi military into a state of chronic decline. Concerned about everything except fighting wars, the cultural and organizational dynamics of the Iraqi military, which once aspired to a Western-like profession of arms, became focused on militarily irrelevant—but for them life or death— issues.

The foremost example of declining Iraqi military effectiveness lay in the condition of the Iraqi Air Force, which failed to launch a single sortie against the Coalition invasion force. According to the commander of Iraq's Air Force and Air Defense Force, failure to launch was the result of Saddam Hussein's decision that the Air Force would not participate in the war. Apparently, Saddam reasoned that the quality and quantity of the Iraqi Air Force's equipment would make it worse than useless against Coalition air forces. Consequently, he had decided to save the Air Force for future needs, ordering his commanders to hide their aircraft.[7] This decision is yet another indication that he did not believe Coalition ground forces would reach into the heart of Iraq and that his regime would survive whatever conflict ensued.

To implement the decision to preserve the Air Force, which Saddam decided only two months before the war, the Iraqis moved most of their aircraft away from operational airfields and camouflaged them in palm groves. They also buried other aircraft literally in sand to hide them from prowling Coalition air forces, where American forces dug them up after the war. The refusal of the Iraqi Air Force to engage is reminiscent of DESERT STORM when Saddam ordered a significant portion of the Air Force to flee to Iran. This time, however, Saddam ruled out the option of seeking Iranian sanctuary. He remarked, "The Iranians are even stronger than before; they now have our Air Force."[8] Even with his regime under dire threat, Saddam's thoughts were never far away from the regional power balance.

Schemes and "Bureaucratic Eloquence"

Besides the regime's political calculus, which constantly worried senior officials and focused on almost everything except resisting a Coalition invasion, another factor reduced military effectiveness: sanctions. For more than a dozen years, United Nations sanctions had attacked the very fiber of the Iraqi military by making it difficult to purchase new equipment, procure spare parts, or fund adequate training. Attempts to overcome the effects of the sanctions led Saddam to the Military Industrial Commission as a means to sustain the military.[9] The Commission and a related series of special organizations steadily promised new capabilities to offset the effects of poor training, poor morale, and neglected equipment. Saddam apparently waited for the delivery of wonder weapons that would reverse the tide of defeat.[10]

One Republican Guard officer described the insidious effect of sanctions on the military in the following terms:

> The government made rapid efforts to limit the negative direct and indirect effects of the savage sanctions on the weapons and activities of the military forces. Unfortunately, they were the wrong kind of efforts. The army continued to fight the schemes of the Military Industrial Commission, which played an important role in promising secret weapons it would never deliver while most types of things we needed were neglected. These people received large amounts of financial support, but the army could not get simple things. As time passed, President Saddam Hussein set aside many resources for the commission departments that were difficult to afford and led to a large amount of administrative corruption in the commission directorates to keep the money coming to them.[11]

The Iraqi naval forces fared no better. According to a former commander of the Iraqi Navy:

> The best we could ever hope to do was defend the beaches with light infantry, artillery, and light weapons. We had a regiment of infantry, which we could only man at a level of 60 percent, maximum. Between 1991 and 1998, the navy's personnel strength dropped from approximately 25,000 to 9,000. We no longer had much equipment, so our need for high numbers of personnel was gone. At one point we tried to get boats made for us. We went to the Military Industrial Commission to get a private company to make boats for us. The commission also promised to get missiles as well. They made the launchers, but were late in making the missiles because some essential equipment was caught in so-called 'procedural delays.' After the two years of this project we still had no boats, and by the end of the third year, the war came and interrupted the plans.[12]

A captured Military Industrialization Commission annual report for 2002–

2003 investments showed more than 170 research projects with an estimated value of more than 320 million Iraqi dinars. The Commission divided projects among areas such as equipment, engineering, missiles, electronics, strategic weapons, artillery, and air forces. One senior Iraqi official alleged that the Commission's leaders were so fearful of Saddam that when he ordered them to initiate weapons programs that they knew Iraq could not develop, they told him they could accomplish the project with ease. Later, when Saddam asked for progress reports, they simply faked plans and designs to show progress when no program existed.

This constant stream of false, or at best optimistic reporting, undoubtedly accounts for why many of Saddam's calculations on operational, strategic, and political issues made perfect sense to him. According to Tariq Aziz:

> The people in the Military Industrialization Commission were liars. They lied to you, and they lied to Saddam. They were always saying that they were producing or procuring special weapons so that they could get favors out of Saddam—money, cars, everything—but they were liars. If they did all of this business and brought in all of these secret weapons, why didn't they work?[13]

However, the Military Industrial Commission members were not the only ones lying. This was particularly true of the most trusted members of the inner circle—especially if negative news reflects poorly on their responsibilities or reputation.[14] In the years before OPERATION IRAQI FREEDOM, everyone around Saddam understood that his need to hear only good news was constantly growing and it was in their best interest to feed that need. As noted earlier, honest reporting of military readiness and capabilities became the exception, not the rule. Many commanders simply became afraid to put their positions, possibly their livelihoods, or even lives at risk by challenging the given truth.[15] One senior minister noted, "Directly disagreeing with Saddam Hussein's ideas was unforgivable. It would be suicide."[16] Another official said that there existed an almost reflexive tendency to pass on good news and to never contradict what they had previously told Saddam. According to one former high-ranking Ba'ath official:

> Saddam had an idea about Iraq's conventional and potential unconventional capabilities, but never an accurate one because of the extensive lying occurring in that area. Many reports were falsified. The ministers attempted to convey a positive perspective with reports, which were forwarded to Saddam's secretary, who in turn passed them up to Saddam.[17]

In another instance, Saddam commissioned a series of reviews and studies of lessons learned after the 1991 Gulf War with the Coalition. One might assume this would have represented a singular opportunity for the military to bring some reality into Saddam's conception of the world. Just the fact he was calling for a lessons-learned discussion could be interpreted that perhaps Saddam recognized something had gone wrong However, these reviews and studies started from the assumption that Saddam's decision to invade Kuwait was militarily sound. Therefore, the "lessons learned" efforts did not take into account the complete scope of Gulf War experiences.

The opportunity was too much for the military commanders to handle. Presented with a one-of-a-kind opportunity to tell the truth, they passed. During one recorded review of a post-DESERT STORM study, the Commander of the Republican Guard strode to the podium with confidence and listed the "great" accomplishments of his forces during the "Mother of All Battles," among them:

- Creating impenetrable and perfectly camouflaged command bunkers.

- Analyzing the battlefield and deploying in such a way as to make the American nuclear-tipped Pershing missiles useless (no mention of the facts that the United States did not deploy Pershing missiles during the war, or that by dispersing their forces to avoid nuclear attack, the Iraqis became easy prey for the massed Coalition armor).

- Determining the specific method and timing of US operations so that "once the attack began, we were clearly expecting it." (Nothing was in the presentation about how the Iraqis were helped by President Bush giving them an ultimatum and countdown.)[18]

According to the then-Republican Guard Commander,

> As a result of all these successful preparations, our losses were not as devastating as the arsenal that was used against the Iraqi Army during the period should suggest. So this clearly shows that the Republican Guard and the other Iraqi armed forces were able to dig in and deploy wisely, and thus minimize the damage of the aerial power...[19]

In Saddam's conception of victory, the ability to escape total annihilation equated to military success.

Fear of Saddam's reaction to bad news was not the sole prerogative of his ministers and soldiers. Its pernicious tentacles even reached into Saddam's immediate family. One former high-level official related the following story about Qusay Hussein and an opportunity for at least a modicum of honest readiness reporting:

> At the end of 2000, it came to Saddam's attention that approximately seventy military vehicles were immobile. Saddam told

Qusay to resolve the problem. Republican Guard mechanics claimed they could repair the vehicles if the funds were made available. Qusay agreed to the work and funds were provided for the task. Once the work was completed, Qusay sent a representative to inspect the vehicles and he found them lined up on a vehicle park thirty five vehicles on each side. The vehicles looked like new, having been freshly painted and cleaned. After Qusay's representative inspected them, a second inspection was conducted to verify that they were now operational. The staff was told to supply drivers to move all vehicles to the opposite side of the vehicle park to ensure they were in working order. None of the seventy vehicles would start. When this was reported to Qusay, he instructed that Saddam not be informed, as Qusay had already told Saddam that the vehicles were operational.[20]

In the end, Qusay did not order mechanics to fix the vehicles—it appears that he was only eager to have this failure be hidden from his father.

As if lying were not enough, there were further impediments to the flow of information within the regime. One such impediment was the requirement to embellish even the simplest fact with fawning over Saddam, as evidenced by the Minister of Defense's relation that a training exercise called GOLDEN FALCON took place:

In reference to your Excellency's instructions regarding the large exercises at the Public Centre, having strong faith in the only God of our hearts, and God's permanent support to the believers, the faithful, the steadfast, and with great love that we have for our great homeland and our Great Leader, our Great Leader has won God's favor and the love of his dear people in the day of the grand homage.

Your enthusiastic soldiers from our courageous armed forces have executed GOLDEN FALCON Exercise number 11. In this exercise we have tested our readiness and confrontation plans against any who attempt to impure the lands of civilization and the homeland of missions and prophets. This exercise is the widest and most successful in achieving the required results. Soldiers from the III and IV Corps have participated in this exercise. And, on this occasion, and on behalf of your heroic men in the great army of Iraq, I have the pleasure and the honor to reaffirm the manhood pledge to confront plans of conspiracy and aggression, and in the name of God, we shall not bargain the truth for vanity, neither let depravity prevail against mortality, nor shall we fear anyone save God, and we shall bow-down only before God.

> The curse and the entire curse shall be put upon Washington, Lon-don, and Tel-Aviv, who are the supporters of the devil, depravity, and corruption and upon whom ever supports them. And, God willing, The Great Iraq shall achieve victory, and with God's help this victory is very near.[21]

More notable was the fact that the Iraqis conducted GOLDEN FALCON in anticipation of an Iranian invasion just months before the Coalition invasion. This was one more indicator of how Saddam actually considered Iran to be the real threat and how little he regarded the potential finality of decisive American action. There was no indication that the two corps actually conducted any significant maneuver or field training exercise during this period.

This kind of bureaucratic "eloquence" extended to every level of military organization. Some documents show that flowery language replaced actual orders to units. One example is a 9 March 2003 instruction marked as a movement order from the Al-Hussein brigade to one of its combat groups:

> The Third Group, al-Quds Army...and other formations attached to it are fighting valiantly, placing their trust in God Almighty, until the end that He proscribes, which God willing will be the enemy's defeat and his withdrawal, and a victory for us that will please our friends and grieve our enemies...[22]

After the war, several of the more capable military commanders commonly noted four other factors that seriously affected military readiness, each of which is discussed in greater detail in the following sections.

- The mostly irrelevant military guidance passed from the political leadership to the lowest level of military operations.

- The creation and rise of private armies.

- The tendency for relatives and sycophants to rise to the top national security positions.

- The combined effects of the onerous security apparatus and the resulting limitations on authority.

Many senior Iraqi military officers blamed this "coup-proofing" of the regime for most of what befell the Iraqi Army during OPERATION IRAQI FREEDOM.[23]

Irrelevant Guidance

According to one Iraqi general, "All military planning was directed by Saddam and a selected few. It was much like Hitler and his generals after 1944."[24] After 1991, Saddam's confidence in his military commanders steadily eroded, while his confidence in his own abilities as a military genius strengthened. Like a number of other amateurs in history who dabbled in military affairs, Saddam began to issue a seemingly endless stream of banal instructions. He could not resist giving detailed training guidance at the same time he became fascinated with the ethereal military capabilities promised by the Military Industrial Commission.

Dozens of surviving memoranda mirrored the 2002 Iraqi top secret document "Training Guidance to the Republican Guard" (described below). They all hint at the guidance military officers received from Saddam on a regular basis. One chapter from the Training Guidance document, "Notes and directions given by Saddam Hussein to his elite soldiers to cover the tactics of war," charged them to train in the following ways:

- train in a way that allows you to defeat your enemy;
- train all units' members in swimming;
- train your soldiers to climb palm trees so that they may use these places for navigation and sniper shooting; and
- train on smart weapons.[25]

Similar instructions were repeated in almost every training manual issued to the armed forces. In time, Saddam's wisdom became a substitute for real training.

In Saddam's view, such simple guidance was necessary to keep his commanders focused on what he considered the important issues in combat. For him, the key to all things military was violence of execution. In discussing the proper employment of the Republican Guard, he reminded his generals that

> it should be kept away from skirmishes. I mean, if it is sent in, I want it to be decisive. The Republican Guard will consider anyone on the battlefield an enemy. I don't want to complicate things for them.[26]

For most Western military organizations, a key to effectiveness rests on its ability to absorb and profit from past battlefield experiences; and one thing Iraq was not short of was recent battlefield experience. However, even if they understood the lessons, the senior leaders in the Iraqi military appeared incapable of either applying them or else extrapolating from their own experiences to deal with future contingencies. For instance, the Iran-Iraq war (1980–1988) appeared to have conditioned Iraq's generals to fight bloody, slow-tempo, slugfests over prolonged periods. Therefore, when the high-tempo Coalition forces smashed into Iraqi forces in DESERT STORM, the Iraqi operational command structure became overloaded and largely collapsed. Whatever lessons Iraq's generals took away from DESERT STORM did nothing to prepare them for the speed and tempo that Coalition forces imposed on them in OPERATION IRAQI FREEDOM.

As usual, this problem started at the top. In the aftermath of the 1991 war, the Iraqis made extensive efforts to "learn" from their experiences on the battlefields in DESERT STORM. These attempts were hampered by Saddam's conviction that his ground forces had performed well in the fighting. This forced officers compiling Iraqi lessons-learned analyses to avoid issues that might involve Saddam's prestige or questioned Iraqi fighting abilities. Instead, they focused on peripheral issues that were almost totally irrelevant to winning wars. We have already seen how these self-imposed restrictions led to such perverse claims as the Republican Guard actually won the war by avoiding annihilation:

> If it were not for these precautions, we would have suffered great loss, but when we compare our losses with the large number of fighter aircraft, missiles, and artillery bombing that the Iraqi Army was subject to we find these losses trifling. That proved that the Republican Guards and the armed forces managed to reduce the danger from air strikes.[27]

This was just one of dozens of briefings on DESERT STORM that drove home the point that in the issues that mattered, Iraq had done well in that conflict. In a short time, the constant repetition of these lessons—dispersing, digging deep bunkers, and hiding the Iraqi Army—became the *de facto* operational doctrine.

Little evidence exists that any of the politicized Iraqi generals understood the advantages in maneuverability, speed, exploitation, command and control, or the training that the US forces enjoyed.[28] However, by the time the military was ready to brief Saddam on the lessons of the Gulf War, they fully understood the danger of presenting Saddam truths other than those of which he had already convinced himself. Truthful analyses, therefore, gave way to belittlement of the American victory and discounting that America had any advantage over Iraq other than in military technology. This comment from a mid-1990s conference is typical:

> After the liberation of our land in Kuwait, and despite the fact that more than thirty countries headed by the occupation forces of the US rushed madly upon our Republican Guard, our performance was heroic.[29]

One author captures well the reality behind these revisions of Gulf War history:

From the ruins, Baghdad radio spoke of the war as "a great achievement" and called the withdrawal "heroic." Baghdad's official version of the events reminded some Iraqis of the story of an Italian general defeated at Al-Alamain by General Montgomery. When reproached for having allowed his forces to flee the battle, he solemnly remarked, *"Yes, we ran away—but like lions."*[30]

The Rise of Private Armies

It is hard to overestimate the effects that the Shi'a and Kurd uprisings in 1991 had on Saddam's outlook. The threat of another uprising consistently remained his top security concern. One of the precautions he took to prevent and, when necessary, quell a future disturbance was to create private armies made up of politically reliable troops: the *Saddam Fedayeen*, the *Al-Quds* Army, and the Ba'ath militia. Most Western analysts have argued that Saddam created these (and spin-off organizations) to help defend Iraq from external attack. This was indeed the case but only much later in their development and after Saddam's growing fascination with the success of the Palestinian *intifadas* and with the American experience in Somalia. However, documents emerging after OPERATION IRAQI FREEDOM indicate that the original and primary purpose of the paramilitaries had little to do with defending Iraq from invasion. Because these organizations had a dramatic effect on army recruiting and stripped the military of needed equipment, they actually had negative impacts on conventional elements of national security. Worse still, when they eventually were committed to battle against the onrushing Coalition forces, they were obliterated in short order.

The Al-Quds Army

The Al-Quds Army was a regional militia created to control specific areas, and after the experience of 1991, to crush as rapidly as possible any disturbance that did occur. Always conscious of Iraq's "historic" mission, Saddam created the Al-Quds (named after the Arabic word for "Jerusalem") and claimed the liberation of Jerusalem as its purpose. Its actual size could not be determined at the time of this writing, but it was likely an order-of-magnitude less than the seven million strong Saddam's advisors claimed it to be. The best estimate is that close to 500,000 joined the Al-Quds, but coming with widely varying degrees of commitment.

Currently available documents on the Al-Quds organization indicate that its leaders never seriously considered marching to liberate Jerusalem. Rather, they exclusively focused on defending specific Iraqi locales listed in various Ba'ath "emergency" plans. For example, the August 2002 emergency plan for the city of Kirkuk, located 50 miles north of Baghdad, described the friendly forces as including the various Governate and local Ba'ath militia commands as well as the Al-Quds force. This detailed planning document described the mission Al-Quds "fighters" as follows:

> The Ba'ath Governate Forces Command—Al Quds, supported by subordinate troops, shall fight the enemy rebels boldly. With deep belief in the Mighty God, our forces shall achieve an earth shaking triumph on that enemy, and will prevent that enemy from achieving any despised goals. We shall keep stability and security.[31]

The specified tasks that flowed from this less-than-specific mission statement provides a glimpse of the national security utility of various Ba'ath military capabilities:

- Defend the sector of responsibility from Al-Hurriyyah playground east to the Laylan Bridge south and...prevent the enemy rebels from occupying it, no matter what it may cost

- Protect vital establishments within responsibility limits by assigning a proper force and identifying the commandant and the assistant.

- Prevent rebels from infiltrating into the town to achieve their goals. Maintain security and stability in town.

- Keep all possible village routes and roads under surveillance to prevent saboteurs infiltrating into town.[32]

One finds the same tone in contingency planning for the Al-Quds in southern Iraq, where the Shi'a represented the main threat. The Commander of the Al-Quds Karbala Division issued a detailed plan on 9 March 2003 for dealing with internal and external threats. His plan took the form of protecting against what he termed "agent-inspired spontaneous disorder against vital targets in order to destroy the infrastructure of Iraq and create pressures against the nation."[33] This commander also worried that this time the Coalition might assist the rebels with "a media and psychological war meant to affect morale" and possibly "a push towards vital targets with the use of infantry supported by air force and helicopters."[34]

In response to the anticipated threats, the order spelled out the following tasks:

- Prepare alternative methods to deal with the possibility of an interruption in communication.

- Combat rumors and hostile propaganda.

- Keep the main roads open at all times and adopt flexible and effective measures if bridges are destroyed.

- Move, camouflage, and hide all weapons, equipment and vehicles to their assigned holes. Disperse and evacuate. Move to alternative head-quarters.

- Avoid using the entire force in the early stages until after the most serious threat has been identified.[35]

As to their value as a military force in time of war, the Minister of Defense best expressed the conventional military evaluation of their capabilities:

> The Quds Force was a headache, they had no equipment for a serious war, and their creation was a bad idea. The Ministry of Defense was required to give them weapons that were taken from the real Army. But the Army had no control of them. Their instructions came only from the President's office and not from normal military channels.[36]

According to another senior Iraqi general, the Al-Quds was not a serious combat force: "It never had anything to do with the liberation of Jerusalem or fighting the Zionists, and was merely another organ of regime protection."[37]

During the war, the system crafted by Saddam continued to pass a stream of boasts, half-truths, and of lies about the abilities and performance of the Al-Quds. Because he fully expected its members to fight like lions and bleed the Americans dry, no one was courageous enough to tell him the truth. A typical report from early in the war was captured by a public release from the Iraqi Army General Command:

> A hostile force backed by jets fighters and helicopters attempted to approach the outskirts of the Al-Muthanna Governate. Our unrivaled men of the Al-Quds Army confronted it and forced it to stop and then retreat. They inflicted on it huge human and equipment losses. This included the destruction of seven vehicles of various types. Congratulations to the Al-Quds Army on its absolute victory over the allies of the wicked Zionists.[38]

That the event never happened as described was immaterial to the Ba'ath Command. It closely mirrored the stream of Al-Quds reporting throughout late March 2003. For the military high command, reality was whatever Saddam expected it to be.

The military advisor to the Commander of the Central Euphrates Region presented a more realistic assessment of the Al-Quds martial spirit on the same day as the above report:

> According to the leadership, the Ba'ath party members were to fight inside the city and had built some sandbagged positions, while the Al-Quds Force was to remain outside. During my in-

spection I could not find even 10 percent of the 30,000 Al-Quds that they assured me were ready. When I asked where they were, I was told they were all locals and at that moment they were either at home or changing shifts—but I was assured that they would be right back. In the Al-Quds fighting positions, where I should have should have found approximately 200 soldiers, there were not even 50 present.[39]

The reality that Saddam's inner circle refused to tell him was that the Al-Quds started dissolving as American tanks approached. By the time Coalition tanks arrived at many Al-Qud defensive positions, Saddam's vaunted warriors had vanished. As another military advisor to the Central Euphrates region noted after the war:

The Quds Force numbers were not fixed. Before the war (in normal times) each regiment had 300 fighters. These numbers started dropping to zero during the war. Some were wounded in action, but most deserted.[40]

This same advisor went on to state that virtually every professional military officer in the field knew what the Ba'athists chose to ignore:

All of these Al-Quds were not prepared to fight because their commanders were civilians who had no military experience... The military advisors to the Al-Quds had no role, because the Ba'ath commanders made the decisions and wouldn't listen to the advisor. But Ba'ath commanders, especially Saddam Hussein, lived an illusion. Commanders told him that we have seen millions in the Quds Army and Saddam Hussein would depend on them."[41]

The Fedayeen Saddam

The Fedayeen Saddam is an even more interesting example than the Al-Quds of Saddam's growing infatuation with popular forces. If the Al-Quds was viewed as a part-time territorial defense force to be used in times of crisis, the Fedayeen Saddam was a permanent force tasked with a number of state security missions. Before the war, Coalition planners believed the Fedayeen Saddam was a paramilitary group with wide ranging missions from counterinsurgency, domestic direct action, and surveillance operations. They also understood that the Fedayeen Saddam served as a backup to the regular army and Al-Quds in case of a local uprising.[42] Such assessments were generally correct, but the real significance of the Fedayeen Saddam and its sometimes bizarre evolution only became clear after the war.

Saddam formed the Fedayeen Saddam in October 1994 in reaction to the Shiite and Kurdish uprisings of March 1991. As previously mentioned, these uprisings, which Saddam called "Page of Treason and Treachery," seared the soul of the regime. Together the Shi'a in the south and the Kurds in the north revealed to Saddam the potentially fatal flaws in his internal security concepts.[43]

- First, the local Ba'ath organs were not capable of crushing an uprising by local populations without external support.

- Second, the Iraqi army, and to a lesser extent the Republican Guard, was unable to act with sufficient speed and ruthlessness to suppress any rebellion.

- And finally, the tribes of Iraq still represented a significant threat even after more than 25 years of Ba'athist pan-Arabic, socialist indoctrination.

The post-DESERT STORM 1991 uprisings as the seminal event in Saddam's rule cannot be overstated. As with the creation of the Al-Quds, he moved rapidly to create other military capabilities to prevent a recurrence—even at the risk of further weakening Iraq's military capabilities to defend against an external attack. The fanatically loyal Fedayeen Saddam was the perfect tool to ensure any future revolt would be rapidly crushed.

A growing challenge that drove Saddam to expand the powers of the Fedayeen Saddam was maintaining civil order as the effects of the United Nations sanctions began to unravel the social contract of the nation. While many in the West may find it difficult to understand how criminal groups could function effectively in a police state, the tribal culture of Iraq made the formation of secret criminal gangs an easy and often lucrative enterprise. After 1991, criminal gangs became involved in a burgeoning black market, growing steadily in power, influence, and, above all, riches. It is ironic that while the Fedayeen Saddam was charged with controlling a growing lawlessness, its members were heavily involved in large-scale criminal activity.[44]

It would be easy to view the Fedayeen Saddam as particularly ruthless state police force, but that would be a mistake. According to Fedayeen Saddam planning documents captured by the Coalition, the mission of the Fedayeen Saddam was to protect Iraq "from any threats inside and outside."[45] To accomplish this mission, the Fedayeen Saddam was to defeat any enemy, defined as whoever sought to sabotage, destroy, or threaten the safety, security, and sovereignty of Iraq, whether from inside or outside, including those involved in the following activities:

- The destruction of Iraq's economic environment.

- Smuggling and forging.

- Spying and being agents.

- Corruption in the armed forces.

- Spreading negative rumors.[46]

Meticulous Fedayeen Saddam records listed numerous operations conducted in the decade after the creation of the Fedayeen Saddam:

- "Extermination operations" against saboteurs in Al-Muthana.

- An operation to "ambush and arrest" car thieves in Al-Anbar.

- The monitoring of Shi'ite civilians at the holy places of Karbala.

- A plan to bomb a humanitarian outpost in Irbil, which the Iraqi secret police suspected of being a western intelligence operation.[47]

The Fedayeen Saddam also took part in the regime's terrorism operations, which they conducted inside Iraq, and at least planned for attacks in major Western cities. In a document dated May 1999, Uday Hussein ordered preparations for "special operations, assassinations, and bombings, for the centers and traitor symbols in London, Iran and the self-ruled areas (Kurdistan)."[48]

Other captured documents indicated that preparations for a regime-directed wave of terror, codenamed "Blessed July," against targets outside of Iraq were well underway. Evidence exists that the Fedayeen Saddam had already conducted a number of early operations, particularly against the Kurds and Shi'a. Evidence supporting this contention comes in a letter to Uday Hussein from a Fedayeen Saddam widow who requested help to secure her husband's pension benefits. According to the letter, her husband, a longtime operative with the security services, had died in July 2000 carrying out a suicide operation for the Fedayeen Saddam against Kurdish opposition parties.[49]

In the final months before OPERATION IRAQI FREEDOM, the Fedayeen Saddam actively began planning operations against the Coalition, including suicide missions aimed at crossing into Kuwait to "explode volcanoes under the feet of the invaders," if Coalition forces were to reach Baghdad.[50] While it appears that they never crossed into Kuwait, a number of Fedayeen Saddam suicide attacks did take place during the war.

Equipping and training the Fedayeen Saddam was a priority mission for the regular Iraqi Army and for the fast-growing bureaucracy of the Fedayeen Saddam. The organization also became a hobby for Uday Hussein when he was not running Iraq's Olympic Committee or the Iraqi Youth Union. Saddam's support and Uday's involvement ensured that the Fedayeen Saddam remained near the top of the priority list for men and materiel. Thus, it became just one more organization sapping the strength and morale of the regular Iraqi Army and focusing the security energy at the internal threat.

Fedayeen Saddam's training focused primarily on small arms, small-unit tactics, sabotage techniques, and military surveillance and reconnaissance tasks. The Fedayeen Saddam also became a primary consumer for many of the "niche" military capabilities that proliferated throughout the regime. One such project was the Iraqi Intelligence Service's "Division 27" that supplied the Fedayeen Saddam with silencers, equipment for booby-trapping vehicles, special training on the use of certain explosive devices, special molds for explosives, and a variety of explosive timers.[51] The only apparent use for all of this Division 27 equipment was to conduct commando or terrorist operations. The Military Industrial Commission also got into the business of supplying—or at least promising to supply—the Fedayeen Saddam with a surprising array of special capabilities. According to a December 2000 memorandum, these capabilities included specially armed helicopters, unmanned aerial vehicles, and specially modified fishing boats capable of firing rockets with a range of 10 to 20 kilometers and torpedoes in international waters.[52]

Beginning in 1994, the Fedayeen Saddam opened its own paramilitary training camps for volunteers, graduating more than 7,200 "good men racing full with courage and enthusiasm" in the first year.[53] Beginning in 1998, these camps began hosting "Arab volunteers from Egypt, Palestine, Jordan, 'the Gulf,' and Syria." It is not clear from available evidence where all of these non-Iraqi volunteers who were "sacrificing for the cause" went to ply their newfound skills. Before the summer of 2002, most volunteers went home upon the completion of training.[54] But these training camps were humming with frenzied activity in the months immediately prior to the war. As late as January 2003, the volunteers participated in a special training event called the "Heroes Attack." This training event was designed in part to prepare regional Fedayeen Saddam commands to "obstruct the enemy from achieving his goal and to support keeping peace and stability in the province."[55]

Less than 30 days prior to the start of the war, the Directorate of General Military Intelligence's Special Mission Unit took charge of the training of a group of Fedayeen Saddam volunteers. They were to form "small kamikaze combat groups, equipped with weapons, and munitions suitable for use behind enemy lines and on the flanks, by causing additional damage in the enemy's armor and helicopters."[56] The volunteers attended a condensed 30-day course, which included physical training, weapons training, planning, map reading, recognizing enemy weapons, using communications devices, military engineering, combat in rough conditions, and swimming, then topped off with a practical exercise.[57] Assuming this group started training in the first week of March 2003, some of them were undoubtedly available to test their new skills against the US 3rd Infantry Division during its "Thunder Runs" into the heart of Baghdad.

Not atypically, corruption soon worked its way into the Fedayeen Saddam. Despite regular showers of cash, on-the-spot bonuses for successful missions, educational benefits, military privileges if injured, martyr privileges if killed, and free land just for volunteering, a number of Fedayeen Saddam still joined the growing underground economy.[58] In 2001, reports surfaced that members of the organization were smuggling weapons to the Saudi border for cash and establishing road-blocks in order to shake down travelers unlucky enough to be caught on the roads.[59]

These failures of discipline elicited a strong response from the regime. After all, the Fedayeen Saddam was the regime's private army—therefore Saddam expected it to possess the highest standards of personal honor and virtue. Beginning in 1996, harsh penalties in some cases resembling the harshest examples of Sharia (Islamic) law became the norm for the Fedayeen Saddam. These punishments included amputating hands for theft, being tossed off towers for sodomy, being whipped 100 times for sexual harassment, stoning for various infractions, and cutting out tongues for lying.[60] Given the mixed missions, it was only a matter of time until military failure also became punishable as a criminal offense. In typical Iraqi bureaucratic fashion, a table of specific failures and the punishment to be meted out was created and approved. In 1998 the Secretariat of the Fedayeen Saddam issued the following "regulations for when an execution order against the commanders of the various Fedayeen":

- Any section commander will be executed if his section is defeated.

- Any platoon commander will be executed, if two of his sections are defeated.

- Any company commander will be executed, if two of his platoons are defeated.

- Any regiment commander will be executed, if two of his companies are defeated.

- Any area commander will be executed if his Governate is defeated.

- Any Fedayeen Saddam fighter including commanders will be executed, if he hesitates in completing his duties, cooperates with the enemy, gives up his weapons, or hides any information concerning the security of the state.[61]

No wonder that the Fedayeen Saddam often proved the most fanatical fighters among the various Iraqi forces during OPERATION IRAQI FREEDOM. On numerous occasions, Fedayeen forces hurled themselves against armored columns rushing past the southern cities of As Samawah, An Najaf, and Karbala; and finally even trying to bar entry into Baghdad itself, long after the Republican Guard had mostly quit the field. In the years preceding the Coalition invasion, their leaders became enamored with the belief that the spirit of the Fedayeen "Arab warriors" could overcome rapid maneuver and precision fires that were the major attributes of military doctrine.[62] In any event, they proved totally unprepared for the kind of war they were asked to fight, dying by the thousands.

Relatives and Sycophants

Saddam only truly trusted one person—himself. As a result, he concentrated more and more power directly in himself. The list of leadership positions he had assumed by the early 1990s illustrates this lack of trust: President, Prime Minister, Chairman of the Revolutionary Command Council, General Secretary of the Ba'ath party, and Commander of the Armed Forces.[63]

However, no single man could do everything. Where he was forced to enlist the help of others to handle operational details, Saddam pursued a unique set of hiring criteria. As one senior Iraqi leader noted, Saddam focused on selecting the "uneducated, untalented, and those who posed no threat to his leadership for key roles."[64] The ability or talent to do the assigned job was never high on Saddam's list of attributes for a new hire. As one of Saddam's closest confidants, Ali Hassan Al-Majid ("Chemical Ali") noted, "Saddam was always wary of intelligent people. While Saddam liked having men around him with strong personalities, he did not like for those men to show off."[65]

Describing Saddam's approach for choosing those charged with making decisions that directly affected the military, one Republican Guard Corps commander commented after the war:

> Saddam Hussein was personally a brave and bloody man. But, by his decisions he threw out the clever men, or the clever men learned not to involve themselves in any decision-making. They were then replaced by hypocrites who cared not for the people or army, but only cared about pleasing Saddam. This was clear in the last war when many relatives of Saddam said they would stay and fight for the honor of Saddam, but they did not. This is the nature of any dictatorship.[66]

Always wary of a potential coup, Saddam remained reluctant to entrust military authority in anyone too far removed from his family or tribe. To Western observers, the Republican Guard represented bulwark of the regime, but for Saddam, it was the military force best positioned to overthrow him. Consequently, in 2001 he placed his youngest son Qusay at its head. According to members of the inner circle, Qusay gradually became the major player in national security after 1995. His rise culminated in his being named "honorable supervisor" of the Republican Guard and Special Republican Guard. In addition, Qusay maintained varying degrees of control over the Special Security Organization and other internal security organizations.[67]

Qusay now commanded the elite combat units of the Iraqi military, but his military experience was limited to a short stint at the Iranian front in 1984, where he had little, if any, real combat. According to the Minister of Defense:

> My working for Qusay Hussein was a mistake; Qusay knew

nothing—he understood only simple military things like a civilian. We prepared information and advice for him and he'd accept it or not. As the ultimate Commander of the Republican Guard, Qusay could take advice from professional military officers in the Ministry of Defense and the Republican Guard or ignore it to make decisions.[68]

Despite his lack of expertise, Qusay exuded confidence and attempted to play a dominant role in the final planning of Iraqi deployments against a Coalition invasion. During a December 18, 2002, Republican Guard planning meeting, Qusay presided over the presentation of a new defensive concept before the corps commanders and their staffs. When several officers gently probed the plan's underlying assumptions, Qusay's lack of military experience forced him to rely on the intellectually weak but very effective retort: "The plan is already approved by Saddam and it is you who will now make it work." He soon followed up with the equally reassuring "there will be no changes to the plan because Saddam has signed it already."[69]

As the "honorable supervisor" and son of Saddam, Qusay had the final say in significant military decisions unless Saddam himself chose to intervene. His purview included such fundamental matters as what key terrain to defend and when and how to shift the remaining Iraqi forces during the war. Several senior officers privately questioned many of his decisions, but few were willing to do so in such an open forum.

After the war, senior military officers constantly remarked on Qusay's lack of military knowledge and his unwillingness to take their "good" advice. However, this is too simplistic a formulation to explain everything that went wrong. The evidence shows that many who were in a position to advise Qusay were, in fact, unqualified to do so, while those who were qualified were often silent even when given an opportunity to speak.

One of those at the heart of the regime who proved incapable of providing sound military advice to Qusay was a Major General Barzan 'Abd al-Ghafur, the Commander of the Special Republican Guard. Before the war, Coalition planners generally assumed that the quality—and loyalty—of Iraqi military officers improved as one moved from the militias to the regular Army, to the Republican Guard, and then on to the Special Republican Guard.[70] It stood to reason that the Commander of the Special Republican Guard would then be a highly competent, loyal, and important personality in Iraq's military system. After all, the regime was entrusting that individual with the duty of conducting the final defense of the homes and offices of the regime's elite. Coalition planners considered the Special Republican Guard the elite of the elite; and by logical extension, their commander would surely be the best Saddam could find. This piece of conventional wisdom was wrong.[71]

After the war, the peers and colleagues of the Special Republican Guard Commander were all openly derisive of Barzan's performance as an officer and commander. Saddam had selected Barzan, as one general noted, because he had several qualities that Saddam held dear, "He was Saddam's cousin, but he had two other important qualities which made him the best man for the job. First, he was not intelligent enough to represent a threat to the regime and second, he was not brave enough to participate in anyone else's plots."[72]

As the Special Republican Guard commander, Barzan was well aware of the tenuous nature of his position. He recalled in a postwar interview:

> I was called to Baghdad from holiday and told that I would be taking command of the Special Republican Guard. I was on a probationary status for the first six months. I was ordered by Saddam to take the command; I had no choice. I was sick at the idea of being the Special Republican Guard commander. It was the most dangerous job in the regime.[73]

This general, the man who was to command the last ditch stand of Saddam's Guards, spent most of the war hiding. The selection of such a man for an important military position appears counter-intuitive, but given the imperatives of Iraqi politics, it was the only possible rational decision Saddam could make.

The case of the Minister of Defense, General Sultan Hashim Ahmad al-Ta'i, is strikingly different. Here, by all accounts, was a competent military commander who, upon reaching the pinnacle of power, apparently decided silence was the better part of valor. A number of senior Iraqi leaders identified General Sultan as one of the best and brightest among Iraq's military leaders. His peers described him as a "mountain of morals" and compared him to Jafar al Askari, Minister of Defense in the 1930s and considered the "father of the Iraqi Army."[74] Judging from just the scope of his military record, he appears to have been an impressive soldier. During his forty-year career, Sultan commanded two brigades, three divisions, and at least two corps of regular army troops. In so doing, he fought in every war after 1968 and developed a reputation as a creative, dynamic military leader.

However, Sultan's elevation to Minister of Defense changed him as well as his colleagues' opinions of him. The specific reasons for the change are no doubt complex, but his actions during the meetings and planning conferences prior to the Coalition invasion suggest an explanation. In one telling event during the final planning, he remained silent when more junior officers voiced concerns over Saddam's new plan for the defense of Iraq. As one corps commander who was present later noted, "Some of the senior military leaders present only competed to please Saddam. The Minister of Defense was an honorable man but he gave up his strategic vision in order to keep Saddam's favor. This, "in his opinion," was very unfortunate for Iraq."[75]

Security and Command Limitations

While most senior military leaders found themselves caught up in the corrupting influences surrounding the regime's inner circle, other factors combined to undermine the effectiveness of subordinate leaders and units. While actual warfighting units at corps and division level also possessed their share of "trusted" officers, many still exhibited a level of professional competence during post-war interviews that seemed inconsistent with their general reputation. They provided two reasons for this incongruity: the limits Saddam imposed on their exercise of authority and the effects of the pervasive internal security apparatus.

The Commander of the Baghdad Republican Guard Infantry Division provided an example of the effects of stripping division commanders of authority necessary to make decisions. The division's mission from 1998 until the Coalition invasion was to defend the area around the city of al-Kut, located southeast of Baghdad. This area has traditionally been the key terrain for defending Iraq against an Iranian invasion from the east; it remains one of the most critical areas in Iraqi defense planning:

> In the Republican Guard, division and corps commanders could not make decisions without the approval of the staff command. Division commanders could only move small elements within their command. Major movements such as brigade-sized elements and higher had to be requested through the corps commander to the staff command. This process did not change during the war and in fact became more centralized.[76]

Such a lack of trust had a direct effect not only on the commander's ability to lead his unit but also the unit's ability to take advantage of its knowledge of the ground to prepare an optimal defense. In many cases, staff officers in Baghdad who had never visited the area still managed to forward precise deployment locations for even the smallest units directly to division commanders. The Baghdad commander continued:

> Only the Republican Guard staff command directed maneuvers and it did not allow subordinate commanders to make suggestions. If a commander made a decision without the Republican Guard chief of staff's approval, he would be punished. The only commanders who had any protection were those from Tikrit. They were allowed to make their own decisions because the government trusted them more.[77]

The Commander of the II Republican Guard Corps echoed the problems described by the Commander of the Baghdad Division. He reported a constant struggle with higher headquarters regarding disposition of "his" units. As the

Commander of the II Republican Guard Corps noted, "I had to ask for permission from the Republican Guard Staff in Baghdad to move brigade-size units and was still doing so up until 2 and 3 April."[78] By then Coalition forces were making their final drive on Baghdad.

The gulf between Iraqi and Coalition approaches to battlefield command and control could not have been wider. Coalition doctrine emphasized distributed operations and battlefield autonomy (or decentralized command and control), while the focus of Iraq's military was on template solutions and centralized control. The nature of Saddam's regime made it impossible to tolerate any other approach. Saddam personally advising a group of senior commanders on how they should react to an enemy helicopter assault offered an example of where the regime's emphasis on centralized control bounded all but the most aggressive commanders' authority:

> If we assume that X is a commander of an armored brigade according to ordinary standards and there was a landing by helicopters 20 km [kilometers] away from him, what are the checks he should make? What should he wish to know about the landing?...What are the sources of information he can depend on?...What are the issues? In all events you have one or two guns near the headquarters brigade. Therefore, the first thing you should do is an immediate reaction by artillery. At the same time, you call by phone and say: Maximum attention. And then you prepare the entire brigade to be ready for a later order and then you report this to the higher headquarters and tell it: A landing at a depth of so-and-so took place in front of us...This will enable the headquarters to operate its artillery. At the same time, as a higher headquarters, it will help you by offering proper advice, orders, or instructions.[79]

Not every operational commander had to endure the restrictions that impeded the Baghdad Division commander and others. In sharp relief to these restrictions were those imposed on the Al-Nida Division. The Al-Nida was a Republican Guard armored division tasked to defend the Baghdad's eastern approaches against possible Iranian attacks along the Dialya River from the northeastern shoulder of Baghdad up to Baquba. This sector was the critical terrain in the conventional defense of Baghdad against an enemy attacking from the east.[80] The division's position would make it the "last-line of defense" for any serious Iranian attack. Given the relatively short 120 kilometers to the Iranian frontier, the readiness of the Al-Nida Division was a national priority.

Both Iraqi and Coalition intelligence organizations considered the Al-Nida Division to be the "best of the best" in the Republican Guard. As described by the Al-Nida's chief of staff, the division's materiel readiness was the best in the Iraqi military:

The brigades were at 100 percent strength or better. The tanks were between 99 percent or 98 percent ready for war. The brigades had all the most modern equipment in the Iraqi armed forces, T-72 tanks, and BMP-2 armored personnel carriers, 130mm artillery cannons...and 155mm cannons. Every battalion had 18 cannons.[81]

According to his Chief of Staff, the division commander planned and conducted training virtually independent of any higher authority. Such autonomy was unheard of in his sister unit, the Baghdad Division.[82] For example, before the Coalition invasion the division moved one of its brigade garrisons and conducted a series of "urban warfare" training drills. The division's Chief of Staff also described adjusting its defensive posture to create a series of "false" brigade fighting positions, while a robust series of new survivability positions were hastily dug along the Diyala River with little or no direction—or interference—from higher headquarters.[83] The Al-Nida Division's commander stated that during the war he often made direct contact with other division commanders to receive battlefield updates and build a picture of what was occurring. For most Iraqi commanders, contacting other commanders even during wartime remained a risky enterprise.

When asked in a post-war interview to explain the disparity between the authority he exercised and that exercised by other divisional commanders, the commander answered in an incredulous tone, "I am a Tikriti and other commanders were not."[84] In Saddam's military, tribal or familial relationships trumped the actual documented authority necessary for effective command at any particular echelon.

Another critical inhibitor of Iraqi tactical performance lay in the effects of the regime's pervasive internal security environment. The almost-Orwellian security environment of the Ba'athist regime stretched from the central offices of the regime's inner circle down to tactical units. According to one senior minister:

> Each ministry or any other government establishment had a security chief who reported to the agency to which he belonged. His section kept an eye on all affairs and actions, encouraging disgruntled individuals to provide information on what was going on. The Ba'ath party members and "aspirants" also wrote reports to the leader of the sector or cell. Rivalries and backbiting were encouraged.[85]

Military officers executed their duties under the constant, intrusive, and, more often than not, uncoordinated supervision of multiple security services.[86] One knowledgeable source claimed, "One officer in five reporting on his peers was the 'desirable' state of affairs, but the Special Security Office often achieved higher ratios."[87] Every senior commander interviewed after hostilities emphasized the psychological costs of constantly looking over their shoulders as a significant constraint on their military effectiveness.

At any one time, each of these commanders had to contend with at least five major security organizations: the Special Security Office, the Iraqi Intelligence Service, the Directorate of General Security, the General Directorate of Military Intelligence, and various "security service" offices within the Republican Guard's bureaucracy.[88] Moreover, the number of security personnel in each of these organizations increased dramatically after 1991. In many cases, new spies were sent to units to report on the spies already there, even those from their own organizations. One former senior commander described the Republican Guard's Security Office as growing from a small office to a battalion-sized element in response to finger-pointing after the 1991 Gulf War and the regime's increasing fears about internal security.[89] In a rambling tirade, this officer outlined the nature of the surveillance from this one organization and corroding effect this spying had:

> The main function of the Republican Guard Security Office was to monitor and ensure the loyalty of Republican Guard forces. All phones in Republican Guard offices were monitored and all meetings were recorded. High-ranking officers were subjected to constant technical monitoring and surveillance in and out of their homes. The Republican Guard Security Office monitored all aspects of senior Republican Guard officers' lives, including their financial affairs and diet. Republican Guard Security Office personnel even questioned the guards at senior officers' houses to see what they could learn about the officers' life styles. Republican Guard security officers were generally despised by the regular Republican Guard personnel. The Special Security Office knew how many times I went to the bathroom. Requesting retirement was impossible because the regime would assume one opposed them politically, and one would be arrested and jailed. Republican Guard Security Office monitoring was thorough; for example, one officer was given six months in jail for telling a joke about the Republican Guard Security Office. This was supposed to ensure that Republican Guard personnel would never become involved in politics. This had a powerful negative affect on Republican Guard morale. Republican Guard commanders were not trusted to conduct any movement or even so much as start a tank without permission.[90]

The Republican Guard II Corps Commander described the influence of the internal security environment on a typical corps-level staff meeting:

> First a meeting would be announced and all the corps-level staff, the subordinate division commanders and selected staff, as well as supporting or attached organizations and their staffs would

assemble at the corps headquarters. The corps commander had to ensure then that all the spies were in the room before the meeting began so that there would not be any suspicions in Baghdad as to my purpose. This kind of attention to my own internal security was required. I spent considerable time finding clever ways to invite even the spies I was not supposed to know about. Failure by the "target" of all of this internal spying to coordinate the surreptitious activities of the various persons spying on him could easily have left one out and resulted in unwarranted and possibly dangerous suspicion by the senior leadership in Baghdad based on his report of being excluded from a "secret" meeting.[91]

This corps commander describes what he believed the impact of all this spying had on military effectiveness:

You must understand that the Republican Guard internal security process was very compartmented, even in normal times. For example, in some cases a subordinate unit could be moved by the Republican Guard headquarters without my permission. In some cases, I would find out just prior to the execution of the move. I could not question it. In fact, security measures like this killed the flexibility in units and made commanders into very "small soldiers." My long experience in the Republican Guard allowed me some flexibility but I was having trouble because the regime security people were always trying to set me up and find some mistake. This is why I always invited all the spies to my meetings. The security situation in the last few years reached the point of incredible. We could have no relationships with fellow commanders. This prevented even friendships. Thank God for my books or I would have felt otherwise a man alone in a cave. During this critical period I was completely uninformed about other unit plans around me. I had the Al Nida and the Baghdad Divisions but officially I could not ask them about any of their missions and plans that were sent to them directly from Republican Guard headquarters in Baghdad.[92]

There were two common reactions to the pervasive security apparatus. The first, taken by the Commander of the II Republican Guard Corps, was to work through the fog of suspicion and maintain as open a process as possible, while still attempting to command a military unit on the brink of war. Operating in this manner often required extreme precautions. The II Corps commander, for instance, held most of his private meetings in the walled garden of a private home where he was relatively assured the regime's spies could not eavesdrop on him.[93] The second reaction, the one more commonly followed by senior leaders, was to avoid any actions, activities, or circumstances that might bring suspicion from the various "eyes" of the regime.

During interviews with the Commander of the Republican Guard I Corps, it was obvious he selected the second method as his preferred way of dealing with the security forces:

> One of the biggest weaknesses of the Iraqi military was that, units were not allowed to independently coordinate with each other for defensive integration. All orders came from the Chief of Staff of the Republican Guard, which ultimately came from Qusay or Saddam Hussein...In order to know where units were located on our flanks, we had to use our own reconnaissance elements because we were not allowed to communicate with our sister units."[94]

The net effect of such reactions to the threat imposed by the security services was that corps-level operational command and control disappeared from the battle-field. This atmosphere of fear and its resulting impact on the performance of Iraqi leadership explain much about the actions of Iraq's military forces on the battlefield. The restrictions imposed on them in peacetime made it impossible to coordinate plans or action during war. The regime had consistently sacrificed military effectiveness for the more important needs of internal security. In effect, it had neutered its military force, which was now incapable of standing up to against a disciplined and competent military force.

Reflections

At the conclusion of Iraqi military operations, one of the most thoughtful senior officers in the Iraqi armed forces provided a list of what he regarded as the major contributing factors to the stunningly sudden collapse of Iraq's military organizations:[95]

- "The persistence of the Commander in Chief (Saddam Hussein) until a very late time in insisting that every branch of the armed forces, in their organizational differences, make independent plans for the defense of their areas of responsibility...

- "The tyranny of the security establishment and justification of any of their whims on security grounds, even though those whims actually harmed the defensive planning operations...

- "The military bureaucracy grew enormous with the constant loss of authority that was a result of the administrative rule, 'There is no responsibility without authority, and there is no authority without accountability...'"

- "The unchecked spread of administrative corruption and bribery, especially in the last few years...

- "A drop in the level of training as a philosophy, and a concrete loss in the foundations for training (because of the sanctions), and a lack of ability to conduct operational planning...

- "Boredom and restiveness within the military career field because of the measures taken by the political leadership by which they alienated the people (the regime was a constant threat to the people for over twenty years straight. There was a prevalence of the negative emotions from huge numbers of families of martyrs, those being punished, and prisoners). The army did not want to confront the people.

- "The weakness of political loyalty between the commands and the personal separation from the political leadership by a lot of those affiliated with the armed forces.

- "Personal egos were behind the behavior of various levels of the high command: this ruled over their moral responsibilities towards the nation and the people and lasted until the final days of the war."[96]

In the end, Saddam determined that the most important factor for military success lay in the sprit of the warrior. Saddam considered the ideological commitment to the Ba'athist cause as the fundamental basis of this spirit and the foundation for preparing Iraq's soldiers for war. Because he perceived the Ba'athist spirit of the "Iraqi warrior" was far superior to anything American soldiers were capable of bringing to the battlefield, he overlooked the many forces eroding the foundations of true military effectiveness. The conclusion of an Iraqi training manual sums up the regime's attitude:

> Military power is measured by the period in which difficulties become severe, calamities increase, choices multiply, and the world gets dark and nothing remains except the bright light of belief and ideological determination...If [the soldier] ignores [his] values, principles, and ideals, all military foundations would collapse. He will be defeated, shamed, and [his] military honor will remain in the same place together with the booty taken by the enemy. The President, the Leader Saddam Hussein asks, "Would men allow for their military honor to be taken by the enemy as booty from the battle?[97]

In March 2003, the regime ordered its military to stop the Coalition invasion. It was not the first army to place "spirit" over the reality of firepower and steel, and it is unlikely to be the last.

Notes

1. Captured document (undated), "Lessons Learned Report."

2. "Perspectives of the II Republican Guard Corps."

3. Captured media file, (approximately 1993) "Saddam discussing issues related to the war in 1991."

4. This is not meant to be a clinical description but is intended to capture the dramatically different definitions of professional competence at work in Iraq. Some generals were purely Ba'athist and political while others displayed a clear understanding of what in the West would be considered military competence. But even this latter group was adept at acting with the former when circumstances demanded it.

5. Captured media file, (10 August 1995) "Saddam Hussein Meeting with Leaders of the Republican Guard Regarding Readiness of the Guard."

6. For example, "The RGFC [Republican Guard Forces Command] maintains a significant capability by regional standards. The size and experience of the RGFC are key advantages over other regional armies in the absence of US support. However, thirteen years of sanctions have prevented Iraq from replacing the massive equipment losses suffered in OPERATION DESERT STORM, and Iraqi forces remain much weaker than they were in 1990." US Central Command CONPLAN 1003-V.

7. Classified Intelligence Report, June 2003.

8. Classified Intelligence Report, July 2004. According to Kenneth Pollack, some 115 frontline Iraqi aircraft sought security in Iran during OPERATION DESERT STORM. Arabs at War, Military Effectiveness, 1948–1991 (Lincoln, NE, and London (UK), University of Nebraska Press, 2002), p. 243.

9. For a detailed description of the history and organization of the Military Industrial Committee, see the Comprehensive Report of the Special Advisor to the DCI on Iraq's WMD, vol. I, (Central Intelligence Agency, 30 September, 2004), p. 17.

10. Captured document, (25 February 2003) Military Industrialization Commission Annual Report for 2002–2003 Investments, Projects, and Plans.

11. Unpublished draft memoirs of LTG Raad Hamdani, Commander II Republican Guard Corps.

12. "Perspectives Assistant Senior Military Advisor." General Taha was commenting about his experiences as the senior naval officer in Iraq before he retired in the fall of 2002.

13. Classified Intelligence Report, May 2003.

14. According to one senior Iraqi source, "The rumor circulating was that if one said no to Saddam, one would be summarily executed; this was particularly true in the year prior to the lead-up to OPERATION IRAQI FREEDOM in April 2003." Classified Intelligence Report, September 2003.

15. Classified Intelligence Report, March 2004.

16. Classified Intelligence Report, July 2004.

17. Classified Intelligence Report, March 2004.

18. Captured document, (approximately 1993) "9th Session on the Role of the Republican Guard."

19. Captured document, (approximately 1993) "9th Session on the Role of the Republican Guard."

20 Classified Intelligence Report, March 2004.

21 Captured document, (8 November 2002) "Letter Addressed to Saddam and Signed by the Minister of Defense Referring to the Summer 2002 Military Exercise 'Golden Falcon.'"

22 Captured document, (9 March 2003) "Movement Order No. 3 for 2003, al-Hussein Brigade General Staff Headquarters."

23 Evidence of Saddam "coup-proofing" his regime through the manipulation of military assignments, rewards, and implementing strict controls over military organizations is clear in a large cross-section of interviews, debriefs, and interrogations. For an accurate description of the underlying civil-military relationship, see Ahmed Hashim, "Saddam Husayn and Civil-Military Relations in Iraq: The Quest for Legitimacy and Power," Middle East Journal, vol. 57, no. 1, Winter 2003.

24 "Perspectives II Republican Guard Corps."

25 Captured document, (25 August, 2002) "Soldiers of the Republican Guards Headquarters of Offensive Mission as Noted in Republican Guards Training Guidance."

26 Captured media file, (29 February 1992) "Saddam Meeting with Military Commanders Discussing 1991 Uprisings."

27 Captured media file, (dated approximately 1993) "Iraqi Command Meeting Regarding the Coalition Attack on Iraq and the 1991 Uprising."

28 The project noted a distinction between most senior officers and a small but surprising group of two- and three-star commanders who possessed a lucid understanding of the capabilities of the Coalition and the qualitative gulf between forces on the eve of OPERATION IRAQI FREEDOM.

29 Captured document, (dated approximately 1993) "Iraqi Command Meeting Regarding the Coalition Attack on Iraq and the 1991 Uprising."

30 Faceh Abd Al-Jabbar, "Why the Uprisings," Middle East Report, May-June 1992, p. 8.

31 Captured document, (29 August 2002) "Correspondence Issued from Al-Ta'mim Branch Command under the Arab Socialist Ba'ath Party to Emergency Regiment Command Secretary." Many similar examples are archived in the captured documents database from areas such as Fallujah, Basra, Al Nasiriyah, and Karbala. They all generally follow the tone and specificity of the Al-Ta'mim Branch document.

32 Captured document, (29 August 2002) "Correspondence issued from Al-Ta'mim Branch Command under the Arab Socialist Ba'ath Party to Emergency Regiment Command Secretary."

33 Captured document, (9 March 2003) "Plan by al-Quds for Defending District Issued by Karbala Division Commander."

34 Captured document, (9 March 2003) "Plan by al-Quds for Defending District Issued by Karbala Division Commander."

35 Captured document, (9 March 2003) "Plan by al-Quds for Defending District Issued by Karbala Division Commander."

36 Project interview of Sultan Hashim Ahmed Al Hamed Al-Tai, Minister of Defense, 13 November 2003.

37 Classified Intelligence Report, December 2002.

38 Foreign Broadcast Information Service, (24 March 2003) "Iraqi Army General Command Issues Statement on Military Operations 23, 24 March" Baghdad Iraqi Satellite Channel Television.

39 "Perspectives Assistant Senior Military Advisor."

40 Project interview of LTG Kenan Mansour Khalil al-Obadi, Senior Military Advisor to RCC Member Mizban Khudr Al-Hadi, 30 November, 2003.

41 Project interview of LTG Kenan Mansour Khalil al-Obadi, Senior Military Advisor to RCC Member Mizban Khudr Al-Hadi, 30 November, 2003.

42 See US Central Command CONPLAN 1003-V.

43 Starting in late March 1991 and continuing through at least November 1995, Saddam participated in numerous conferences, sponsored studies, and directed analyses of both the 1991 Gulf War and the rebellions that followed. See captured audio tape, (5 May 1991) "Saddam Hussein's Meeting with High-Ranking Iraqi Officials, Evaluating the Iraqi Military Performance on the Battlefield during the First Gulf War 1991."

44 A large volume of captured Fedayeen Saddam documents deal with internal criminal investigations for activities ranging from smuggling to armed robberies.

45 Captured document, (2 November 1995) "Military Directorate Correspondence Reports About Fedayeen Saddam Troops and Their Organizational Structure."

46 Captured document, (2 November 1995) "Military Directorate Correspondence Reports About Fedayeen Saddam Troops and Their Organizational Structure."

47 Captured documents: • (11 July, 1999) "Plans and Analysis Reports by the Fedayeen Saddam Secretariat"; • (14 March, 2000) "Memo from Office of the Fedayeen Saddam Chief of Staff about Special Operations Against Car Thieves"; • (20 March 2002) "Security Plan for Karbala Force of Fedayeen Saddam from Fedayeen Secretariat"; • (16 November 2000) "Military Orders for Fedayeen to Blow up a Building."

48 Captured document, (25 May 1999) "Fedayeen Saddam Instructions."

49 Captured document, (1 July 2001) "Correspondence Between Fedayeen Saddam and Iraq National Olympic Committee Regarding a Letter from a Widow." The widow's letter goes on to note her husband's many successful missions, including the July 6, 1992, car bomb attack against a convoy near Halabjah carrying the wife of a former French president.

50 Captured documents: • (25 March 2003) "Correspondence from Fedayeen Saddam to Uday Regarding Fedayeen Saddam Suicide Mission Team"; • (15 March 2003) "Letter from Qusay to Saddam Regarding the Preparation of Fedayeen Forces to Strike Deep Within Kuwait if American Forces Converge on Baghdad."

51 Captured document, (approximately 1999) "1999 IIS Plan for Training Fedayeen Saddam Using IEDs."

52 Captured document, (23 December 2000) "Fedayeen Saddam UAV and Special Boat Plans."

53 Captured document, (2 November 1995) "Military Directorate Correspondence Reports about Fedayeen Saddam Troops and Their Organizational Structure."

54 Captured document, (7 October 2000) "Correspondence from Presidential Office to Secretary General of the Fedayeen Saddam Regarding Foreign Arab Volunteers."

55 Captured document, (16 January 2003) "Training Exercise 'Heroes Attack' Plan for Kadhima Command, Al-Muthana Force of the Fedayeen Saddam."

56 Captured document, (23 February 2003) "Special Unit in Fedayeen Organization Formation Orders from Military Intelligence Director."

57 Captured document, (23 February 2003) "Special Unit in Fedayeen Organization Formation Orders from Military Intelligence Director."

58 Captured document, (14 June 1995) "RCC Decision About Fedayeen Saddam Rights and Privileges Forwarded to MIC."

59 Captured document, (9 May 2002) "Correspondence Issued by Secretariat of Fedayeen Saddam Regarding Cutting Off Hands of the Fedayeen Saddam Members Who Were Smuggling Weapons to the Saudi Side During 2001."

60 Captured documents: • (21 August 1996) "Reference File of the Laws of the Fedayeen Saddam"; • (11 October 2002) "Memos within Fedayeen Saddam General Secretariat regarding disciplinary actions and punishment orders."

61 Captured document, (15 January 1998) "Memos Issued by the Head of the Fedayeen Saddam Passing Down Regulations for Executions."

62 In a 1995 discussion with senior military commanders, Saddam requested a study of such non-Arab struggles, "especially their military sides...[w]e can gain a lot from...Rommel and De Gaulle." However, Saddam cautioned them to "avoid propaganda books" and above all do "not concentrate on the leaders." In this context, perhaps examining operational and tactical decision-making cut too close to Saddam's exclusive domain. After all, military history is as much a review of mistakes made as it is successes achieved. Captured document, (8 October 1995) "Saddam Meeting with Senior Military Leaders."

63 Comprehensive Report of the Special Advisor to the DCI on Iraq's WMD, vol. I, (Central Intelligence Agency, 30 September 2004), p. 5.

64 Classified Intelligence Report, April 2004.

65 Classified Intelligence Report, August 2003.

66 "Perspectives II Republican Guard Corps," p. 37.

67 Classified Intelligence Report, April 2004. Also Comprehensive Report of the Special Advisor to the DCI on Iraq's WMD, vol. I, (Central Intelligence Agency, 30 September 2004), pp. 87–88.

68 Project interview of Sultan Hashim Ahmed Al Hamed Al-Tai, Minister of Defense, 13 November 2003.

69 "Perspectives II Republican Guard Corps," p. 7.

70 The Special Republican Guard (SRG): The SRG was a division-sized internal security force of approximately 15,000 men. Its primary mission was to protect Saddam and control the civilian population of Baghdad. The SRG troops were organized into approximately 12 battalions, but were normally deployed in platoon- and company-sized elements.

71 There was an exception to the conventional wisdom. A Central Intelligence Agency study, The Iraqi Senior Officer Corps: Shaped by Pride, Prejudice, Patrimony, and Fear, was released on 18 March 2003 (one day prior to the beginning of OPERATION IRAQI FREEDOM). It noted the following about the SRG Commander: "He reportedly drinks heavily and has sexual relation-ships with numerous women." (p. 27)

72 Project interview of Sultan Hashim Ahmed Al Hamed Al-Tai, Minister of Defense. 13 November 2003.

73 Project interview of Barzan Abd Al-Ghafur Sulayman Al-Tikriti, Commander, Special Republican Guard, 16 November 2003.

74 Iraqi Survey Group Notes, (September–October 2003).

75 "Perspectives II Republican Guard Corps," p. 8.

76 Project interview of Salih Ibrahim Hammadi Al Salamani, Commander, Baghdad Republican Guard Division, 10 November 2003.

77 Project interview of Salih Ibrahim Hammadi Al Salamani, Commander, Baghdad Republican Guard Division, 10 November 2003. The correlation between political power and the town of

Tikrit goes back to the 1968 Ba'ath revolution. Men from Tikrit, two of them relatives, dominated the new Revolutionary Command Council. The deputy to the new President was Saddam Hussein who spent the next decade ensuring men from Tikrit (al-Tikriti) held the critical positions of trust.

[78] Project interview of LTG Raad Hamdani, Commander of the II Republican Guard Corps, 17 November 2003. The contrast in command and control authority between the commanders of the US V Corps and I MEF (Marine Expeditionary Force), and their opponent, the II Republican Guard commander, cannot be overstated.

[79] Foreign Broadcast Information Service, "Saddam Discusses Possible 'Enemy' Landing Operations with Military Commanders," Republic of Iraq Television, 1 February 2003.

[80] Historically this enemy was always the Persians (modern day Iran). In the past decade, it included the significant threat posed by the Badar Corps (Iraqi Shi'a expatriates supported by Iran) based in southwestern Iran.

[81] Project interview of Staff Brigadier General Muhammad Sattam Abdullah Al Hamdani, former Chief of Staff, Al Nida Division, 19 November 2003. This officer insisted that these were not inflated readiness numbers but reflected the priority enjoyed by his division.

[82] According to Intelligence information, no significant training occurred in the Baghdad Division during the fall of 2002. By contrast, one armored brigade of the Al Nida Division trained for a period that was several weeks longer than previous training cycles, and another brigade of the Al Nida Division conducted urban warfare training.

[83] It should be noted that based on their actions the priority for this division, despite its orders, reputation, and location, was on survivability and not defense. In some cases, up to four survivability positions were prepared for every one fighting position.

[84] Project interview of Abd Al-Karim Jasim Nafus Al-Majid, Commander, Al Nida Armored Division, 21 November 2003. According to open source and intelligence reporting, Al-Karim's father is Saddam's cousin.

[85] Classified Intelligence Report, April 2004.

[86] One captured document describes a directive from Saddam in 1996 forbidding employees of the various security organizations from communicating with each other without a "direct order" from Saddam Hussein or his secretary. Captured document, (13 July 1997) "Letter from Secretary of the Presidential Office to SSO Director and Others Ordering Security Employees not to Address Secretary."

[87] Classified Intelligence Report, May 2004. The source was a high-level official of the Iraqi regime with direct access to the reported information.

[88] The Special Security Organization (SSO) within the Republican Guard was extensive and included 1 SSO officer and 15 to 20 support staff at divisional headquarters; and 1 officer at each brigade and at the regimental level. Republican Guard military intelligence officers reported directly to SSO and not their operational commanders. While SSO did not "infiltrate undercover officers into the RG [Republican Guard]," it did rely on "informal" sources within the commands. Classified Intelligence Report, April 2004.

[89] Classified Intelligence Report, June 2004.

[90] Classified Intelligence Report, June 2004.

[91] "Perspectives II Republican Guard Corps."

[92] "Perspectives II Republican Guard Corps."

[93] Classified Intelligence Report, September 2003. The source was a senior Iraqi officer who had direct knowledge of Iraqi war planning, operations, and information reported.

[94] Project interview of Majid Hussein Ali Ibrahim Al Dulaymi, Commander, I Republican Guard Corps.

[95] Unpublished draft memoirs of LTG Raad Hamdani, Commander, II Republican Guard Corps.

[96] Unpublished draft memoirs of LTG Raad Hamdani, Commander, II Republican Guard Corps. Additionally, thousands of captured documents and personnel files attest to the treatment repatriated Iraqi prisoners of war received from numerous security services. Actions included things such as arrest, constant surveillance, denial of employment, and even denial of marriage permits

[97] Captured document, (date unclear; from late 1980s) "Handbook on Ideology and Requirements on Being an Iraqi Soldier."

IV. CRIPPLED OPERATIONAL PLANNING

قيادة فرقـة كربلاء
جيش القـدس
لواء الحـــين
الفوج الأول

ومجاهدوا في الله حق جهاده هو اجتباكم

جيش القدس

سجـــل

الهيكل التنظيمي

لدورة القائد المنتصر

And the stand of the troop and the people under the leadership of the party in the cities, and denying the enemy from occupying and city, is the principal base for the failure of the aggression, and that was accomplished to thank God, but that alone is not enough to evicting the enemy from Iraq...[1]

—Saddam Hussein
29 March 2003

Al-Quds Army (Al-Husayn Brigade) Military plans during 2002 and 2003[2]

IV. CRIPPLED OPERATIONAL PLANNING

> With this incredible simplicity and stupidity...Qusay said that the plan
> was already approved by Saddam and "it was you who would now
> make it work."[3]

> — LTG Raad Hamdani, Republican Guard

Conventional wisdom has depicted the Iraqi professional soldiers as being incapable of adequately training or preparing an army for war, a conclusion drawn from their poor showing against Coalition forces in two wars. Iraqi performance in combat spoke for itself. As previously discussed, this view is supported when looking at the highest levels of the regime where sycophancy was the rule rather than the exception. Furthermore, as realistic training for combat became a distant memory, the quality of lower-ranking officers and non-commissioned officers also degenerated.

Yet between the senior levels of the regime and the tactical leaders, significant pockets of competence still existed at the operational level of command, the corps and division commanders. Examples abound of Iraq's operational-level military leaders tasking their senior staffs and consultative bodies (e.g., universities, ad-hoc groups) to conduct studies and analyses of current and past operations in attempts to understand what went wrong in 1991, OPERATION DESERT STORM, and how to fix it.[4] After the obligatory paeans to Saddam in the beginning, most of these documents demonstrated some facility to identify shortcomings and outline steps to overcome them. In post-war interviews after OPERATION IRAQI FREEDOM, a number of operational commanders expressed considerable frustration over the gulf between knowing what was required and what Saddam would accept or allow.

Still, many officers and their staffs were determined to make the best of a bad political situation. They worked hard towards identifying their own shortcomings, and attempted to predict the course of a future war. These efforts eventually led to a single operational plan to defend Iraq that remained constant until late 2002, when it was discarded for an entirely new concept promulgated by Saddam. This chapter will examine two facets of the Iraqi military's planning for war. First, it looks at how Iraqi's operational planners understood their situation and the plans they made to defend Iraq based on that understanding. Second, it examines the effects of Saddam's sudden decision in December 2002 to ignore nearly all of the previous effort and change the entire war plan only three months before the Coalition invasion.

The Operational Concept Before 18 December 2002

Immediately following the 1991 Iraqi "victory" in the "Mother of All Battles" and continuing through late 1995, the senior military and political leadership directed and participated in a series of after-action reviews, military seminars, and studies on the conflict and the ensuing Kurd and Shiite rebellions in the north and south, respectively. These reviews aimed to identify and fix the perceived tactical weaknesses of the Ba'ath Party and the Iraqi military. From the start, the senior generals assumed that given the strategic decision to invade Kuwait, any confrontation with the Americans—while not desirable—was survivable.[5] In the end, this self-imposed challenge to intellectual honesty coupled with the growing impact of the sanctions ensured that most of these reviews had little practical results. In fact, many of the earlier preparations to crush real and possible rebellions actually played into the strengths of a potential invader, all of which were identified in these Iraqi military studies.

As was so often the case in the 30 years of Ba'ath power, Saddam constantly influenced the planning process by providing guidance that bore little resemblance to the actual operational and combat conditions his troops would confront. A typical example of his military genius, which he was never reluctant to impart, came from a 1995 meeting between Saddam, his youngest son Qusay, and a group of senior officers:

> The principle of agglomeration is the ability to regroup within 10 to 20 days or a month even if we distribute the Republican Guard throughout Iraq. The principle of agglomeration is a very old one. It means dispersing our brigades and maintaining their ability to regroup into a whole. The Republican Guard is the reserve of the great commander [Saddam]. So we must not build it on one concept. If we build on one concept by distributing our troops as a way of managing some battles of a certain size and using certain methods of regrouping, and then face something else, we will be in a bad situation. For example what will happen if we build the Republican Guard's concept around the idea of national security [in other words against internal enemies] and then face air and land attacks from outside? We should build it around the concept of national security and include the possibility of outside and air attacks.[6]

While most of this guidance seemed contradictory to an outsider, the meaning was clear to Saddam's politically attuned generals: priority one was crushing internal revolts. After making sure that the planning process had distributed forces to put down any rebellion, then and only then were army commanders to consider what to do against external invaders. With this mantra constantly reinforced by thousands of smaller decisions, military planners undertook steps to stop a future American invasion.

According to the senior generals and operational plans captured by Coalition forces, Iraq's defense gradually evolved from a conventional defense-in-depth in 1995 and toward a slightly more urban-centric defense concept until December 2002. The earlier defense plans relied primarily on conventional ground forces augmented by trained and untrained militias. They expected mobile air-defense systems, surface-to-surface missiles, and a reliable national command and control system to be available to support the ground forces.

The defense in-depth would begin with the border guards on the frontiers backed up by regular Iraqi Army units. Behind the regular Iraqi Army units would be the two corps of Republican Guards centered on Baghdad. Finally, any invader would have to confront that Special Republican Guard if he were foolish enough to try and enter the capital.

In the wake of the December 1998 Coalition bombing offensive, the Iraqis slightly adjusted their base plan and developed several contingencies. One was the development of a corps-level plan that aimed at mitigating the impact of air attacks. One such plan was completed in 2001, OPERATION HOLY CONQUEST: The Plan for Evacuation and Dispersal.[7] As the name implied, the plan called for the "near" and "distant" dispersal of forces and equipment. The formulation was based on the acceptance of Saddam's absolute belief that Iraq would only have to endure a Coalition air campaign while his international allies by diplomatic means forestalled a Coalition ground assault. After accepting Saddam's wisdom on this issue, military planners put the "lessons learned" of Kosovo and their own experiences to use.

The best way to survive an aerial assault is to disperse and hide. Unfortunately, it is the worst possible solution if one is also confronted with a massive ground assault. Thus, Iraqi forces were on the horns of a dilemma. If they remained in position, they would be attacked either from the air or else by the advancing Coalition ground forces. If they tried to move, they made themselves extremely vulnerable to patrolling Coalition aircraft, including attack helicopters.[8]

Saddam's security priorities were centered around internal threats (rebellions and coups), followed by regional threats (e.g., Iran), and finally external threats (the United States, Coalition forces). Despite Saddam declaring that a Coalition invasion was the least of the threats confronting the nation, his military planners continued refining plans for that possibility. A major change to the base plan after OPERATION DESERT FOX dealt with the problem of responding to a ground invasion supported by air power. The Commander of the II Republican Guard Corps described the major elements of this plan in the following terms:

> If the Americans came from the north, they would face I and V Regular Army Corps. Each of these corps was supported by a Republican Guard division formed behind it (The Adnan Division stood behind V Corps and the Nebuchadnezzar Division stood behind the I Corps).
>
> Upon an attack, the Adnan Division and remnants of the V Corps would conduct a fighting withdrawal back to and across

the Euphrates River, while the Nebuchadnezzar Division and remnants of the I Regular Army Corps would fall back behind the Tigris River. They would defend along strong defensive lines between Bayji to Al-Hadithah with a fallback line from Samarra to Al-Fallujah.

If the Americans attacked from the west (Jordan), I and II Regular Army Corps would defend along the Euphrates River, while the III Regular Army Corps was to form a strong defense around point K160.[9] I Regular Army Corps would establish a strong defensive line from Al-Hadithah to Ar-Ramadi. II Regular Army Corps would deploy from Ar-Ramadi to Karbala. II Regular Army Corps would be in front of my command, II Republican Guard Corps, which would stand behind them for support

If the Americans attacked from the south, III Regular Army Corps could defend from Basara to Nasiriyah, IV Regular Army Corps from As-Samawah to Al-Amarah. II Republican Guard Corps would defend from Karbala to An-Najaf to As-Samawah and I Republican Guard Corps from Ar-Ramadi to Karbala.[10]

To command and control these forces during a conflict, Saddam carried out a reorganization of military boundaries, focusing on maintaining political control rather than military efficiency. He divided Iraq into four regional commands, each representing a new ad-hoc organization, to ensure the regime's internal control over critical sections of Iraq in the event that Coalition air attacks disrupted communications with Baghdad.[11] Because this change was foremost an arrangement for continued political control, Saddam appointed a close and trusted confidant to command each region:

- Southern region: Ali Hasan Al-Majid (Chemical Ali), Saddam's cousin and member of the Revolutionary Command Council.

- Northern region: Izzat Ibrahim Al-Duri, Saddam's deputy prime minister.

- Middle Euphrates region: Mizban Khatar Hadi, a member of the Revolutionary Command Council.

- Baghdad (central) region: Saddam's son Qusay.[12]

None of these men had any significant experience maneuvering ground forces in combat, a weakness that would have huge consequences for the Iraqi armed forces.

Only four days before the Coalition's invasion, Saddam finalized details for this new regional command structure after making minor adjustments in boundaries and personnel during a meeting of national leadership.[13] According to the Revolutionary Command Council decree of 15 March 2003, Saddam ordered the regional commands to carry out the following orders:

> Engage in defense within the confines of the concerned terri-
> tory and lead and utilize all of the state's material and human
> resources, including party organizations, the people, and mili-
> tary troops to confront any external aggression targeted against
> Iraq's sovereignty, independence, and security, and protect
> internal security.[14]

Perhaps aware of their lack of military experience, the regional command-ers did not make many changes to the basic defense plans already established for their regions. Some, however, took their new responsibilities seriously. For example, at a meeting in October 2002 in Kirkuk attended by Izzat Ibrahim Al-Duri, the Northern Region's Ba'ath leader designee, the Minister of Defense, the Army Chief of Staff, and the commanders of the I and V Regular Army corps met to review the basic plans. The group conducted sand-table exercises to test the existing plans against various Coalition scenarios.

The assembled commanders had sensed a chance to use these "trusted" men as a conduit to funnel some of their professional military advice to Saddam and accordingly recommended some changes to the plans approved by Saddam.[15] It is uncertain if their advice actually went up the chain of command or what effect it had. Time was running out, and they were soon to discover that Sad-dam was already enthralled with an entirely new plan.

For the Iraqi military, the dangers of trying to repel an invasion using the command and control arrangements originally intended to maintain internal control became obvious early in the campaign. According to the Minister of Defense, the new arrangement dramatically reduced the quality of battlefield reporting and leadership situational awareness. With the regional commands now directly under Ba'athist control, Baghdad received its reports on the course of military operations along the Euphrates River from politicians and not professional military officers. In addition, the arrangement effectively cut key military leaders and their staffs out of the chain of command. As the Minister of Defense noted after the war:

> During the war, the role of the Minister of Defense was compli-
> cated in that there were four subordinate regional heads who
> had independent authority and control over military forces in
> their areas. My deputy collected information and reports from
> these regional commands to form a picture of the unfolding
> operational situation. I effectively became an assistant to Qu-
> say—only collecting and passing information.[16]

One could best summarize planning and preparations prior to December 18, 2002, as pessimistic pragmatism. Commanders focused their limited re-sources on local training, preparing survivable combat positions, and making every effort to survive the impending conflict. They knew their forces did not have any optimum solutions for stopping a Coalition invasion, but they were certain they had developed the best one possible, given the conditions they were forced to work with.

But on December 18, Saddam once again asserted his priorities for self-preservation, putting into place his own operational concept that would have hastened the destruction of the Iraqi armed forces. How the generals reacted is discussed in the following section.

The Operational Concept After 18 December 2002

On December 18, 2002, the Chief of Staff of the Republican Guard gathered his commanders together and announced a new concept for the nation's defense. It was both original and bold in conception—and totally impractical. The new plan centered on the defense of Baghdad, which was the focus of all military efforts, and hardly a surprising development in a country where the leader considered his survival as the paramount interest of the state.

In a post-war interview, the Commander, II Republican Guard Corps, reported how the news of the new plan was reported and received:

> On 18 December 2002, the Republican Guard Chief of Staff called all the commanders (Republican Guard Corps, division, and air defense commanders) to meet at the Republican Guard Command Center.[17] When I asked why, I was told that they had a new plan for the defense of Baghdad. I thought to myself that we were supposed to be defending all of Iraq, not just Baghdad. When we got there, we found that Qusay Hussein was also present.

> The Republican Guard Chief of Staff briefed in front of a large wall map that covered just the central portion of Iraq. The map showed Baghdad in the center with four rings. Every ring had a color. The center ring was red. Approximately ten kilometers out from the red ring was a blue ring. Then approximately seven kilometers out from that one was a black ring. Finally, the last circle was marked in yellow which was designated for reconnaissance forces only. The Republican Guard Chief of Staff explained the plan in a very crude and ugly way.

> Things like "the Republican Guard Hammurabi Division defends in the north of the city, the Republican Guard Medina Division in the south, the Republican Guard Al Nida Division in the east, and special forces and the Special Republican Guard

in the west."[18] When the Americans arrived at the first ring and, on order from Saddam, the forces would conduct a simultaneous withdrawal. The units would then repeat this "procedure" until reaching the red circle. Once in the red circle, the remaining units would fight to the death.

With this incredible simplicity and stupidity, the assembled Republican Guard officers were told that this was the plan for the defense of our country.

Qusay said that the plan was already approved by Saddam and "it was you who would now make it work." I disagreed and told Qusay that a proud Army with an 82-year history cannot fight like this. We were not using our experience. I was told by Qusay that there would be no changes because Saddam had signed the plan already.[19]

Suddenly imposing an entirely new concept without debate where it could receive serious consideration from professional officers was typical modus operandi of Saddam. It was hardly surprising that the new plan suffered from a number of weaknesses, not the least being devoid of a realistic understanding of the coming war with the Coalition, as it seemed to many in the room. Compared to previous concepts and plans that had been drawn up by a professional military staff, this new plan represented an amateurish attempt to cobble together a defense. It also failed to pay the slightest attention to basic military major factors such as geography: in Saddam's eyes, the rivers, swamps, and canals simply did not exist. Worse, the new plan did not take into account how units could all simultaneously retreat from one ring to the next while being engaged on the ground and simultaneously assaulted from the air.

Several officers gently voiced their concerns during the meeting. Taking the lead, the Commander of the II Republican Guard Corps pointed out that the Iraqis did not yet know the nature of the coming Coalition attack, and that concentrating forces around the cities and in the face of Coalition air power would not help matters.[20] Other senior military officers offered their own criticisms of the plan, among them:

- The failure to account for the terrain around Baghdad (specifically, rivers and bridges).

- The optimistic assessment of the combat power and training of the Iraqi forces.

- The conviction that such a "simple" plan would pose few difficulties in terms of command and control.

- Finally, the expectation that the Coalition would wear itself out prior to arriving at Baghdad.

These plans would call for a high degree of coordination and synchronization between units that security restrictions (both real and perceived) made impossible. Add this reluctance to coordinate activities among themselves, under the inevitable stress of combat against a massive Coalition attack, it is difficult to imagine Iraqi commanders being able to orchestrate anything this complicated. None of these concerns convinced Qusay or the Republican Guard Chief of Staff, General Sayf al-Din al-Rawi, so no one ever addressed them in a serious fashion after the meeting broke up.

The lack of coordination or deliberate planning prior to the new plan's announcement suggests in many ways how disconnected the regime leadership had become from the real world. It is still hard to discover exactly the origin of such a radical departure from established operational plan or how the new approach became official policy. Detailed discussions and long-winded debates over the optimal use of Iraq's conventional military had become commonplace after 1991. The idea of an "urban-centric" offense had appeared at several high-level meetings such as described in this 1995 description by Izzat Ibrahim Al Duri (a long-time member of the Revolutionary Command Council, and future Commander of the Northern Regional during OPERATION IRAQI FREEDOM):

> The first rule is adherence to the cities, which would require that our units be somehow close to the cities in order not to allow the enemy to attack or affect them. We deduce from this two things: First, to protect our units and...to control the cities and impose in them security and order. Second, it means the Republican Guard...should not get out and carry out maneuvers on a large scale so that they would be the target of an attack.[21]

Of course, the movement of army units close to or within key cities would also better position them to take part in a coup. Al-Duri understood this risk and advised against early implementation of any city defense plans. He also emphasized the need to keep those units that did move closer to cities isolated from any possible coup influences.

> Forces located so near population centers are always possible to be subjected to security penetration. For this reason of security, it is important that the leadership make sure the Guard is inaccessible and under control. They must not mix with the locals or even be allowed to receive any visits from [either] an administrative official nor a Party official.[22]

It is possible that the idea for the "ring defense" of Baghdad had always been part of Saddam's operational concept for the nation's defense, but for security reasons he did not want to implement it until absolutely necessary.

According to another Iraqi general, the basic tactical concept of a "ring defense" was a standard element in Iraqi doctrine. The general noted,

The 5th Div planned to face Kurdish forces as their primary adversary. The defense plan that called for the exact location of these defensive circles was dependent on the enemy axis of advance. When the war started, we abandoned all defensive lines except the innermost red line, which collapsed after two days of bombing. The doctrine of four concentric circle defensive lines is standard doctrine taught at the Iraqi Army Staff School. The original doctrine comes from Sandhurst military academy, in the United Kingdom."[23]

Whatever its origins, it still was mainly just an idea and far from being a true military plan that would have required much more detailed study and preparation. According to the Minister of Defense, the plan was delivered to the military without any guidance on how to implement it:

The month before the plan was agreed to and delivered, there was a meeting to discuss a general plan for the defense of Iraq with the Chief of Staff, the operations officer, and the planning directorate office. The plan we had relied on for years was not accepted. But the only agreement between the office of the president and the military staffs that came out of this meeting was a general idea that the cities had to be defended. The cities then became the critical things to defend and the military was withdrawn into the cities to protect them. This was on the instruction from the president. There was an attempt to complete a plan to defend these cities because the military understood things like how to create defensive obstacles. There were a number of tasks to complete to ensure the city defenses, but there was no agreement as to what they were or how to get them done.[24]

Even after Qusay and the Republican Guard Chief of Staff had briefed the final operational concept in December 2002, the senior military leadership failed to achieve any agreement on how to implement the plan. According to Ali Hassan Al-Majid ("Chemical Ali"), who was present at the some of these discussions:

Military planners met five more times before the war but only tried to coordinate strategic defensive plans in one of the meetings following the December 2002 meeting. They met again in February 2003 and discussed defensive measures to use against the US and Coalition forces, but nothing was resolved or agreed to.[25]

There is little reason to doubt that to Saddam the mere issuing of a decree was sufficient to make the plan work. For him the Iraqi army required neither coordination nor further planning to make his conception effective.

Notes

1   Captured document, "Saddam's Letter/Speech Written on 29th March 2003 to his Generals and People.

2   Captured document (2002) "Al-Husayn Brigade Military Plans.

3   "Perspectives II Republican Guard Corps."

4   For example, a captured document disclosed a group of senior Republican Guard officers (including the future Republican Guard Chief of Staff during OPERATION IRAQI FREEDOM) participated in an series of extensive staff studies between April 1991 and August 1995 on the conduct of DESERT STORM (8 January 1995, "Iraqi Study on the 1991 Gulf War in Kuwait"). Public sources reported that after 1991, the Iraqi War College focused on lessons on how to create an indigenous psychological operations capability (to counter the United States) and how to defend against precision weapons by using the urban environment.

5   The number and variety of documents and tapes relating to the various Iraqi after action reviews of the events of 1991 are extensive. A representative sample includes the following: • captured audio tape, (1 May 1991) "Saddam Meeting with High-Ranking Officials Evaluating Iraqi Military Performance in the 1991 War"; • captured media file, (15 March 1992) "Meeting of High-Ranking Military Officials Supervised by Minster of Defense Regarding Lessons of the 1991 War"; • captured media file, (15 May 1992) "Seminar Held by Al-Bakir University for Military Studies on the Strategic Role of the Um Al-Ma'arik Battle"; • captured document, (30 August 1993) "Chief of the Seventh Section and Chief of the First Section Correspondence Regarding Desire for a Study About the Role of Air Forces in the Gulf War 1991"; • captured video tape, (20 November 1995) "Military Scientific Conference by Air Force and Armored Forces Command on Um Al-Ma'arik Battle." Finally, some of the "lessons" were turned into training vignettes, for example, captured document, (5 September 2002) "Military Training Manual Based on Lessons from the Al-Khafji Battle."

6   Captured media file, (8 October 1995) "Saddam Hussein Meeting with Qusay and Leaders of the H-J Operation Regarding Republican Guard Movements."

7   Captured document, (9 September 2001) "Republican Guard Plan Report Entitled 'Operation Holy Conquest: Evacuation and Dispersal.'"

8   This is the same dilemma Iraq faced in the 1991 war. US Department of Defense, Conduct of the Persian Gulf War: Final Report to Congress, April 1992, p. 197.

9   On a 1:500,000 scale map, the general pointed to a location approximately halfway between the Jordanian border and the city of Ar Ramadi.

10 "Perspectives II Republican Guard Corps," pp. 7–8.

11 Project interview of Ali Hasan Al-Majid ("Chemical Ali"), 10 November 2003. According to "Chemical Ali," "the basic plan for defense was established in 1998. Around the time of "DESERT FOX," the four regions and the plans were understood. [I]t did not change much since then."

12 Captured document, "Iraqi Strategic Defense Plan of the Four Regional Commands." In addition, according to various open source media reports, the commands were active from 16 December 1998 and suspended on 25 June 2000.

13 Classified Intelligence Report, December 2003.

14 Foreign Broadcast Information Service, (15 March 2003) "Iraq RCC Decree Forms Four 'Commands of Regions' in Case of War," Baghdad Iraqi Satellite Channel Television, translated from Arabic, 2000 GMT.

[15] Project interview of Kamal Mustafa Abdullah Sultan Al-Tikriti, Secretary of the Republican Guard and Special Republican Guard, 14 November 2003.

[16] Project interview of Sultan Hashim Ahmad Al-Jabburi Al-Tai, Minister of Defense, 13 November 2003.

[17] The Republican Guard Chief of Staff during OPERATION IRAQI FREEDOM was Lieutenant General Sayf Al-Din Al-Rawi.

[18] "Perspectives II Republican Guard Corps." Lieutenant General Raad Majid Rashid Al-Hamdani provided a sketch of the defensive plan from this briefing to the authors of this study, which was very similar to one obtained by Coalition forces in February 2003.

[19] "Perspectives II Republican Guard Corps."

[20] "Perspectives II Republican Guard Corps," pp.7–8.

[21] Captured media file, (5 November 1995) "Saddam and Senior Leaders Discuss the Republican Guard."

[22] Captured media file, (5 November 1995) "Saddam and Senior Leaders Discuss the Republican Guard."

[23] Classified Intelligence Report, March 2004.

[24] Project interview of Sultan Hashim Ahmad Al-Jabburi Al-Tai, Minister of Defense, 13 November 2003.

[25] Project interview of Ali Hasan Al-Majid ("Chemical Ali"), 10 November 2003.

V. The Regime Prepares for War

Cover of Iraq's July 2002 Military Magazine[1]

Early Muslims were trained for warfare, the Believers fought with their faith, therefore, faith was the basics; skill established on faith is ideal. — Saddam Hussein[2]

V. THE REGIME PREPARES FOR WAR

America might be the most powerful but it is not the strongest country because strength is given by God. When the enemy is more advanced in communication technology, it is better to use a simple, basic, and natural communication technology like camels. It is necessary to learn horseback riding. Get 10 horses and train 50 people or more per day. The important thing is to prevent the enemy from getting to its goals. No peace without strength.

— Saddam Hussein, 9 March 2003[3]

Iraq found itself once again in the crosshairs of America's military and diplomatic power following the collapse of the Taliban regime in Afghanistan in late 2001. As the United States and Britain steadily turned up the diplomatic pressure, Saddam also confronted stepped-up Coalition air strikes, which could easily have sparked another Shi'a uprising, as well as new resolutions from the United Nations. Additionally, Iraq's Intelligence Service, reporting from Iraqi embassies in Jordan, Turkey, Qatar, Yugoslavia, Russia, and other countries, warned Saddam of the Coalition's increasing deployment of military forces to the region.[4] In response, Saddam marshaled his diplomatic, economic, military, and propaganda organizations to deter, or failing that, to minimize the consequences of an attack from a US led coalition.

The Diplomatic Campaign

An unstated premise of most diplomatic communications is that one party is capable of delivering a message that the other party clearly understands. In this regard, Iraqi diplomacy *vis-à-vis* the United States failed right from the start. However, developing an understanding of Iraq's diplomatic maneuvering prior to the war requires the observer to recognize the constraints Iraqi diplomats faced when trying to deal with the United States. In describing Iraq's failed attempts at direct communication with the three successive American administrations, Tariq Aziz explained,

We didn't have any opportunity to talk to a US official during Bush, Clinton, or the new Bush administration, so there was no opportunity to talk face-to-face and address matters of concern. They always rejected us...We knew that the Poles had a representative in Baghdad who looked after the interests of America; secretly, not in the open. But no, we didn't go through them. Sometimes we talked to the Algerians about it, but not much. The Iraqi Intelligence Service tried in its own way to work the issue...they tried to pretend they were doing something to move relations along, but no one took them seriously; they were incapable of the simplest of tasks.[5]

Unable to engage the United States, Iraq turned to the one consistently effective diplomatic lever that it possessed—oil. As United Nations sanctions wore on him, Saddam displayed less restraint in using oil as both a weapon and a tool. With prudent application, oil allowed the regime to buy considerable influence with nations that would be key players in any Western military coalition.[6] By leveraging their long-standing ties with Russia, and by using oil to influence France's support, and to a lesser extent China's, the Iraqis hoped to influence the UN Security Council and stymie American and British resolutions.[7]

In the run-up to war, Iraq's strategy was to use its oil reserves to gradually alleviate UN-imposed sanctions and eventually have them lifted.[8] This policy of gradualism had made some progress over the decade before the war; and by mid-2002, some in the regime were placing great stock in the influence of its "bought friends." Most external observers would agree that elements of Iraq's influence campaign did succeed in reducing the impact of sanctions, shifting much of the international debate away from Iraq's failure to comply with UN Security Council resolutions and to the humanitarian effects of non-compliance. In many ways, the Iraqis had succeeded in isolating the United States and the United Kingdom from the regional allies it had enjoyed in the Middle East during the 1991 Gulf War.

In the end, these efforts were not enough. The Iraqi regime's constant overplaying of its hand meant it could never muster enough international support to break completely free of the sanctions regime. Actions such as publicly supporting suicide bombers in the Israeli-Palestinian conflict and harassing UN weapons inspectors were enough to keep the Americans and some of its allies highly suspicious of Saddam's motives and intent. Iraq also had to face the fact that its erstwhile friends would defend it only so far. Ultimately, they calculated only their self-interest. As Tariq Aziz explained to an interviewer after the war:

> France and Russia did not help Iraq, they helped themselves
> ...We had attempted to win favor with the French and the Russians through the oil and other contracts, but our relationship with the French began to suffer after 1998, when the Iraqi government began charging a 10 percent cash surcharge on each oil-for-food contract. The French refused to do it; they ended up doing it through intermediaries. Their contracts would be made through Jordanian firms but filled by the French, and this was not as profitable as before. [Prime Minister Lionel] Jospin[9] told me in 1998 the profit [had] reached 400 million by then. After the surcharge went into effect, the French started making negative statements about Iraq. Jospin and [President Jacques] Chirac[10] made anti-Iraqi statements, and we began to reconsider our relationship. The French are dubious; they are Westerners...

Their opposition to lifting sanctions was in their national interest, just as their support for it was in their national interest prior to the war—they know that the post-sanctions contracts will go to US companies, and they will lose millions. Their opposition proves that their interest in lifting sanctions was not genuine. The French were defending their position, not defending Iraq... We both realized that France could not sacrifice its relationship with the United States to the extent that Russia did, although even Russia did not go too far. The Russian foreign minister was also careful not to displease the Americans. Russia continued to support us in the Security Council, but for the same reasons as the French. Iraq gave Russian companies huge contracts in irrigation, agriculture, electricity, machinery, cars and trucks. Before oil-for-food, some of it was paid in crude oil guarantees, which would be paid after sanctions were lifted. After oil-for-food, we paid them cash.[11]

Though diplomacy, often lubricated by substantial bribes, had been successful in the past, Saddam credited most of Iraq's past diplomatic success to its willingness to back up diplomacy with armed might.[12] Sensing that oil was not sufficient means to solve his problems, Saddam had to convince numerous competitors that Iraq was a powerful country and a potentially dangerous entity with which to tangle. Intentionally or not, Iraq's weapons of mass destruction (WMD) program became a crucial component of both Saddam's maneuvering to prevent war and its proximate cause.

The technical extent of Saddam's WMD capabilities is beyond the scope of this book and is covered in the report of the Iraqi Survey Group from September 2004.[13] But the tension created by the regime's steadfast refusal to "come clean" with regard to WMD shaped the actions and interactions of both sides leading up to war. Saddam walked a tight rope with WMD because as he often reminded his close advisors, they lived in a very dangerous global neighborhood where even the perception of weakness drew wolves. For him, there were real dividends to be gained by letting his enemies believe he possessed WMD, whether it was true or not. On the other hand, it was critical to his survival and his plans to end sanctions that the West, particularly the United States, be convinced that Iraq no longer possessed such weapons. He had placed himself into a diplomatic and propaganda Catch-22.

Saddam privately had commented that "the better part of war is deceiving."[14] When it came to WMD, Saddam was simultaneously attempting to deceive one audience that they were gone and another that Iraq still had them. Coming clean about WMD and using full compliance to escape from sanctions would have been his best course of action for the long run. Given the international situation, the growing concern over the humanitarian effects of sanctions, and the world's thirst for oil, it probably would have been difficult to impose new sanctions even if Saddam subsequently resurrected Iraq's WMD program. However, Saddam found it impossible to abandon the illusion that Iraq possessed weapons of mass destruction—especially since the illusion played so well in the Arab world. As Saddam boasted in an April 1990 conference with Yasser Arafat:

> Iraq has chemical weapons and successfully used them on the Iranians and Iraq won't think twice about striking Israel with chemical weapons; when you ask Israel, why would the Iraqis use chemical weapons against you? The answer is to restore Palestine for the Arabs and that is it!...Israel owns the atomic bomb, this is not a big deal.[15]

"Chemical Ali," who received his sobriquet for using chemical weapons on Kurdish civilians in 1987, was convinced Iraq no longer possessed WMD, but claims many within the ruling circle always believed they did. Even at the highest echelons of the regime, when it came to WMD there was always some element of doubt about the truth. According to Chemical Ali, Saddam was asked about having WMD during a meeting with members of the Revolutionary Command Council. He replied that Iraq did not have WMD, but flatly rejected a suggestion that the regime remove all doubts to the contrary. Saddam went on to explain that if Iraq made such a declaration, it would not only show Israel that Iraq did not have WMD but might actually encourage the Israelis to attack.[16]

For many months after the 2003 war, a number of senior Iraqi officials continued to believe it possible (though they adamantly insisted they possessed no direct knowledge) that Iraq still possessed a WMD capability hidden away somewhere. In addition to Saddam's purposeful ambiguity on the issue, coalition interviewers discovered three other mutually reinforcing ideas as to why this possibility might be true:

- Iraq possessed and used WMD in the past. Given the growing danger from Iran's emerging WMD program, Iraq would likely need them again.

- While none of the Iraqi officials admitted to personally knowing of WMD stockpiles, the idea that in a compartmentalized and secretive regime other military units or organizations might have WMD was plausible to them.

- Finally, and ironically, the public confidence of so many Western governments, especially based on CIA information, made at least one senior official believe the contention that Iraq possessed such weapons might be true.[17]

By late 2002, Saddam finally tilted towards pursuing policies designed to persuade the international community that Iraq was cooperating with the United

Nations Special Commission (UNSCOM) and that it was free of WMD programs. This small but significant move away from ambiguity also aimed at solidifying the promise of more substantial French and Russian efforts on Iraq's behalf. As 2002 drew to a close, the regime took active measures to counter anything that might be seen as supporting the Coalition's assertion that WMD still remained in Iraq. Saddam was insistent that "in order not to give President Bush any excuses to start a war," Iraq would give full access to UN Inspectors.[18] But by this point, after years of purposeful obfuscation, it was difficult to persuade anyone that Iraq was not once again being economical with the truth.

Ironically, it now appears that some actions resulting from this new policy of cooperation solidified the Coalition's strategic and operational case for war in the eyes of the many. In the decade prior to the 2003 war, the Western intelligence services had obtained many internal Iraqi communications, among them a 1996 memorandum from the Director of the Iraqi Intelligence Service directing all subordinates to "insure that there is no equipment, materials, research, studies, or books related to manufacturing of the prohibited weapons (chemical, biological, nuclear, and missiles) in your site."[19] When UN inspectors went to these research and storage locations, they inevitably discovered lingering evidence of programs relating to WMD.

So in 2002, when the United States intercepted a message between two Iraqi Republican Guard Corps commanders discussing removal of the words "nerve agents" wherever mentioned "in the wireless instructions," or when it learned of instructions to "search the area surrounding the headquarters camp and Al-Madinah battalion for any chemical agents, make sure the area is free of chemical containers, and write a report on it," US analysts viewed this information through the prism of a decade of prior deceit.[20] Western intelligence analysts would have no way of knowing their information this time indicated an attempt by the regime to ensure it was in compliance with UN resolutions.

This flurry of last-minute activity "to remove all traces of previous WMD programs" did not go unnoticed in the West. However, what was meant to prevent suspicion actually served only to heighten it. Military actions to remove lingering traces of weapons fielded in the past appeared to Western intelligence agencies as attempts to conceal current WMD assets or operations. For instance, the already mentioned Republican Guard order, or one like it, to remove the term "nerve gas" from radio instructions likely precipitated the signal intelligence intercept referenced in Secretary of State Colin Powell's 5 February statement:

> Just a few weeks ago we intercepted communications between two commanders in Iraq's [II] Republican Guard corps. One commander is going to be giving an instruction to the other. You will hear as this unfolds that what he wants to communicate to the other guy, he wants to make sure the other guy hears clearly to the point of repeating it so that it gets written down

and completely understood. Listen. Let's review a few selected items of this conversation. Two officers talking to each other on the radio want to make sure that nothing is misunderstood. 'Remove, remove. The expression, the expression, I got it.' 'Nerve agents, nerve agents.' 'Wherever it comes up.' 'Got it.' 'Wherever it comes up.' 'In the wireless instructions.' 'In the instructions.' 'Correction. No, in the wireless instructions' 'Wireless, I got it.' Why does he repeat it that way? Why is he so forceful in making sure this is understood? And why did he focus on wireless instructions? Because the senior officer is concerned that somebody might be listening. Well, somebody was. 'Nerve agents.' 'Stop talking about it.' 'They are listening to us. Don't give any evidence that we have these horrible agents.' But we know that they do and this kind of conversation confirms it.[21]

The constant focus by America and Britain on possible WMD in Iraq greatly heightened Saddam's concerns, which now verged on paranoia, over UN inspectors finding traces of WMD programs. He became convinced that because there were no WMDs were to be found in Iraq, the Americans or the Israelis were not beyond planting fake evidence. In several directives, he issued what amounted to all points bulletins for signs of United States or "Zionist" infiltration and planting of WMD "evidence." A warning memorandum from the Ba'ath Party Secretariat in January 2003 is typical:

> The evil American authority stepped up their [sic] accusation of Iraq hiding chemical agents or biological labs on moveable trucks and trailers or inside containers. The American authorities are planning on bringing such trucks and containers into Iraq across the Iraqi borders or the border of the self-ruled areas or smuggling areas to provide it to the weapon inspectors to be used against Iraq in order to launch their wicked invading against our precious country.[22]

The following procedures will be followed to prevent the evil American authority from achieving their purpose:

1. Perform detailed inspection on all trucks and containers entering the country through the borders using the super vision of the intelligence agencies not [already] working at the borders. Place more inspection points and provide them with all needed supplies.

2. Monitor all smuggling routes and increase patrolling areas and inform all organizational party and country agencies at areas [bordered by] self-ruled areas, Kuwaiti, and Jordanian borders, and cease the entrance of all trucks through main and side roads leading to the self-ruling

areas during the next few months.

3. National agencies that have open warehouses or containers, must inspect...contents to prevent any hostile act or accusation Iraq [is] storing forbidden agents at these locations.

Please, review and pass the information to all comrades responsible for security agencies in all provinces to take proper precautions.[23]

Similar directives provide a qualified explanation for the many examples of suspicious imagery, incriminating intercepts, and other reporting, but they fail to fully explain away every event. A December 15, 2002, memo from an undercover Iraqi Intelligence escort for the UN inspection team notes, "Inside Bader WMD inspection site, there are Russian and Turkish scientists. When we visited the site, they were forced to hide from inspectors' eyes. We request your guidance if International Atomic Energy Agency (IAEA) [should] confront our foreign scientists."[24] Even when viewed through the post-war lens, documentary evidence of messages are consistent with the Iraqi Survey Group's conclusion that Saddam was at least keeping a WMD program primed for a quick re-start the moment the UN Security Council lifted sanctions.

Countering Psychological Operations

Even as Iraq burnished its international image, it confronted a new set of internal problems. In the days before the 2003 invasion, the Coalition intensified its psychological operations (psyops) aimed at the regime, its military, and the general population. Saddam responded by having the party direct a new wave of pro-regime, pro-Ba'athist, pro-Arab, and increasingly pro-Islamic propaganda.[25] Such propaganda was already routine within Iraq. What was different this time was that the regime's message now had to contend with an increasing volume of messages delivered by the Coalition. The regime noticed with alarm that the focus of Coalition psyops campaign included not only traditional leaflets and broadcasts, but also new individually targeted messages directed at key military personnel.

Prior to the war, Coalition planners had considerable difficulty measuring the would-be effectiveness of the leaflet campaign. However, Iraqi sources have confirmed that at the national level this campaign caused tremendous concern.[26] The regime's security services went as far as establishing a special psychological operations committee for "collecting US air-dropped propaganda leaflets, to study the psychological results, to make recommendations, and destroy them when complete."[27] It was a priority task for local Ba'ath party leaders to keep the leaflets out of circulation.[28] One Iraqi noted soon after the start of OPERA-

TION IRAQI FREEDOM:

> Citizens of Iraq were forbidden to possess or pass along leaflets dropped around Iraq. Military and political representatives threaten to either imprison or kill anyone possessing any leaflets. Military and political representatives had orders to collect and burn all leaflets dropped. The government did not want the people to see the promises the US armed forces were offering the Iraqi soldiers and civilians.[29]

One of the almost Orwellian aspects of Iraq's attempts to get ahead of and counter Coalition psyops was government monitoring and initiation of rumors. In a society that tightly controlled information, rumors and conspiracy theories often fill the void. Many rumors had operational significance and the regime did its best to monitor and control them. Found among the files of the intelligence services were official "Rumor Forms" used to track the source, analysis, and effect of new rumors.[30] Some of the more colorful rumors tracked by the regime in late 2002 included an Iraqi scheme to mix anthrax-laced leaflets with the ones the Americans were distributing; Iraqis dressed as Americans killing Iraqi civilians for propaganda effect; Russia evacuating its citizens on the eve of war; and the families of high-ranking Ba'athists leaving the country.[31]

Logistical Preparations for War

Publicly and privately Saddam appeared confident that his diplomatic and propaganda campaign would limit the use of force by the United States to air strikes. Nevertheless, he still took steps to meet a Coalition ground assault. But war with a new Western Coalition loomed, his primary concern remained how any attack would once again exacerbate the threat of internal revolt, which would in turn make dealing with the Coalition all the more difficult. In a meeting held on the eve of OPERATION IRAQI FREEDOM Saddam told attendees to:

> ...ensure the people of Iraq were ready for the attack. Saddam also instructed the members of the Special Security Organization and Mukhabarat to "keep the internal situation under control," and that it was very important to "keep the people satisfied..." Saddam was concerned about internal unrest amongst the tribes before, during, or after an attack by the United States on Baghdad.[32]

As a further hedge against the possibility of a ground assault, the regime undertook massive logistical operations in preparation either for a ground war or to withstand a prolonged aerial assault. The following pre-war logistical guidance to the militia demonstrates that the regime expected any conflict with America to be prolonged:

> For the purpose of implementing an emergency plan and for precaution from the possible invasion and for the fact that our war is expected to be a long one with our American enemy and for the purpose of providing the movement with supplies, we emphasize...finishing storing fuel for a six-month supply, depending on available sources.[33]

A post-war interview with an Iraqi Regular Army colonel bore further evidence of the kind of war the regime expected. However, it also provided a clear indication of the kind of war even relatively senior army officers were hoping for, which was distinctly at odds with the regime's expectations.

> They told us to bring provisions in for a long war. Our commanders told us to expect an air attack, followed by a ground war. We reserved water. We planned to be immobilized by air attacks, so there would not be a lot of movement on the ground (avoiding the exposure of movement). We wanted the Americans to come quickly and finish the war rapidly...There was no plan other than setting aside provisions.[34]

In the months leading up to the war, and even during major combat operations, Saddam continued to stress the need to store provisions for a prolonged struggle. Ba'ath Party officials and military leaders were tasked to ensure the establishment of food, fuel, and ammunition caches in a variety of "safe places" (e.g. buried or in mosques, schools, churches). An Iraqi Army plan signed on March 14, 2003, provided an example of the deliberate nature and scope of the ammunition distribution plan. It presented a detailed ammunition priority list (beginning with 122mm munitions and ending with 14.5mm munitions) to be moved from the Al Najaf arsenal to more than 59 military schools and training areas around Iraq. Under this plan, the ammunition was to be pre-loaded on trucks no later than March 16 and the distribution completed by April 14, 2003.[35]

As with most Iraqi plans prior to OPERATION IRAQI FREEDOM, the actual execution under pressure was not without its problems. The commander of one of the schools on the aforementioned ammunition distribution list wrote on March 20:

> Referencing your letter number 64, dated March 20, 2003, concerning sending munitions to our school, we would like to explain the following:
>
> 1. The place that was assigned for your military munitions has been recently occupied by another military unit.
>
> 2. The ammunitions which you have sent to us so far, was put in bedrooms, halls, and in the training warehouse.
>
> 3. The school cannot receive any more munitions since the place is con-

stricted and old. Please do not send any munitions to our school in the future.[36]

After the war the Coalition collected and destroyed thousands of tons of these munitions, but enough escaped monitoring and detection to help fuel the insurgencies. Much of the post-war debate on the origin of the insurgencies has centered on whether the regime placed munitions around the country to support a future guerilla war against an external foe. At this point, there is no significant documentary evidence to support this contention. Rather, it is clear that the regime ordered the distribution of ammunition in order to preserve it and possibly fight a prolonged conventional war with Coalition forces. A prolonged conventional war forced the wide dispersal of ammunition away from logistical bases, primary targets for Coalition airpower. That these munitions were available to insurgents was fortuitous for them, but available documentation provides no evidence that dispersal was part of any pre-war master plan to support such actions.

War and the Oil Wells

Pre-war American intelligence and even media reporting contained many warnings that in the event of a Coalition attack, Saddam would immediately torch the country's oil infrastructure.[37] This concern rested on several assumptions, among them:

- Experience during the first Gulf War when the Iraqi army had torched hundreds of oil wells in Kuwait as it retreated.

- The practical advantage the military would gain by creating a physical barrier of burning wells to block Coalition movement and obscure targeting efforts.

- The widespread idea that Saddam was not beyond ordering a *Gotterdammerung* ("Twilight of the Gods") as he went down to his final defeat.

Captured Iraqi documents indicated that at a regional or even local level plans had been made to destroy the northern and southern oil fields, and that some preparations were underway at the end of 2002. Accounts of movements of critical equipment, the preparation of demolition charges, and military units moving into position before major combat operations commenced were numerous not only among Coalition commentators but among the Iraqis as well. However, Saddam, for a variety of reasons, was loath to embark on such a path.

> Al-Duri [RCC member and Northern Area commander] ordered planning for setting explosives on the oil infrastructure. Within 48 hours after the meeting ended, an order came to Al-Duri

from Saddam directing him not to do anything to damage or destroy the oilfields...Saddam felt that destroying the oil fields would affect the morale of the soldiers and the people. Saddam worried about history indicating that he had destroyed the wealth of Iraq.[38]

Other senior leaders confirmed that Saddam viewed oil as the primary source of wealth for the Iraqi people and that he specifically directed them not to destroy the oil fields.[39] In this case, Saddam was in agreement with President Bush who admonished the Iraqi leadership "not [to] destroy oil wells, a source of wealth that belongs to the Iraqi people."[40] As a practical matter, of course, Saddam saw no distinction between his own person and the Iraqi people.

The Ba'ath Party and Its Militia

Ba'ath party preparations focused on refining the various emergency plans developed during the 1990s.[41] These included organizing units to patrol for infiltrators, find deserters, locate insurgents, monitor inter-city travel, and counter any airborne assault by the Coalition.[42] The following captured document highlights examples of local Ba'ath party preparations:

Al-Zubair Bin Al-Awwam Branch Headquarters [Vicinity of Basra] – Implementation of Defense Methods over Villages

...[T]he branch headquarters, the nation's party headquarters and other groups have executed the procedures and actions as follows:

1. Discussions were completed with regard to the implementation of the defense methods over the villages in three consecutive meetings at branch headquarters.

2. [A] meeting was conducted on 26 December 2002 for tribal chiefs, family, and religious leaders to clarify resistance to American hostility and devilish intentions, and the role of every citizen to cause the retreat of the enemy and his shared involvement in the defense of the villages.

3. The nation's party and other group members held many public speeches throughout the area, to explain and clarify the objective of the defense methods for the villages and responsibility of each citizen.

4. Table layout was prepared for exercise purposes based on party groups; and committees were appointed for inspection. This was implemented among [the] main groups and the inspection procedures are still ongoing.

5. The party group headquarters completed tunnel construction in each quarter and village borders and main roads.

6. Protective shelters have been constructed on the main roads within the

people's and Party group's positions.

7. Tribes were united to perform the plan; the district and area leaders were distributed as follows:

   a. Force commander is the corps commander member, or the senior member working in respective cell.

   b. Assistant force commander will be the tribe chief or the religious leader or the respective public figure.

   c. One of the members will be part of the force command and at the same time a deputy commander.

   d. Member of the party group along with one citizen will be part of the force command.

8. Detachments were assembled in each district as follows:

   a. First aid detachment supported with women.

   b. Intelligence detachment supported with women.

   c. Drinking water supply detachment.

   d. Supply rations detachment transport food supplies to citizens.

   e. Cooking detachment for the fighters selected from the women.[43]

Other party leaders, however, were not always as focused on the possibility of a Coalition invasion. Ba'ath Party correspondence from the Diyala Governorate dated 19 March 2003 complains that the emergency plan budget does not contain enough funds for a new office building or the furniture to go in it. At the time this letter was written, Coalition forces were already crossing Iraq's borders.

Immediately prior to the start of hostilities, the Commander of the Middle Euphrates region sent his deputy to "inspect training on the emergency plan" in the southern zone of the region. The resulting report underlines the kind of bluff that eventually came to dominate actual combat reporting:

- The emergency plan training, which took place on 10 March, began with a meeting of all the commanders in the operations center where we revised all the plans and checked...the maps, it was good.

- A detailed field inspection of the local sand tables, the cooking facilities, the fighting trenches, the group prepared for fighting air drops. They were all good and ready.

- The raised spirits of the tribes is shown by all and the men all pronounce that they were good and ready to deal with any emergency.[44]

The inspecting officer noted that local authorities should give more attention to such things as night training, preparing for enemy airdrops, collecting and sending information "as fast as possible," and ensuring the command was ready to deal with "areas which are expected to have riots and troubles."[45] Finally, the report offered that the area should be presented as the regional example to be shared with other zones since "the people are dealing as if they belong to one big united family...the role of the local party supervisor and the esteemed governor is very obvious."[46]

Similar to much of the reporting up the chain of command, this account failed to reflect the true condition of local militia readiness or actual preparations. An extensive post-war interview with the retired head of Iraq's navy (and a military advisor to the Ba'ath regional leader in the Central Euphrates region of southern Iraq) better illuminated the reality of Ba'ath Party "preparations" in the months immediately preceding the Coalition assault:

> Around the first week of March 2003, the high command sent for me. I was told that the Minister of Defense appointed me to the [Central] Euphrates Region as the military advisor to Mizban Khudr Al-Hadi, the Commander of the [Central] Euphrates Region. This was one of the mistakes of the political leadership: taking a man with almost forty years of experience in the navy and assigning him to a non-military man to advise him on a ground campaign. I was assisted in this task by a Major General Kan'an from the military college.[47]

> Before the war began I arrived in the [Central] Euphrates Region and found that there were no significant preparations being made. The [Central] Euphrates Region is an area that's responsible for Karbala, Najaf, As-Samawa, and Ad-Diwaniyah.[48]

> In each area there is a party member who commanded the governorate of the individual city. These local party heads and the Al-Quds force answered to the regional governor, Mizban. Governor Mizban was the highest commander in the region, something like a corps commander. He told all his city governorates, 'you're like my division commanders.' All forces in the region were under his command—even the regular army forces answered to him. Each Ba'ath commander had full authority inside each city.[49] They controlled the police, party functions, the Al-Quds force, etc. They did not, however, control the Fedayeen Saddam, which was controlled by Uday Hussein, or the Republican Guard, which answered to Qusay Hussein. There was no interaction of any type among the different forces.

> In As-Samawa on 24 or 25 March, I met with the As-Samawa

Governorate Ba'ath leader Saif Al-Din Al-Mishadad, and his political assistant, Zaiki Faidhi, and asked them about the preparations for the defense of As-Samawa. They explained to me that they had divided the Ba'ath members into two branches: the As-Samawa Branch in the east part of the city and the Muthena Branch in the west. The As-Samawa Branch had an Al-Quds force division whose members were all from As-Samawa. I asked the assembled leadership for total numbers of fighters and what they gave me added up to 120,000 soldiers from the various tribes, police forces, military units, etc. This was the number before the start of the American bombing. I asked for a conference with the Ba'ath local leadership and each reviewed his situation. I asked for the numbers of deployed soldiers again. This time they said most of them were gone, but there were 30,000 loyal members who would fight. I took a map showing the Ba'ath and the three brigades of Al-Quds positions and set out on a personal inspection.

According to the leadership, the Ba'ath members were to fight inside the city and had built some sandbagged positions, while the Al-Quds Force was to remain outside. During my inspection I could not find even 10 percent of the 30,000 troops [that is 3,000] they told me were ready. When I asked where they were, I was told they were all locals and at that moment they were either at home or changing shifts—but I was assured that they would be right back. In the Al-Quds company-level fighting positions, where I should have found approximately 200 soldiers, there were not even 50 present. I did not complete my inspection because it was growing dark and due to security concerns from American bombers, etc., I couldn't use my lights to continue.[50]

Back at the Ba'ath headquarters in As-Samawa, I told the Ba'ath leadership about the scarcity of numbers I had seen, and they promised to fix the problem by morning. I was hopeful and thought that since most were civilians that they had matters to attend to during the evening and would be ready in the morning.[51]

On the morning of the 25th, I continued my inspection and the situation was even worse. The Ba'ath leadership was giving speeches like 'we'll punish them; we'll fix it all...' They called the tribal chiefs in As-Samawa to try and get more men, but the tribes said, 'We have no weapons, so how can we fight?'[52] I sensed we were losing control of the situation—and the American forces had not yet arrived; there were only air attacks. I told the regular Army Chief of Staff that if the Coalition comes, they'll invade the city without any resistance.[53]

Regular Army Preparations

Except for several regular army units attached to Qusay's Republican Guard Command after the 2003 war started, the Iraqis deployed the regular army mainly to repel an Iranian attack from the east and south and to contain the Kurds in the north. The Chief of Staff of the Armed Forces noted that there was a growing consensus in the general staff on the escalating Iranian threat.[54] When the army command turned to address the growing Coalition threat, local commanders complained that the divided focus on Iran and the possibility of a new Coalition assault was more than they could prepare for.[55] The army's command handled this by taking worries about the Coalition off their list of concerns; after all, Saddam was certain such an attack would not happen.

Units, such as the 11th Infantry Division, which was directly in the path of a Coalition invasion, never seriously progressed preparations beyond the point where they presented more than a minor challenge to the US Army's 3rd Infantry Division. According to the Chief of Staff of the Iraqi Armed Forces, the regime had hastily positioned many regular army units on the eve of war and never tied them into any coherent concept of maneuver or defense.

> Prior to February 2003, Iraq had no military forces in Umm Qasr and southern Rumaylah. Saddam ordered military units placed in southern Rumaylah and Umm Qasr in February to prepare a defense against US and Coalition forces attacking Iraq. The forces were placed there to guard the Iraqi port and petroleum resources. The 45th Infantry Brigade guarded Umm Qasr. The 704th Infantry Brigade guarded southern Rumaylah... There were no Republican Guard units in the southern sector... The 51st Mechanized Division was to protect the entrances to Basra by ways of Umm Qasr, Safwan, and southern Rumaylah, and to establish defensive lines around Basra. The 6th Armored Division was to protect the entrances of Al-Qurnah [and the] bridge in north Rumaylah near Al-Qurnah toward Basra and al Dayr, by establishing defensive lines. The 18th Infantry Division was tasked to defend the strategic city of Al-Qurnah. It was to prevent the enemy from occupying Basra, continue to communicate with the IV corps to the north, and prevent any enemies along the supply and communication routes.[56]

None of this hurried movement and preparation escaped Coalition attention, which made such hastily prepared defensive positions easy targets for Coalition firepower.

While a listing of Iraqi regular army units gives the impression of considerable military strength, in reality most of these units were in a state of poor readiness. Besides crippling morale and manning problems, the state of frontline equipment had deteriorated greatly in the decade since the 1991 Gulf War. The chronic effects of sanctions drastically affected the availability of spare parts. By the time the war started, only a fraction of Iraqi armor and artillery was still functioning.[57] Heroic attempts at smuggling spare parts into Iraq continued right through the onset of the war, but such efforts never came close to meeting the army's dire needs.[58] As the regular Army's II Corps Commander noted:

> Of the 250 tanks at the start of the war, about 220 were usable. About 130 to 145 tanks were in good shape, characterized as 75 to 80 percent operable. No tanks were in very good or excellent operating condition, characterized as 85 to 90 percent and 90 percent operable, respectively; the balance of tanks were between 50 and 75 percent operable. No night vision capability or any other modifications had been made to any II Corps tanks. No new tanks could be purchased after 1991. Spare parts were hard to get, so repairs were made with whatever parts could be found. Furthermore, tanks were not sheltered from the elements, contributing to their degradation. The tank force was never as good after 1991 as it was before.[59]

Overtasked, poorly equipped, badly supplied, and undermanned, regular army troops had little optimism in facing the threat of combat with the Coalition. Still, some elements of Iraq's military attempted to conduct serious planning activities even if they simply went through the motions in the end. These nascent plans provide critical insights into how Iraqi military leaders interpreted their strategic guidance and subsequently developed their underlying planning assumptions.

Providing a window into Iraqi regular army preparations were a series of staff planning documents exchanged between the Minister of Defense, the Office of the Chief of Staff of the Army and the Headquarters for the Regular Army. One document from late January 2003 details the planning concept for the defense of Basra.[60] The concept, as articulated, was a logical extension of the urban-centric defense plan briefed by the Republican Guard Chief of Staff in Baghdad. The overriding assumption was that if the Coalition attacked along either the Tigris or Euphrates from Kuwait, its ground forces would expose their flanks to Iraqi forces attacking from cities all the way to Baghdad.

Apparently, Iraqi army planners never seriously considered the possibility of an American attack that would isolate and bypass the southern cities.

- They thought the Coalition military forces would be loathe to leave strong pockets of armed resistance along their 400-mile supply line.

- They had no true appreciation of American logistical capabilities and did not believe it was possible to sustain an attack to Baghdad without opening up the all the major roads that ran through major southern cities.

- Most had bought into a general belief that even if the Coalition did launch a ground assault, its forces would stop after liberating southern Iraq and not push on to Baghdad.

Additionally, there was a good portion of wishful thinking throughout the officer corps. Senior Army leaders remained convinced that Iraqis were superior warriors when compared to the Americans. All their soldiers needed was a chance to prove their mettle in combat where the conditions would nullify the Coalition's technological superiority. Some believed that urban battles might enable a confrontation to be fought on their own terms. The perception that Americans were averse to close combat made some confident that if they could not defeat them, they could at least bloody any American units that dared to enter the cities. During the course of OPERATION IRAQI FREEDOM, Ba'athist reporting from the south supported the planner's hopes for a series of slow urban fights. This "confirmation" of a key planning assumption made it almost impossible to entertain notions that Coalition forces would be doing the opposite.

Specific plans to defend the cities followed the regime's dictates that operations should inflict the "greatest possible losses on the enemy from the first moment of exposure" and "assure the city is held for the longest period of time possible."[61] Both of these fit neatly within Saddam's tenets that the Americans would not continue if they sustained heavy losses. Most of Saddam's inner circle believed that time was on their side.

Defending Basra

Basra is the largest city in southern Iraq and the Iraqis planned that it would be a key Coalition objective. By studying the Iraqi concept for the defense of Basra, it is possible to extrapolate how the Iraqi army planned to defend the other cities along the Euphrates and Tigris rivers.

Forces available for the defense of Basra included conventional military formations of the Regular Army's III and IV Corps, elements of the small Iraqi Navy, the local Al Quds militia, members of the General Military Intelligence directorate, and Fedayeen Saddam formations.[62] The military concepts employed for the defense represented the traditional military doctrine of a defense-in-depth, anchored on fixed strong points throughout the sector. The defensive scheme included the use of fixed obstacles, delaying and resisting units, reinforced by tanks and armored personnel carriers, defensive minefields, a mechanized "corps strike-force," artillery kill-sacks, and a series of prepared fall-back positions. Like all local city commanders, the Basra commanders were ordered to stockpile a minimum of 60 days of supplies and munitions. These orders emphasized the need to hide and protect such stockpiles "to sustain units in the event of their isolation."[63]

The written plan for the defense for Basra reflected both the intellectual predilection of an officer corps determined to sit on the defensive, and in some cases, their naiveté in believing that their plans contained a realistic depiction of either the Iraqi or the Coalition force. The local authorities in Basra sent excerpts of the plan for defending the city to Saddam for approval:

> The chief objective of the defense consists in forcing the enemy to be exposed, to... delay [him], and to...inflict...the largest possible losses, by driving [him] into kill zones, and paving the way to launch a mortal blow against him, based on completion of a fundamental reorganization of the defense. To achieve this objective, it is necessary to distribute the units within the defensive position from the frontline to the rear depth in the following manner:
>
> First. Units for protecting and observing the defensive minefields—composed of fixed patrols [with] strong cover and concealment; occupy fortified defensive positions and locations, with the necessity of insuring secure passages for them within the fields to perpetuate their movement.
>
> Second. Resistance and hindering forces take the form of autonomous, self-sufficient infantry companies, reinforced with a variety of anti-tank and anti-aircraft weapons. It may be that a suitable composition will appear as follows:
>
> (1) An infantry company.
>
> (2) A platoon organized with guided anti-tank weapons.
>
> (3) Anti-aircraft weapons (57mm-caliber guns/shoulder-carried rocket launchers).
>
> (4) Tanks and armored personnel carriers.
>
> (5) A network of compatible and redundant communications.
>
> (6) Transformation of these units, as to the manner of the way they fight, into the defense through attrition, by distributing them into small groups assigned to observe the enemy and take advantage of opportunities to divert and delay him during hours of darkness, in addition to transmitting information.
>
> (7) As appropriate, composition of headquarters mobilized to

command these forces, in accordance with exposure of their frontlines.

Third. Blocking and surrounding forces, reinforced with a variety of anti-tank weapons, opening up behind the protective minefields, in the form of a corps battle group or fighting groups hidden in secured and concealed positions and capable of firing on their targets, by exiting from their hiding positions to firing positions (with the body concealed). These units will be able to conduct their fighting in earnest and, with the assistance of the impeding minefields, drive the enemy into kill zones, which have been chosen and prepared in advance.

Fourth. A main strike force, which takes the form of a corps battle group of prevailing armor distributed in refuges to hide its mission of launching the strike against the forces of the enemy, after they have been driven into kill zones by the blocking and surrounding units. Here it is certainly to assure that these opening units at the front possess the capability of avoiding the effects of the enemy air forces, by reinforcing the line with field air defense weapons.

Fifth. An opening line of artillery, including both principal and alternate sites of medium and heavy artillery, distributed in the form of batteries in accordance with their being positioned for the benefit of facilitating the concentration of fire...with the assurance that the sites of these batteries will be protected and capable of defense from all directions an island of resistance), and noting the designation of a section its resources for resisting the enemy's tanks by using appropriate barrage.

Sixth. Special administrative zones for the initial advances for the purpose of filling deficits in the supplies for supplying the fighting of the artillery units. Here it behooves us to assure the protection of them from any possible hostile land or air threats.

Seventh. A variety of units to confront the invasion and the enemy air assault, composed of elements of reconnaissance, reinforced by mechanized infantry and appropriate anti-tank and anti-aircraft weapons.

Eighth. It is necessary to cover each part of the defensive position with a network of observation posts equipped with compatible and redundant communications working with each unit from the front to the depth of the rear.

Ninth. It behooves us to put in place a detailed and researched plan for the distribution of consolidated, monitoring radars in the areas of our opening units.

Tenth. It is assumed that groups of Fedayeen, will work in front of the lead artillery units, under the command of the general directorate of military intelligence, which has previously conducted research into their composition and methodology, the study of which has been forward to your Excellency.[64]

Besides the requirement to plan and prepare for a possible Coalition attack, Saddam tasked local commanders and party leadership to "deal with all the situations that may occur such as outside aggression from countries or adjacent governates, acts of sabotage, internal rioting, or any other action that requires decisive action or fighting...For all until death to defend Iraq and its Revolution, Party, and the President."[65] This direction created a command emphasis on securing critical facilities, specifically the homes of Ba'ath officials, as well as controlling the roads and bridges between the governorates (so a revolt in one area did not spill over into adjacent areas). Once again, concerns about the internal situation were clearly impeding preparations to meet a Coalition invasion.

To ensure that those involved in the defense were fully committed to carrying out their duty, the plan concluded with a typical effort to motivate by threat.

Fighters from specified forces in the plan will not retreat, whether in yards, streets, or headquarters, for any reason, except by a written and clear order from the emergency force command...severe punishment by way of summary execution will be carried out immediately following insubordination in front of the fighters.[66]

On 23 February, the Army's Chief of Staff issued the results of a planning directorate meeting on the possible course an American invasion might take and the steps necessary to meet such an eventuality.[67] For the first time, the regime informed Iraqi forces in the south to prepare to engage in offensive operations. The new orders included:

First: Executing operations against the enemy during their assembly which was ordered by the central decree in accordance with direction from the President, Commander in Chief of the Armed Forces. The aims of the operations are to make trouble for and to intimidate the enemy during their assembly and also during the beginning of the attack on our troops.

Second: Form small Fedayeen commando fighting groups from special forces, deep reconnaissance and commando companies equipped with weapons and suitably prepared. The duties of these groups are to inflict maximum damage to the enemy defensive lines, positions, and helicopters.[68]

Yet, as is the case with many Iraqi military documents, the Chief of Staff's missive was long on ideas and short on the specifics required to implement the plan. Moreover, with only weeks left before the Coalition assault, it was too late to imbue the Iraqi army with a renewed offensive spirit. Besides presenting a rich target set for Coalition aircraft, any Iraqi attack into Kuwait would have run directly into the massed firepower of American and British armored units.

In the end, such plans seemed designed to show activity and confidence rather than actual defensive preparation. The 'hope that the invasion wouldn't happen' was a common thread in planning and preparation efforts undertaken by the Iraqi regular army in the days immediately prior to the war.[69] Given the nature of the regime, it was understandable that many planning staffs produced documents that were focused on the rhetorical at the expense of the practical.

Republican Guard Preparations

As indicated in the previous chapter, Saddam and Qusay provided the Republican Guard corps and division commanders with a shell of a defense plan on 18 December—the ring plan. One of the division commanders present at a later planning meeting claimed that the commanders who were expected to put the ring plan into effect were not allowed to have actual copies of the plan, but could only make notes.[70]

Saddam's new plan called into question 12 years of previous military planning and the underlying operational assumptions. In the absence of clear implementing instructions, Saddam and Qusay counted on the Republican Guard commanders to display considerable initiative to make the plan work.[71] Unfortuantely, initiative was not a trait valued or even encouraged among Republican Guard officers. In effect, serious planning for the defense of Iraq simply ceased in the months before the invasion. The Republican Guard II Corps commander later commented to interviewers:

In January 2003, during the resumption of United Nations in-spections, the Republican Guard commanders kept wondering which plan we were supposed to be preparing. Very little was being passed to us from the Republican Guard Chief of Staff. I kept asking him, 'Which plan?' and he kept putting me off by issuing confusing or partial answers. I spoke to my counterpart in the I Republican Guard Corps and asked him to try and get some clarity from the Republican Guard Chief of Staff. He was unable to help. By late February and into early March 2003, we watched the military build-up in Kuwait and Turkey, and the mobilization of forces in the United States on the news. We still had no clear guidance from Republican Guard headquarters. So I started meeting with my commanders and staff officers to plan for the coming war. I included in these meetings the security officials (Special Security Organization, Directorate of Military Intelligence, etc.) assigned to my headquarters, because I did not want there to be any suspicions in Baghdad as to my purpose. There was already a kind of "cloud" around me.[72]

From mid-February we started preparing extensive defensive positions. We made preparations and in some cases spread out forces away from their garrison locations. Most of this movement was from 15 February to approximately 1 March 2003. I recall that we prepared over 7,000 armored vehicle fighting positions during this time.[73] We moved tons of ammunition, changed the storage locations, and extensively camouflaged our fuel and ammunition stocks. I gave guidance to the commanders to save their ammunition for helicopters and not to engage fixed-wing aircraft, [because] we expected an extensive air campaign by the Coalition. I also instructed them to begin making extensive reconnaissance from North to South in front of their positions.[74]

Sometime in mid- to late-February 2003, I met with Qusay and the Republican Guard Chief of Staff because the Special Security Organization Chief had reported on my staff meetings and said that I was deploying my forces without authority. I was able to convince them of my honest intentions.[75]

On about 1 March, I ordered all remaining II Republican Guard Corps units to deploy out of garrison locations. The Republican Guard Chief of Staff called and told me I was deploying forces too early. I replied that I was personally responsible as a commander for over 70,000 men, 1,000 vehicles, and hundreds of cannons. How could I wait while the Coalition has the capability to strike? I told the Republican Guard Chief of Staff that as commander I was responsible for my decisions, and we ended the conversation without conclusion.[76]

About three days before the war, approximately 16 March, but I cannot be sure, I met with the Republican Guard Chief of Staff. He and his staff were reviewing news on the Internet, and all the news was very bad.[77] I was upset and told him that it was immoral that I was a corps commander and yet he had not told me anything about what was happening. He did not even notify me when units moved from the I Republican Guard Corps. We were close to war and there were no planning meetings![78]

For example, an order was issued by the Republican Guard staff for the Republican Guard's Adnan Division to move from Mosul to the area of Bayji-Tikrit about a week prior to the war. Additionally, there was the order for the Republican Guard's Nebuchadnezzar Infantry Division to move from the area of Kirkuk to an area northeast of Tikrit also about a week prior to the war. I was never told of these moves beforehand and they had an impact on my planning for the II Republican Guard Corps.[79]

I had strong confidence in everyone around me including staff officers, commanders, leaders, and soldiers. We tried to beat time, imagining the war and working out the specifics of how it would go. We set up realistic training programs and broad operational agendas to make the preparations. I had set 15 February 2003 as the drop-dead time for completing all of these actions. We finished deploying all of the corps' troops starting from that date, and on my personal responsibility. Many, especially political and security officials, asked about the source of this conduct since one tank moving outside its barracks is considered a crime in the Republican Guard. I attributed all of this activity to myself in light of our analysis of the political and military situation. The strange thing was that no planning meetings were held. No meetings to investigate the political and military positions and to analyze them were conducted. It was as though the war was not about to start. Where were the intelligence assessments to supply us with the information we needed? Most of what was available was superficial.[80]

Despite the fact that my suggestions to the commanders, leaders, and soldiers in every one of my meetings did stray from the essence of the national political and media dialog, I tried to approach the images of reality one way or another even for the lowest ranking warriors. There were priorities that I set in directing operations at the end of February, like so:

I. Finish the necessary preparations for combat and make sure they are well-set all the way down to the rank of private. Pay constant attention to cover and concealment.

II. Do not use the alternate locations unless the primary locations have been exposed to enemy bombardment.

III. Send reconnaissance patrols and open observation posts. Establish ambushes with air defense weapons.

IV. Rely on wired communications and runners and prohibit the use of radio communications except in battle.

V. Specify the operations in the artillery field, and specify locations for mobile artillery.

VI. Direct freedom of action to deal with emergency situations if the enemy surprises us with deep-penetration patrols, and notifying higher headquarters of any developments in the situation.[81]

The Secretary of the Republican Guard painted a similarly bleak picture of preparations prior to the invasion:

The Republican Guard did not perform any special training to defend Baghdad. Republican Guard units only had their typical individual and small unit training. There was never a war game of the defense of Baghdad because Saddam Hussein thought there would be a fight away from Baghdad and closer to the borders. In anticipation of the war, units were ordered to dig in and reinforce their defensive positions. They were issued enough ammunition, food, fuel, and supplies for one month. Soldiers were paid three months' salary.[82]

Besides issuing his simplistic ring plan, Saddam's supervision of the planning process appears to have been minimal. His participation was limited to giving his commanders inspirational speeches that bore no relationship to the gathering storm. On 30 December 2002, he spoke to his senior military leaders in the following fashion:

We do not want this war, but if it is forced on us, we will force America to her knees. We will destroy her armies on the border of the desert, and if God wishes, the great evil force will fail before the forces of righteousness, no matter how small. If America [had] crumbled before the former Soviet Union, people would have said that a superpower had triumphed over a superpower, and there is nothing amazing about that. I am confident in our victory and that America will be made to kneel if she comes with her army, because God does not have any army left to fight for his cause other than the army of Iraq.[83]

With Saddam's optimistic predictions ringing in their ears, the Iraqi regime and its military forces prepared to confront the armed forces of the Coalition. The attitude of those around was summed up when the President's Secretary, Abid-Hamid, announced to the assembled officers before they met with Saddam, "My brothers, the President is tired of the way things are. Do not mention any problems, concentrate on the positive."[84] Even General Hamdani, the plan's most vocal critic up until that point, went silent.

Final Events Prior to 19 March

As military and paramilitary preparations continued into March, the prospect of a diplomatic "win" for the regime ebbed. Despite Iraq's commitment to renewed inspections, new declarations and documentation, and the destruction of Al-Samoud missiles, Saddam's international "allies" had not been able to halt the massive build-up of Coalition forces. Nevertheless, even though President Vladimir Putin had ordered the evacuation of Russian citizens from Iraq, the Russian ambassador assured Iraqi officials that:

> Russia, together with France and Germany, and expectedly joined by Syria and China, had prepared a resolution responding to the American-British resolution presented to the Security Council. Also, he stated that voting on the two resolutions was scheduled for March 9. The ambassador, also, indicated that a number of the Security Council's countries, including Pakistan, Chile, and Kenya are expected to refrain from voting.[85]

These developments gave Saddam hope that the international community could dissuade the Coalition from attacking. In mid-March 2003, Saddam held a meeting with intelligence service officials. A post-war account of the meeting shows that Saddam seemed sure he could avert war, even at this late date:[86]

> A few weeks before the attacks Saddam still thought that the United States would not use ground forces; he thought that you would only use your air force...Of course he was aware [of the build-up of forces in the region], it was all over the television screen. He thought [the Americans] would not fight a ground war, because it would be too costly to the Americans. He was over-confident. He was clever, but his calculations were poor. It wasn't that he wasn't receiving the information; it was right there on television, but he didn't understand international relations perfectly.[87]

In the end, Saddam finally understood that the Coalition assault was only days or hours away and he took decisive measures to protect what mattered to him most—his position. In a discussion with the head of the Central Bank of

Iraq and other senior leaders about ten months before the Coalition invasion, Saddam expressed concern that if a war started, the Central Bank would be bombed and all the country's hard currency would be destroyed.[88] In order to secure the cash, Saddam ordered what was essentially a raid on the Central Bank of Iraq:

> On or about March 19, 2003, Saddam arranged a meeting be-tween the presidential secretary, Qusay, and the finance minister ... Saddam ordered the withdrawal of one and a quarter billion dollars and euros...The money was taken in approximately 300 metal cases. Each metal case held 3 to 4 million in [U.S. dollars] and euros for a total amount of approximately one billion and 30 million. The gold was left behind at the Central Bank of Iraq because gold is gold, even if it burns down. Saddam agreed to leave it at the Central Bank of Iraq. The amount of gold at the Central Bank of Iraq was 4.5 tons in brick form. Saddam was waiting at the main presidential palace for money because it was taking all night, and he was expecting the [Americans] to begin attacking Iraq.[89]

It is clear that even as he led Iraq into military defeat, Saddam prepared for the internal security aftermath of the coming battle. One lesson from 1991 was while the use of force was still the stock and trade of this regime, cash was an increasingly effective form of ammunition to either confront or motivate the tribes.

Notes

[1]   Captured document, (July 2002) "Military Magazine."

[2]   Captured document, (9 March 2003) "Saddam's Speech to IIS Directors."

[3]   Captured document, (9 March 2003) "Saddam's Speech to IIS Directors."

[4]   Project interview of Zuhayr Talib Abd al-Satar Al-Naquib, Director of Military Intelligence, 16 Nov 2003.

[5]   Classified Intelligence Report, May 2003.

[6]   As noted by Tariq Aziz, the Iraqis often overstated the degree to which their influence campaign had any tangible effects. In several cases they adjusted the targets of their campaign in order to get more impact (See captured document, (5 February 2002) "Memo from the Assistant of Intelligence Service for Operations, 4th Directorate, to Director of the IIS regarding French-Iraqi Relations.").

[7]   Classified Intelligence Report, June 2004. It should be noted that none of the contracts were executed "...Iraq concluded a contract with a Russian oil company to exploit the Majnoon oil field in southern Iraq. However, the Russian company could not raise the required capital (20—30 billion USD) to execute the contract. In response to the failure of the Russian company, Iraq approached China and France and offered them a contract. The company involved was probably the Total oil company. France agreed to the contract in principle, but with the stipulation that it would not be executed until sanctions were lifted. Negotiations with China were still on-going when the Iraqi regime fell."

[8]   Classified Intelligence Report, June 2004. Additionally, for an extensive and authoritative description of the Oil-for-Influence program see also Strategic Intent section, Vol. 1 of the "Comprehensive Report of the Special Advisor to the DCI on Iraq's WMD" (CIA, 30 September 2004).

[9]   Lionel Jospin was the French Prime Minister from 1997–2002.

[10] Jacques Chirac has been the President of France since 1995.

[11] Classified Intelligence Report, May 2003.

[12] For more information on the way Saddam's regime attempted to influence foreign politicians and officials through the issuance of oil allocations under the U.N. Oil-for-Food Program, please see the United States Senate Permanent Subcommittee on Investigations, Committee on Homeland Security and Governmental Affairs, Report on Oil Allocations Granted to the Russian Presidential Council, Report on Oil Allocations Granted to Vladimir Zhirinovsky, and Report on Oil Allocations Granted to Charles Pasqua & George Galloway, May 17, 2005.

[13] See Strategic Intent section, Vol. 1 of the "Comprehensive Report of the Special Advisor to the DCI on Iraq's WMD" (CIA, 30 September 2004).

[14] Strategic Intent section, Vol. 1 of the "Comprehensive Report of the Special Advisor to the DCI on Iraq's WMD" (CIA, 30 September 2004) p.34.

[15] The Palestinian Liberation Organization leader, Yasser Arafat, then replied: "Israel has 240 nuclear warheads for Arab countries, 12 nuclear warheads for every Arab country, [but] these things won't threat[en] Arab security." Captured video tape, (19 April 1990) "Video Containing a Recorded Meeting that took place among President Saddam Hussein, the Iraqi Cabinet, President Yasser Arafat, and the Palestinian Delegation."

[16] Classified Intelligence Report, March 2004. Also project interview of Ali Hasan al-Majid, 10 November 2003. Chemical Ali believes there were no WMD in Iraq and the entire issue with Saddam and WMD was to scare neighboring countries.

[17] Classified Intelligence Report, June 2004.

[18] "Perspectives II Republican Guard Corps."

[19] Captured document, (2 July 1996) "IIS Memorandum 945/712: Secret Instructions When International Inspection Teams Check Sites."

[20] Captured document, (25 November 2002) Republican Guard Intelligence Command Log Book.

[21] United States Secretary of State Colin Powell, Statement in the Security Council on Iraq, 5 February 2003.

[22] Captured Iraqi document, (11 January 2003) "Ba'ath party Memo Number 460." Additional examples include document, (1 Dec 2002) "Memo from Ali Libi Hajil to All Party Commands," which states "It's mandatory to assign the party unit in the west side to be on the look-out and detect any infiltration attempts or reconnaissance planes flying over the restricted area and notify the authorities about any attempts by the Zionist foe or the American enemy to bury any proscribed material and then accuse Iraq with it. Please review and pass it on to all party organizations and give the matter great urgency and importance." Another memorandum, (27 Dec 2002) "Memo To All Party Commands Regarding Outsiders Planting Sanctioned Materials in Iraq" notes, "take precautions from the enemy implanting material prohibited according to U.S. sanctions which could lead to a justifiable attack against Iraq and please take all precaution in protecting all borders, especially Iran and Kuwait borders, and to watch for any movement and not give the enemy a chance."

[23] Captured Iraqi document, (11 January 2003) "Ba'ath party Memo Number 460."

[24] Captured document, (15 December 2002) "UN Inspection Visit."

[25] Captured document, (Jan—Mar 2003) "Meeting Minutes: Hussein Military Branch Command, Sinhareeb Division." A good example can be found in the 13 January 2003 directive to substitute in all instances of the phrase "American strike" with the phrase "American aggression."

[26] In the next chapter we will see the effect they had on the morale of the Iraqi soldiers.

[27] Captured document, (8 March 2003) "Correspondence Between Air Force Command and the Office of the Commander Regarding Orders for Psychological Operations Units."

[28] "Perspectives Assistant Senior Military Advisor."

[29] Classified Intelligence Report, March 2003.

[30] For example, the official Ba'ath Party "Rumor Form" had such data categories as type, source, setting, analysis, response, and official opinion. Captured document, (15 December 2002) "Correspondences and Circulations of Ba'ath Party, Fallujah Branch Including Emergency Plans."

[31] Captured document, (11 March 2003) "Information Letter from the Iraq Military Intelligence Directorate about Anthrax; Leaflets; American Forces Impersonation, and Oil Barrel Trenches."

[32] Classified Intelligence Report, 21 April 2003.

[33] Captured document, (December 2002) "Memo From Iraqi Secretary of State Office to Commanders in Charge of All Parties Organizations Regarding Emergency Plans."

[34] Joint Forces Command interview of COL Jamal Altaaey, Iraqi prisoner of war, Camp Bucca, 10 July 2003 .

[35] Captured document, (16 March 2003) "Memorandum from Army Chief of Staff: Subject—Mov-

ing Munitions."

[36] Captured document, (21 March 2003), "Memorandum from Commander, Combat School of the 1st Corps to BUI Arsenal."

[37] For example see MEMRI Iraq News Wire—No. 14, 6 March 2003. See also Gregory Hooker, Shaping the Plan for Operation Iraqi Freedom: The Role of Military Assessments, (Washington Institute for Near East Policy, 2005), p. 79.

[38] Project interview of Kamal Mustafa Abdullah Sultan Al-Tikriti, Secretary of the Republican Guard and Special Republican Guard, 14 Nov 2003.

[39] Project interview of Zuhayr Talib Abd Al-Satar Al-Naquib, Director of Military Intelligence, 16 Nov 2003.

[40] Address by the President of the United States to the Nation, 17 March 2003.

[41] Captured document, (19 March 2003) "Correspondence Among High Level Officials Regarding the Amount of Money Needed for Emergency Plans for the Various Governates."

[42] Captured document, (December 2002) "Ba'ath Military Branch Memorandum—Emergency Plan B."

[43] Captured document, (Date undetermined, but after 26 December 2002) "Ba'ath Implementation of Local Defense Plans."

[44] Captured Document, (17 March 2003) "A Report on the Emergency Plan Training of Al-Muthanna Governate."

[45] Captured Document, (17 March 2003) "A Report on the Emergency Plan Training of Al-Muthanna Governate."

[46] Captured Document, (17 March 2003) "A Report on the Emergency Plan Training of Al-Muthanna Governate."

[47] "Perspectives Assistant Senior Military Advisor."

[48] "Perspectives Assistant Senior Military Advisor."

[49] Taha used the full name for the Ba'ath party which was the Arab Ba'ath Socialist Party or the initials ABSP.

[50] "Perspectives Assistant Senior Military Advisor." Based on other documents and examining the Coalition timeline it is possible that the actual dates for this inspection tour should be at least a week earlier. See captured document, (17 March 2003) "Report on Emergency Plan Training of Al-Muthanna Governate." Also project interview of LTG Kenan Mansour Khalil Al-Obadi, Senior Military Advisor to RCC Member Mizban Khudr Al-Hadi, 30 Nov, 2003.

[51] "Perspectives Assistant Senior Military Advisor."

[52] As-Samawa is in the predominantly Shiite area of Southern Iraq and tribal loyalties to the regime have been suspect since the 1991 uprising in the area.

[53] "Perspectives Assistant Senior Military Advisor." The Iraqi Army Chief of Staff was LTG Ibrahim Ahmad Abd Al-Sattar Muhammad Al-Tikriti.

[54] Project interview of Zuhayr Talib Abd Al-Satar Al-Naquib, Director of Military Intelligence, 16 Nov 2003.

[55] Project interview of Major General Hamid Isma'aeli Dawish Al-R'baei, Director General of Republican Guard General Staff, 18 Nov 2003.

[56] Project interview of Zuhayr Talib Abd al Satar Al Naquib, Director of Military Intelligence, 16 Nov 2003, and project interview of Ali Hasan Al-Majid (Chemical Ali), 10 Nov 2003.

[57] Note: This was not as true of the Republican Guard formations, which had first call on available spare parts.

[58] For example, see captured document, (6 March 2003) "Contract for the Tank Engines and Spare Parts." The MIC was facilitating a $5 million shipment of spares for T22 and T55 tanks as well as BMP-1 fighting vehicles from a Bulgarian firm through a Syrian corporation and family across the Syrian border.

[59] Project interview of Raad Hamdani, Commander II Republican Guard Corps, 10 Nov 2003.

[60] Captured document, (20 February 2003) "Report by the Office of the Chief of Staff of the Army on Iraq Battle Plan."

[61] Captured document, (20 February 2003) "Report by the Office of the Chief of Staff of the Army on Iraq Battle Plans."

[62] The general officers interviewed for this project all denied any direct knowledge of the Fedayeen Saddam to include the integration of Fedayeen forces into conventional planning. The planning document referred to in this section identified Fedayeen and other unspecified "commando" forces operating both "inside and outside" and being used to "strike the enemy's rear and his assembly areas and his means of communications." Captured document, (20 February 2003) "Report by the Office of the Chief of Staff of the Army on Iraq Battle Plans."

[63] Captured document, (20 February 2003) "Report by the Office of the Chief of Staff of the Army on Iraq Battle Plans."

[64] While there appears to be a disconnect between what most of the Regular Army and Republican Guard officers interviewed for this project stated about conventional force and Fedayeen Saddam integration and what documents like this one imply, the difference is more linguistic than real. When translated, the word Fedayeen can be "one who sacrifices." But this term is also used in reference to "commando" or "special forces" in general as opposed to the very specific organization known as Fedayeen Saddam. See captured document, (20 Feb 2003) "Report by the Office of the Chief of Staff of the Army on Iraq Battle Plans."

[65] Captured document, (2003) "Emergency Plan for Al-Basrah Governate."

[66] Captured document, (2003) "Emergency Plan for Al-Basrah Governate."

[67] Captured document, (8 March 2003) "Top Secret Letter of Army Chief of Staff # 2195 dated 23 February 2003."

[68] Captured document, (8 March 2003) "Top Secret letter of Army Chief of Staff # 2195 dated 23 February 2003."

[69] Captured document, (8 March 2003) "Top Secret letter of Army Chief of Staff # 2195 dated 23 February 2003."

[70] Interview of Salih Ibrahim Hammadi Al-Salamani, Commander, Baghdad Republican Guard Division, 10 Nov 2003.

[71] Captured military planning documents in the period before the 2003 war indicate a military staff planning and orders process that routinely produced very detailed logistics, command and control, medical, and security annexes for even minor military operations.

[72] "Perspectives II Republican Guard Corps." Numerous senior leaders discussed the danger of meetings outside the visibility of the senior leadership.

[73] According to the Al-Nida Division's chief of staff there were four positions dug for the more than 500 armored vehicles in the Al-Nida. This does not include complete dummy brigade

positions 5-10 km away from the actual locations. Project interview of Al-Nida Division Chief of Staff, 28 Nov 2003.

[74] "Perspectives II Republican Guard Corps."

[75] "Perspectives II Republican Guard Corps."

[76] "Perspectives II Republican Guard Corps."

[77] Numerous senior Iraqi leaders have indicated in interviews that open source information (Internet) about the disposition and intent of the Coalition was a primary source of information.

[78] "Perspectives II Republican Guard Corps."

[79] "Perspectives II Republican Guard Corps."

[80] Unpublished draft memoirs of LTG Raad Hamdani, Commander II Republican Guard Corps.

[81] Unpublished draft memoirs of LTG Raad Hamdani, Commander II Republican Guard Corps.

[82] Interview of Kamal Mustafa Abdullah Sultan Al-Tikriti, 14 Nov. 2003.

[83] Unpublished draft memoirs of LTG Raad Hamdani, Commander II Republican Guard Corps.

[84] Unpublished draft memoirs of LTG Raad Hamdani, Commander II Republican Guard Corps.

[85] Captured document, (Date unclear—probably first week of March 2003) "Russian Report on American Troop Dispositions in the Gulf." References place the document date sometime during the first week of March 2003.

[86] Classified Intelligence Report, June 2003.

[87] Classified Intelligence Report, May 2003.

[88] Classified Intelligence Report, June 2003.

[89] Classified Intelligence Report, May 2003.

VI. DOOMED EXECUTION

Soldiers of the Special Republican Guard - 2002[1]

There are conflicting reports and no one can confirm the veracity of the US story that US forces have made a breach in one of the combat points...The Iraqi Information Minister said that these reports are part of a confused method and a military strategy that seeks to create a propaganda clamor.
—Al-Jazirah reporter[2]

VI. DOOMED EXECUTION

> Everyone in whose body the Hulegu's intent and action has settled down—will commit suicide at the walls of Baghdad and Iraq towns, as was the case with those who died at the walls of Jenin and Palestinian towns.
>
> — Saddam Hussein, 13 January 2003[3]

Reconstructing the events of the final days of Saddam's regime remains and likely will remain a challenge. From the Iraqi government viewpoint, the war was a series of events that it could never get ahead of and rarely comprehended. In the midst of an increasingly chaotic situation, both the regime and its military institutions lost control. Moreover, Saddam's peculiar leadership style, the operational concept employed by the Coalition, and the rapid collapse of major Iraqi forces all tend to obscure contemporary analysis of the war from an Iraqi perspective. The difficulty in building a precise picture lies in the fact that though individual sources were well placed by position and background to describe events, they rarely possessed a complete view of the battle.[4] The final Iraqi military collapse came so fast that no one on Iraqi command side could grasp a complete picture.

Nevertheless, based on numerous post-war interviews with the Iraqi commanders and the recovery of hundreds of thousands of contemporaneous documents, an outline of events that is plausibly accurate is coming into view. While the incomplete nature of this evidence should temper the finality of judgments, one must remember that much has already been written and many judgments have been made about the war without the benefit of any Iraqi perspective at all.

Though several key Iraqi commanders were interviewed for this book, this account of the operations centers on the interviews of a few key officers, well-placed to view many key events, and relatively perceptive and honest with interviewers. The most impressive of these interviewees was one of the few truly competent officers Saddam tolerated near the top ranks of the regime, Lieutenant General Hamdani, who served during the war as Commander of the Republican Guard II Corps. Hamdani provided considerable insights into the efforts of the Republican Guard II Corps to defend such areas as the Karbala Gap and the nature of Iraqi military plans and preparations.

Hamdani's views on the conduct of the defense of the Karbala Gap suggested that an adversary not hampered by the restrictions imposed by Saddam could have posed serious difficulties to a modern attacking force. Hamdani himself had had a long and distinguished career in the Iraqi Army, possessing extensive combat experience beginning as a platoon commander during the 1973 Yom Kippur War, in which the Iraqi forces were sent to reinforce the Syrians at the end of that conflict. More recently, he served in the front lines for much of the Iran-Iraq War as a battalion commander and was a brigade commander during DESERT STORM.[5]

His long war service in front-line units identified him as both a competent officer and an individual Saddam could trust. Given the regime's paranoia, military competence was no guarantee of advancement or even survival. What protected General Hamdani from a fate that befell some of the military leaders from the Iran-Iraq War was the fact that Saddam's sons, Qusay and Uday, as well as Tariq Aziz's son, served in his battalion during the war with Iran.[6] In a regime where social connections sometimes counted for more than competence, the relationship the general established with those three individuals undoubtedly helped to propel him to the top of the Republican Guard and protected him from Saddam identifying him as a danger to the Ba'ath regime.

General Hamdani was particularly well placed during the OPERATION IRAQI FREEDOM to present an account of the Iraqi view of the war.[7] His Republican Guard II Corps was responsible for defending the southeastern approaches to Baghdad along which both the US 3rd Infantry Division and the 1st Marine Division advanced. In short, he commanded the Iraqi troops facing the American main effort and supporting ground attacks.

As stated earlier, the Iraqi military commanders charged with their nation's defense found themselves hamstrung by a number of interrelated factors. Quite simply, Saddam trusted no one with the possible exception of his sons. Thus, Iraqi commanders were not able to make the necessary preparations and deployments to meet a Coalition ground invasion. Moreover, Saddam's fear of a coup continued to make it impossible for even corps commanders to do any significant collaborative planning.[8] The final effect of such distrust made it impossible to create coherent plans above the corps level for Iraq's defense.

It is worth re-stating the handicaps that hobbled Iraqi generals even within the purview of their individual commands. Incessant spying, suspicion, and interference by often militarily incompetent superiors—political and military—was a constant psychological stress as well as a serious impediment to making military preparations. Saddam's threat calculations, as well as the inability and/or unwillingness of most of his subordinates to provide accurate information, exacerbated the planning difficulties throughout the system. A combination of mutually exclusive political assumptions and a national security system where truth was in short supply conspired to make adequate preparations for war virtually impossible—especially a war that Saddam repeatedly announced would not happen. Finally, there was the negative impact of the change in war plans on December 18, 2002. Barely three months before the onset of hostilities, Hamdani and his colleagues found themselves saddled with an unworkable and unrealistic plan for the defense of central Iraq and Baghdad—a plan that Saddam had drawn up at the last moment without regard to military realities and apparently without the advice of any of his more competent senior military commanders.[9]

The Coalition Psychological Campaign—Effects of Precision Weapons

From the Iraqi perspective, it appeared, as in 1991, that any Coalition attack would begin with lengthy air operations.[10] Saddam, it seems, believed that air attacks would be the primary military means the Coalition would utilize against Iraq. Most of his senior military officers still using the template of the Gulf War believed Coalition efforts would open with a sustained air campaign possibly followed weeks later by ground operations.[11] It was a shock to many of them when the Coalition offensive began with a simultaneous air and ground attack, coupled with a comprehensive psychological operations campaign aimed at undermining the willingness of Iraqi soldiers to fight. It is likely that at the time, Coalition planners underappreciated the psychological effects precision firepower had on Iraqi combat units. Lieutenant General Majid Husayn Ali Ibrahim Al-Dulaymi, Commander of the Republican Guard I Corps, told interviewers after the war, "Our units were unable to execute anything due to worries induced by psychological warfare. They were fearful of modern war, pin-point war in all climates and in all weather."[12]

The general then added that psychological operations were "the bullet that hits the heart before hitting the body.... When it hits, it makes a fearful man; he walks without a brain. Even the lowest soldier knew we couldn't stop the Americans."[13] Besides the normal tools of a psychological campaign such as leaflets and radio broadcasts, the general emphasized the impact of precision weapons on the psychology of Iraqi soldiers. He himself received a severe shock during a visit to the Adnan Republican Guard Division shortly after a series of precision air attacks had obliterated one of its battalions that moved in the open. In his words, "The level of precision of those attacks put real fear into the soldiers of the rest of the division. The Americans were able to induce fear throughout the army by using precision air power."[14]

The story of the Al-Nida Division, which as we have seen earlier was the best-equipped division in the Iraqi military, underlines the devastating psychological effects of Coalition airpower. Considering that the Al-Nida Division was never really engaged in the ground fighting during the course of the war, what happened to it suggests that psychological operations, integrated with precision fire, created a generalized dread of seemingly inevitable destruction; this combination quite literally broke the will of many Iraqi units subjected to it. In the eyes of the average Iraqi soldier, Iraq's inability to stop the United States from "flying 8,000 miles to drop its trash (pamphlets)" on them proved the regime's military impotence. The fact that the Coalition seemed to know exactly where to drop the "trash" made every soldier in the Republican Guard feel as if they were in "a sniper's sight." Witnessing the effects of precision weapons that devastated exposed positions did not help already poor morale.[15] The Al-Nida commander offered the following opinion on the psychological effects of Coalition air attacks on his troops:

The air attacks were the most effective message. The soldiers who did see the leaflets and then saw the air attacks knew the leaflets were true. They believed the message after that, if they were still alive. Overall they had a terrible effect on us. I started the war with 13,000 soldiers. By the time we had orders to pull back to Baghdad, I had less than 2,000; by the time we were in position in Baghdad, I had less than 1,000. Every day the desertions increased. We had no engagements with American forces. When my division pulled back across the Diyala Bridge, of the more than 500 armored vehicles assigned to me before the war, I was able to get fifty or so across the bridge. Most were destroyed or abandoned on the east side of the Diyala River.[16]

In effect, precise airpower and the fear it engendered made an entire division of the Republican Guard combat ineffective. In this case it was not so much destroyed as dissolved. For the average Iraqi soldier the Americans appeared to be blowing up every hole that they could find. It must have been an unnerving realization when each of them realized they were hiding in a hole.

The Air Campaign

Regime High-Value Targets

The opening salvo of "The Defining Battle" was an American air strike on Saddam's suspected location. Although the attack missed Saddam, it did confuse him about US intentions. According to Saddam's personal secretary, the first US missiles hit a Baghdad residence called "Dora Farm." While Saddam's wife and daughters had at times used this residence, Saddam himself had reportedly not set foot on Dora Farm since 1995. The morning of the opening attack, at approximately 0330 Baghdad time, Saddam and his bodyguards went to his personal secretary's house. It was an attempt to try and discover what had happened and determine if this were the start of the impending Coalition offensive. After gathering what information they could, Saddam and his personal secretary relocated to a safe house in the Al-Mansur neighborhood in central Baghdad. Upon arriving in Al-Mansur, Saddam anxiously recorded a video message for the Iraqi people. Because they had no staff, Saddam wrote the speech in his own hand, which required him to appear for the first time on television wearing his oversized glasses.[17]

The attack on Dora Farm signaled the start of the Coalition air campaign and caused the Iraqi air defense command to immediately swing into action. Despite a profound inability to limit the ferocity of the Coalition air attacks it did demonstrate a determination to appear effective. Which to some extent was all that really mattered. As Saddam often reminded his officers, effort in the face of overwhelming force was the key to success. For instance, early in the war, the Commander of the 1st Air Defense Region, in a typically optimistic over-statement, reported that his forces had either "averted or downed" more than 130 enemy cruise missiles, helicopters, or fighter aircraft.[18] This report was not just the hopeful bluster of the combat uninitiated as evidenced by the tone of air defense reporting within hours of the final regime collapse. On 8 April, the day after American forces entered Baghdad to stay, a field report to the Minister of Defense from the Air Defense Command noted indignantly that "the enemy continues to violate the sanctity of our air space," and proceeded to describe success against enemy aircraft.[19] Memories of the reported execution of the air defense commander in the early days of DESERT STORM undoubtedly had an impact on the new commander's willingness to be entirely forthcoming.

Before the war, Iraqi leaders had every reason to expect they personally would become targets of any air campaign. If there were doubts about the Coalition's intent to decapitate the regime, the opening night attack on "the farm" dispelled them. To improve his chances of survival, Saddam added a final layer of security measures to his now-routine "coup-proofing." He and his inner circle attempted to counter precision attacks targeted at regime leadership by stepping up secrecy, varying the locations of meetings and stop-overs, instituting elaborate electronic signature reduction measures, and using "safe" sanctuaries. Combined, these measures generally proved successful against Coalition efforts to eliminate key regime personnel, although they also significantly degraded the regime's ability to maintain a clear awareness of or provide any relevant command and control to the battlefield.

Saddam's personal security included elaborate measures designed to keep his location and movements a secret from even close associates and advisors. The security services had worked out and rehearsed most of these arrangements prior to the start of the war. The inner circle's wartime communications network included only the most senior cabinet ministers and government officials. The security services assigned these ministers three low-ranking but trusted employees to provide a 24-hour alert team (8-hour shifts) at a central headquarters. During the war, when Saddam wished to meet with a minister, he sent a representative by car to inform the alert teams. These alert teams then traveled by car to the hidden location of the respective minister, informed him of Saddam's orders, and transported him to a secret link-up point. At the link-up point, a special Presidential Guard detail transported the minister to a new transfers point and from there a new detail took him to a presidential safe house. All presidential vehicles were equipped with black curtains to block the minister's view of the route of travel. As a final measure to prevent tracking devices, all cellular phones, watches, calculators, personal pens or pencils, and/or any battery-operated devices were prohibited at all meetings.[20]

In addition, the security services had designed the hide locations as sanctuaries, not bunkers. Bunkers took a major construction effort and attracted the attention of American intelligence sensors during their construction. In fact, not many bunkers remained unscathed by the end of the war. Designating a civilian-constructed building or residence as a sanctuary required no extra work that might be noticed by the ever-prying eyes. Throughout the war, Saddam moved between various safe-houses centered on the upscale district known as Al-Mansour. This area provided other targeting challenges beyond the problem of uncovering Saddam's hide-sites. By placing many of these hide-sites in heavily populated civilian districts or by being sure they shared a common wall with "protected" sites like foreign embassy property, religious sites, or medical treatment facilities, Saddam sought to create foolproof sanctuaries from Coalition air attacks.

Military Targets

Precision air attacks in the first days of the war may have failed to decapitate the regime, but they had a devastating effect on the Iraqi armed forces–even when they missed. The Commander of the Al-Nida Republican Guards Division, whose division dissolved from the psychological impact of the air attacks, commented to an interviewer after the war:

> The early air attacks hit only empty headquarters and barracks buildings. It did affect our communication switches which were still based in those buildings. We primarily used schools and hidden command centers in orchards for our headquarters—which were not hit. But the accuracy and lethality of those attacks left an indelible impression on those Iraqi soldiers who either observed them directly or saw the damage afterwards.[21]

For the most part, the brigades of the Al-Nida Republican Guard Division escaped attack during the first week of the war. But one air attack during this period did find and strike the 153rd Artillery Battalion, located in the 41st Brigade area. The battalion had dispersed itself in three distinct locations: it had hidden its artillery pieces in an orchard, the soldiers in a second hide position, and the ammunition in a third location. The division commander said he was shocked when "The air attack hit all three locations at the same time, and annihilated the artillery battalion."[22] Such experiences became commonplace as Coalition air power chewed up Iraqi ground forces that attracted the attention of satellites or other aerial reconnaissance.

During the course of the conflict's first week, the other two brigades of the Al-Nida escaped serious damage from air attack by remaining hidden in prepared positions. Nevertheless, at the beginning of the second week, Coalition air power found and hit both the 42nd and 43rd Brigades. The Al-Nida Division's commander noted the effect of these air attacks on his forces:

> In the 42nd Brigade sector, the troops were in their prepared positions and were hit very effectively for five days. The continuous nature of the attacks did not allow us to track the number

of losses. After the attacks many of the soldiers "escaped" [a euphemism for deserted]. By the end of the war more than 70 percent of the Al-Nida Republican Guard Division "escaped," [while at the conclusion of hostilities] between the air strikes and desertions only 1000-1500 soldiers remained out of more than 13,000.[23]

Matters were no better with the division's 43rd Brigade. This brigade started the war with three mechanized battalions and one tank battalion. But after one particularly heavy air strike, virtually all of the troops abandoned their positions and ran away. By the time the brigade made its final move to Baghdad on April 1, when the division was transferred to the Republican Guard I Corps and ordered to defend the "red line," the unit had simply ceased to exist as an organized combat unit. Its soldiers had abandoned virtually all of their vehicles east of the Diyala River and walked away rather then risk moving them and becoming targets for Coalition air attacks.[24]

Even before the war, the mere threat of air or missile attack had degraded the Al-Nida division commander's ability to coordinate his brigades, due to a regime mandate that all units and headquarters seek shelter in isolated hide sites. The Al-Nida commander therefore placed his primary headquarters just outside Baqubah, some distance from his fighting forces, and made its primary focus seeking and maintaining protection from air attack. To improve its chances of survival, "the headquarters was dug into underground shelters with reinforced walls and iron plates on the ceilings.... A separate larger shelter was co-located in a nearby orchard for meetings."[25]

The division's headquarters possessed no computers—wall maps with manual plots were the primary means of keeping track of the division's units. Primary communication was by land lines, and radio communications were kept as limited as possible. The division commander did possess a Thuriya [satellite phone], but was afraid to use it for fear of attracting an air attack on his headquarters.[26] When Coalition attacks eventually destroyed the main communications system, the division established a relay system to maintain contact between its headquarters and the various units under its command. To communicate, the division commander was forced to spend much of his time moving among his units.

Nevertheless, for some Iraqi commanders, Coalition air attacks on Iraq's ground forces were less successful in the early days than they were to be later in the war. As General Hamdani reported in post-war interviews, Iraqi forces were generally safe as long as the troops were not moving:

> During this time there were heavy air attacks on the Medina Division, but we were surprised at how few fell on the Al-Nida Division. The attacks were effective against fixed sites such as communications and logistic facilities, but much less so on the

forces themselves. We had multiple positions for each vehicle, and the troops remained dispersed. The Nebuchadnezzar Division took some damage from air attacks during its move into position during this time, but it was not seriously hurt. The real effect was on the morale of the troops. At this point morale had not broken. My soldiers were still prepared to fight.[27]

The Defense of the Southern Cities and Confusion Out West

The View at the Top

As Coalition air attacks ravaged Iraq's military forces and installations, ground forces rolled over the Iraqi regular army units in their way. The British 1st UK Armored Division, supported by the US Marine Corps' 23rd MEU, drove north and then east to seize the Ramallah oil fields and close off the southern city of Basra. Meanwhile the 3rd Infantry Division, followed by the 1st Marine Division, sliced up the desert roads west of the Euphrates River. The 1st Marine Division then turned in to cross the Euphrates at An-Nasiriyah. After fighting its way through the outskirts of Nasiriyah, the 1st Marine Regimental Combat Team (RCT) drove to the northeast towards Al-Kut, while the 5th and 7th Marine RCTs crossed to the north of Nasiriyah with the objective of driving up the Tigris-Euphrates valley towards Diwaniyah. The 3rd Infantry Division continued its advance, bypassing An-Nasiriyah, As-Samawaha, and An-Najaf to gain a position from which it could drive through the Karbala Gap and attack Baghdad.

As the American advance reached toward the northwest, it came under increasingly heavy attack from Ba'ath militia and Fedayeen Saddam. To the Americans, these attacks appeared fanatical and beyond reason. In fact, they were suicidal; in the 3rd Infantry Division, unit after unit reported going "black" on ammunition (almost empty) as they dealt with Fedayeen Saddam, who charged tanks in small groups or in the back of Toyota pick-ups.

However, the picture of the war forming in the Iraqi high command was entirely different from what was actually happening. The regime assumed that Coalition forces would attack, or at the very least invest, each of the cities along the Euphrates and not leave their supply lines open to attack by Iraqi forces operating from these cities. The reports reaching Baghdad of heavy fighting around the outskirts of the southern cities reinforced this pre-conception. As Iraqi units attacked out from the cities, their commanders reported exactly the message that Baghdad expected to hear: that everything was going wonderfully and that Iraqi forces were slaughtering the invaders in surprisingly large numbers.

Throughout the war, the quality of the reporting from the military and security channels to the regime leadership was mixed. Reporting through political channels was almost uniformly bad. An operations log from the General Military Intelligence Directorate (GMID) provide a detailed, if somewhat confusing, hour-by-hour picture of events from 20 March through 2 April 2003. The first entry notes simply say, "At 0532 hours the beginning of the enemy's aerial hostilities, with enemy airplanes bombing the city of Baghdad."[28] Soon thereafter, other cities, particularly in the south, were reported to have "thick aviation" over them.[29]

On that first full day of war, the majority of the entries in the 37th Division's log referred to the loss of "monitoring stations" throughout the county.[30] Of particular note was the emphasis placed on the rapid loss of monitoring stations in the western border areas (near Jordan). The GMID log noted that Coalition attacks had destroyed, attacked, or cut off at least 34 of these monitoring stations on 20 March alone.[31] Iraqi concern undoubtedly heightened when multiple reports received that evening indicated that several groups of as many as 16 enemy armored vehicles were on the road between the Jordanian border and Kilometer 160.[32] Log entries on the evening of 22 March noted that "Enemy has a massive presence of armor in the Al-Kasarat region [Jordan] 90 kilometers from Ar Rutbah."[33] The impression of these reports was that a large American armored force was driving from Jordan and across the western desert. This impression would have profound implications later in the war. Over time, these and other reports helped to fix in Saddam's mind the idea that the main Coalition attack was coming out of Jordan.

One of the more interesting encounters in the western desert during this period occurred as the lead elements of a massive Coalition special operations effort swarmed across the Jordanian border and ran into an isolated Iraqi unit near the village of Al-Hibaria. According to an intelligence report to Saddam's secretary on 23 March, early on the previous morning an American patrol consisting of "four armored cars and a small vehicle" attacked the Iraqi patrol which had resisted "until the ammunition ran out" and was then captured.[34] During questioning, the senior Iraqi present identified himself to his American captors as a sergeant from the border forces. Questioned by the Americans, he convinced his captors of his military ignorance, signed a "local cease-fire agreement," and was released.[35] Unknown to his American captors, the sergeant was actually an officer from Iraqi's elite Special Mission Unit 111 sent to the region on 17 March to gauge the situation in the west.[36] In a clear grasp of the obvious, the Director of Military Intelligence added at the bottom of the report that "we should notify the chiefs of the regional military leadership and the Minister of Defense to tell our soldiers to sign this type of pledge [military cease-fire agreement]."[37]

These and other reports continued to fixate the regime's elites on a Western approach. Losing their early warning outposts in the opening moments of the war could only have one meaning: the Americans were doing something big in the western desert and they did not want it seen. An early assessment in a

GMID operations log notes that the enemy, in addition to attempting to move on An-Nasiriyah in the south, "has utilized all of his present forces and it is possible that he will undertake to reinforce them with additional forces or that he will open up a front in the northern region."[38] By 25 March the reports noted a "military force composed of approximately sixty tanks and armored vehicles...20 kilometers southwest of the Ar Rutbah region...and they had begun to move in a strategic direction...and that according to the commander of the Al-Qa'im border group individuals coming from Syria told him that 'the intention of the enemy is to open a front by way of Jordan.'"[39]

According to these reports, Coalition "armor" was not the only thing crossing the western borders—friends were arriving as well. The operations log notes on 21 March at 0015 hours, "eight Syrian persons surrendered themselves to the Al Qa'im border troops...according to them they came to serve as Mujahideen with the Iraqi people against the American enemy and...more would be arriving soon."[40] Support and promises of support from foreign fighters like this continued throughout the war. According to a memorandum to the Director of the Iraqi Intelligence Service dated 27 March:

> We have been contacted by Dr. Abid Al-Aziz Al-Rantisi [senior Hamas leader in Gaza] ...during the past few days to ensure his and Palestinian support against the barbaric American enemy. He requested us to open the check points at the border to let the volunteer fighters participate in the war.[41]

This offer was apparently part of a first trickle of foreign fighters, which would soon thereafter become a flood.[42] The memorandum went on to say, "Hamas is willing to carry out demonstrations and suicide attacks to support Iraq." The intelligence services reported that they were "pleased with the Hamas stand in this situation as we always expected the movement's support." The memo concluded by saying how "helpful it would be if Hamas was to conduct operations against American and Israeli interests in the occupied lands."[43]

From the Iraqi perspective, though the situation in the west was troubling, the fact that they still controlled the major southern cities meant that their overall strategy was working. The Minister of Defense announced in a news conference on March 27:

> The enemy encircled the town of Al-Samawa from the direction of the desert and is now in the back of the town. The tribes of Al-Muthanna, the Ba'ath Party, Saddam Fedayeen, and military units are now implementing special operations aimed at these American units....Now, as to the situation in the mid-Euphrates sector; in the past three days, the enemy's losses were very heavy, as they are losing tanks and personnel carriers; they are firing at civilians in more than one place and in more than one sector. The performance of our units is very good and there is

very good cooperation in the mid-Euphrates sector between the Saddam Fedayeen, the Ba'ath Party fighters, and the tribesmen. Before I came to the news conference, I talked to Staff Lieutenant General Salah Abbud, deputy commander of the region. He told me that the enemy had withdrawn because they sustained heavy losses.[44]

Since this optimistic assessment was going out the same time the 3rd Infantry Division and 1st Marine Division were rapidly destroying all Iraqi units that challenged them, it was easy to believe that the Minister of Defense was simply parroting regime-generated propaganda. But a close study of the documentary evidence indicates that many of the regime elites truly believed these misconceptions. Ba'ath Party commanders were reporting accurately that they were still holding the cities though their reports of inflicting heavy losses on the Coalition forces were false. No one in Baghdad had any reason or desire to doubt them.[45] Typical of the reporting reaching Baghdad was this March 21 report from the Southern region command's control center:

> The enemy is advancing toward the airport in An-Nasiriyah... a counter-attack force of the 11th Infantry Division made contact with the enemy and [was able to] destroy six enemy tanks...one Iraqi tank has been destroyed.[46]

The fact that most of the 11th Infantry Division had effectively evaporated under the first ground assaults of the Coalition was something that neither Saddam nor those around him had any way of knowing. They were receiving similarly optimistic reports from the militia forces to complement those from trusted party officials. For instance, a report from the security officer of a Basra-based Fedayeen Saddam unit enthusiastically reported on March 24:

> The latest attack...by the Fedayeen and the heroic men of the Party on the remnants of the enemy...on the Az-Zubayr Bridge and fired up two tanks with their crews and the enemy was routed to the rear...the routed force of the enemy is estimated to be more than fifty tanks.[47]

A week into the campaign, perhaps sensing that he was receiving inflated reports, the Minister of Defense displayed a glimpse of the professionalism his peers credited to him. He established a committee to explore exactly how American ground forces were fighting the campaign. On 27 March, this committee forwarded its report titled "The Methods of the US Enemy During the Aggression Against Our Steadfast, Fighting Country."[48] It was a mixture of already well-understood generalizations of American capabilities and some fanciful conjecture to explain events that were not making sense in Baghdad.

This report stated that the Americans were avoiding entering the cities, "while capturing important communications nodes to control entry and exit points for towns and cities, with the objective of preventing the arrival of re-inforcements..."[49] The committee also warned that US forces would attack at a number of places at the same time, "in order to dilute our effort and confuse our troops, coupled with a propensity to withdraw in case of casualties and to hold onto land in case of any success."[50] Both of these items might have provided the regime hints as to what was actually happening, but it appears the report was either not widely circulated or it was ignored. Possibly the Minister of Defense failed to take it seriously because of bizarre elements. One of its explanations for how the Americans could appear at so many different places was that Chinook helicopters were capable of air-landing heavy battle tanks—which Chinooks were not.[51]

The View of Local Ba'athists

The high command had one vision of the war's progress, but that largely reflected the reports it was receiving from the battlefront. It is therefore instructive to take a close look at what the local officials were actually dealing with as opposed to what they were reporting. The best source on what local Ba'athists were seeing in one region was Lieutenant General Yahya Taha Huwaysh-Fadani Al-Ani, the assistant military advisor to the Ba'ath commander in the Central Euphrates region. In his previous career, General Yahya had reached the pinnacle of Commander, Naval and Coastal Defense Force, managing to reach retirement. However, in January 2003 he had been pressed back into service. By his own admission, General Yahya knew he had only limited experience in coordinating a land battle. He did, however, have a front row seat to events as they occurred. General Yahya had a particularly good view of the impact the apparent two-pronged Coalition advance on Ad-Diwaniyah and An-Najaf had on local Ba'ath officials. In fact, those perceived threats were actually American feints designed to confuse the Iraqis as to the Coalition's true objectives— and they worked.

On 28 March, General Yahya first came into contact with American forces. According to his account:

> On the 28th, after the Coalition had rested and resupplied some distance away, the Bradley armored personnel carriers arrived at the outskirts of As-Samawa, but did not enter the city. They covered and penned us in the city while their supply columns moved to the north behind a screen of tanks. Some Fedayeen Saddam patrols attacked with RPG-7s, while the Al-Quds force fired some 120mm mortars. I went to the roof of the As-Samawa hospital to see what I could outside the city. I saw tanks and armored personnel carriers approaching, covered by eight helicopters.[52]

Around 29 or 30 March, we learned that the fighting in An-Najaf had started. I lost communications with my boss, regional governor Mizban.

I contacted Ad-Diwaniyah and An-Najaf and asked them to contact the governor, but they said they had not heard from him for two days. We then heard that regional governor Mizban had been dismissed and sent back to Baghdad, but we did not know who his replacement was. We thought it was Lieutenant General Salah Abboud as the new regional governor of the Central Euphrates region.[53]

Clearly, he was able to see that the Americans were making no effort to enter As-Samawah and that since their supply columns were heading north, he could have reasoned that most of the Coalition's combat power must be proceeding ahead of it. If he needed any confirmation that Coalition forces were bypassing the area, then the fighting around Najaf (100 miles north of his position) the next day should have done the trick. Still, no evidence of any such reasoned analysis traveled up the chain of command.

Of course, the confusion over who was actually in charge of the region at this point may have a considerable amount to do with faulty reporting to Baghdad. This command confusion was due in part to the Ba'ath regime's security bureaucracy. In addition to regional governor Mizban's dismissal on 29 March, the local head of the governorate of As-Samawah, Saif Al-Din Mishadad, also received his walking papers and was replaced by a regular army officer, Major General Ali Al-Hababi. Nevertheless, Baghdad reversed its decision three days later and Mizban was returned to office, quite fittingly on April Fool's Day.[54]

Governor Mizban's difficulties with the defense of As-Samawah were not his only ones. At the same time the defenders of An-Najaf (also within his area of responsibility) were in equal difficulty. By the time Saddam received accurate reports on the situation it was already too late to take effective action. Iraq's former trade minister records Saddam's anger in the following terms:

Saddam appeared upset with the events in An-Najaf, telling the ministers that the situation in An-Najaf was "difficult," that it appeared the city was about to fall to Coalition forces, and that "even the Ba'ath Party was facing difficulty in An-Najaf." After a brief discussion, Saddam ordered that Mahmoud Dhiab Al-Ahmad [Minister of Interior] to leave the meeting and contact Mizban Khuthair al-Hadi, the Central Euphrates regional commander, and direct Mizban to order Iraqi forces to withdraw from An-Najaf. Al-Ahmad returned shortly thereafter and reported that he was not successful in contacting Mizban.[55]

By now the US Army's 3rd Infantry Division had already moved north of

An-Najaf in preparation for its drive through the Karbala Gap. The 3rd Infantry Division was replaced at As-Samawah by units of the 82nd Airborne, reinforced by Abrams and Bradleys. For the defenders of As-Samawah, the situation became increasingly desperate. General Yahya continues his account of events:

> On 31 March I noticed that there were only approximately 200 fighters left in As-Samawah. The Al-Quds fighters complained that they no longer had any soldiers. The Ba'ath Party said they no longer had any men."[56]

By this time, communications with Baghdad were all but cut off. In one last communication with local authorities, Baghdad ordered the replacements of their party leader and the commander of the local Fedayeen Saddam. Both men were immediately ordered to Baghdad.

On 3 April, the local leadership of As-Samawah decamped. As General Yahya indicated, "No one knew where they had gone. Their guards didn't even know where they had gone."[57] At this point the general and his staff decided that discretion was the better part of valor and left for Ad-Diwaniyah on the morning of the fourth. With the departure of the Ba'ath officials, civic order quickly disintegrated. General Yahya recalled, "In the morning...when we started out, the mobs started looting everything. They came to steal our cars, but my guards scared them off."[58] It took almost a full day to get to Ad-Diwaniyah, and once there he again found himself in the midst of chaos. The Defense Ministry, shocked to hear that As-Samawah was about to fall, ordered Yahya to organize the impenetrable defense of Ad-Diwaniyah. Inexplicably, the Defense Minister reversed himself two days later and ordered General Yahya to return to his former post in Baghdad as the head of the military academy.[59]

Putting aside the fact that the Ministry of Defense was worried about staffing its military academies as the Coalition was approaching Baghdad's suburbs, General Yahya's account suggests a complete breakdown of military-political cooperation in the Euphrates region. The authorities in Baghdad had little sense of what Iraqi forces were confronting near the cities, while local authorities clearly had no control of their subordinates. While local Ba'ath leaders dithered, fought amongst themselves, and then finally ran off, thousands of Fedayeen Saddam continued to sacrificed themselves to maintain the regime. While their attacks caused US soldiers some local difficulties as they sped towards Baghdad, their tactical impact on the course of the conventional war was virtually nothing.

The Military View

At the start of the war, Lieutenant General Hamdani was responsible for defending Baghdad from attacks originating from the southeast. Units under his command were spread from Ba'qubah northeast of the capital, to Al-Kut southeast of the capital and then in an arc that generally ran to An-Nasaf and up to Karbala. The Al-Nida Division (41st, 42nd, and 43rd Brigades) deployed in the area around Ba'qubah. The 3rd Special Forces Brigade deployed at the Al-Rasheed airport—to protect the regime from internal rebellion as to defend against external threats. The corps artillery was located southwest of the capital at Sarabadi. The Medina Division (2nd and 10th Armored Brigades and the 14th Mechanized Brigade) was deployed nearby immediately south of Baghdad at As-Suwayrah. The Baghdad Division was deployed in the area of Al-Kut, where it could move either south in case of trouble in the Sh'ia regions, or attack the flanks of an Iranian drive on Baghdad. Finally, the start of the war found the Nebuchadnezzar Republican Guard Division in the midst of quietly moving from the area around Kirkuk through Tikrit to Al-Hillah. This involved subjecting the division to a 300 mile movement under constant threat of Coalition air attack. To accomplish this task, the Division had to leave all of its tanks and artillery behind and move in small groups. It still lost over 10 percent of its men to air attack. And when it was put in the line without its heavy equipment, it had no better prospects of stopping the tanks of the 3rd Infantry Division than did the Fedayeen Saddam.

Hamdani first learned of the start of the Coalition's offensive when reports of air attacks throughout his area of responsibility flooded into his headquarters. During the war's initial phase, he spent much of his time trying to divine the Coalition's intentions. From the earliest reports he understood that a substantial portion of the Coalition's forces was moving up the west side of the Euphrates River. Consequently, he ordered elements of the Medina Division to cross the Euphrates to take up positions guarding the Karbala Gap.

Before his forces could execute the order, General Hamdani's superior, the Republican Guard Chief of Staff, countermanded the order. Hamdani recalled, "Saddam had declared that no Republican Guard forces would deploy west of the Euphrates River. Apparently he was afraid that forces west of the river would become trapped if the bridges were destroyed and would not be available for defending Baghdad."[60] What Hamdani failed to inform the Chief of Staff was that he had already moved two battalions of the Medina Division across the Euphrates. Though his superiors denied him the use of a third battalion, which he had intended to move into the Karbala sector, he was determined to make the best of a bad situation. Sensing that "if the Coalition were going to strike up the west side of the Euphrates, the critical point or the 'neck of the bottle' was the gap between Karbala and the lake. To cover this key terrain, General Handani "stretched the two Medina battalions to cover the road between Al-Musayyib and Karbala."[61]

At the same time that Hamdani was moving troops to cover the Karbala Gap, he ordered the Baghdad Division, which was defending Al-Kut, to prepare to move up the Tigris River to defend the bridges near An-Numaniyah. Meanwhile, as the final units of the Nebuchadnezzar began arriving in his area, he took advantage of the regime's inattention to place some units on the "west" side of the Euphrates.

By 24 March, as the vicious sandstorm closed in, Hamdani took advantage
of the Coalition's tactical pause to discover and assess the true overall situation.
That task was not a particularly easy thing to do. Reports from the southern
cities were almost uniformly optimistic, but Hamdani knew that such reporting
rested on what the locals could see from very limited vantage points. His own
tactical reporting told him that Coalition logistics convoys were sweeping past
the cities, and it was not hard to deduce that heavy armored formations were
moving with them. That he was able to develop a realistic appraisal of ongoing
events demonstrates that intuition, knowledge, and training often count for as
much as the best sensor technology:

> By this time, I thought that the Coalition would focus on a Eu-
> phrates axis of advance and would simultaneously isolate the
> forces in the south on a line from An-Najaf to Al-Kut. Once the
> south was cut off, they would maneuver west of the Euphrates
> River toward Baghdad. My estimate of the situation was that
> it would not be in the Coalition's interest to fight a number of
> battles before Baghdad. Coalition forces would use air power
> to make up for the limited forces on the ground. They would
> move rapidly up the west side of the Euphrates River and at-
> tack Baghdad from the southwest. I expected they would use
> airborne and air assault forces, false and real, to isolate and
> confuse the defenses around the cities.[62]

Based on his estimate of the situation, Hamdani moved his 3rd Special
Forces Brigade from the Rasheed district to Al-Hillah. By 25 March, it had
moved into its assigned positions unscathed by American airpower, which the
sandstorm had partially blinded. The brigade commander reported back that
the Al-Hillah Ba'ath officials were near panic and confused about the state of
affairs to the south. More troubling to Hamdani were reports that "The Al-Quds
units were in chaos and abandoning their posts." According to Hamdani, this
information provided a strong indication that matters were spinning out of the
regime's control.[63]

Even though Hamdani clearly divined Coalition intentions, those above
him did not share his certainty. In Baghdad, rumors persisted that the Israelis
were on the verge of joining the assault with one airborne and three armored
divisions. This force was said to be ready to attack through Jordan.[64] Continuing Coalition special operations throughout the western desert region also
worked to keep the regime's attention focused on the west rather than on the
main Coalition attack coming from the south.

Significantly, the regime was also receiving intelligence from the Russians
that fed suspicions that the attack out of Kuwait was merely a diversion. An
example of this intelligence was the following document sent to Saddam on
24 March:

The information that the Russians have collected from their sources inside the American Central Command in Doha is that the United States is convinced that occupying Iraqi cities are impossible, and that they have changed their tactic; now they are planning to spread across the Euphrates River from Basra in the south to Al-Qa'im in the north, avoiding entering the cities. The strategy is to isolate Iraq from its western borders...Jordan had accepted the American 4th Mechanized Infantry Division; they were supposed to enter through Turkey, but after the Turkish parliament refused, they changed direction and are now in the Suez Canal heading to Al-Aqaba.[65]

Such external sources of information were only one of the fog-generators obscuring the minds of Iraq's senior leadership. The bizarrely optimistic reporting coming up the chain of command from Fedayeen Saddam authorities in the south continued to add to Baghdad's and Saddam's misunderstanding. One Fedayeen Saddam report claimed the destruction of 42 tanks and 49 armored personnel carriers near Karbala on 25 March.[66] Hamdani did his best to draw a more accurate picture of the situation for the regime, but was constantly stymied by Saddam's and his close associates' refusals to entertain comments contrary to what they wanted to believe. Long after the war ended, Hamdani's frustration was still palpable:

Part of the problem with reporting the conditions on the ground was the political leadership. The Ba'ath officials in command of the local units in the Middle Euphrates Region did not understand what was happening. [Nevertheless] Saddam gave great credit to an idealized vision of tribal warfare. In Saddam's eyes this kind of close combat was what the Ba'ath Party could deliver. Saddam thought that the Ba'ath commanders knew more than the professional military. The Ba'ath destroyed the army.[67]

The US seizure of the bridge at Al-Kifl 30 miles north of An-Najaf convinced Hamdani that he was facing the main US attack. However, he remained perplexed by the purpose behind the assault on Al-Kifl. His earlier assumptions were that the Coalition would attack through the Karbala Gap and then cross the Euphrates north of Al-Kifl. Now it appeared they were crossing the river a hundred miles south of the point he had predicted.

To find out what was going on, he decided to carry out a personal reconnaissance of the bridge area along with the commander of his 3rd Special Forces Brigade:

A retired soldier from Al-Kifl met me along the way and told me the Americans were close to the bridge. I sent the commander of the 1st Battalion of the Special Forces Brigade ahead to the bridge site to confirm the report. He told me, when he returned, that when he climbed the wall of the canal next to the bridge, he could reach out and touched the side of an American Bradley fighting vehicle. This meant that I was personally only 300 to 500 meters away from the American units.[68]

Hamdani became convinced that this was a serious threat and immediately concentrated artillery from the Medina and Nebuchadnezzar Divisions to carry out what he termed an artillery raid against the American position. The artillery was a mix of 152mm cannons, BM-21 rocket launchers, and light artillery. Hamdani allocated 10 rounds to each weapon for the mission. His plan was to have them fire the 10 rounds as rapidly as possible and then run for cover before American counter-fire came in. While the Iraqis believed they had destroyed seven vehicles, the attack barely registered with Americans around the bridge. On the other hand, the American counter-fire plastered the surrounding area. As Hamdani later said, "The American reaction to our Kifl attack was very strong. We were somewhat overwhelmed by the volume of the counterattack fire."[69]

As Hamdani attempted to organize counterattacks to dislodge the Americans from the Al-Kifl bridgehead, he was also trying to build a clearer picture of what else he was confronting. The lack of clear information from the south continued to hamper him, while intelligence from Baghdad was proving useless. He later stated, "I was told by Qusay that American forces were in An-Najaf and were quickly moving on Ad-Diwaniyah."[70] This would suggest that the Americans were going to attack up the east side of the Euphrates and not the west as Hamdani was still predicting. However, contrary to information coming from Baghdad, the Americans were doing exactly what Hamdani predicted. The 3rd Infantry Division was moving away from Najaf, which the 101st Airborne Division was now investing, and racing towards Karbala—on the west side of the Euphrates.

It is almost hard to fault Qusay for sending out this misleading information as optimistic reports streaming out of the Central Euphrates Regional Command Headquarters were still bombarding Baghdad. These reports, while generally accurate as to the location and timing of enemy activity, completely missed every other detail. For example, on 28 March, the Central Euphrates Regional Command Headquarters reported that "an enemy force...headed from the Afak intersection toward Diwaniyah" but that a regiment of the Al-Quds "engaged them and forced them to withdraw."[71] The report got the location of the American forces correct, but rather then being forced to withdraw, the Americans smashed the Al-Quds force and continued to roll. It appears that since the Al-Quds force was destroyed, no report reached Baghdad informing them that the Americans had changed direction and were now rolling towards Al-Kut and not Diwaniyah.

A deluge of other reports that same day listed numerous American attacks throughout southern Iraq, but almost every one examined to date reported that the Americans were "forced to withdraw by the brave party units and fighters for Saddam."[72] However, the true import of what was happening was not lost on local Iraqi military officers. For instance, in a post-war interview the senior military advisor to the regional commander, Lieutenant General Al-Obadi, described the action outside Ad-Diwaniyah:

> The style of the American attacks was to attack and withdraw immediately...they did not fight in the cities...all the time Coalition convoys were moving north on the highway to Baghdad, while we were locked up."[73]

Lieutenant Colonel Al-Obadi clearly understood that the American attacks aimed to pin the Iraqis to the cities.

As Hamdani suggested, "Republican Guard headquarters in Baghdad was providing information of very little value."[74] To get a clearer picture of American intentions, he began sending Republican Guard patrols into the zone south of his area of responsibility. In each case, they soon ran into the Americans. Those who survived reported that the Americans were in strength on both sides of the Euphrates. Hamdani later stated, "As the reconnaissance reports began to come into my command post in Al-Hillah, I assessed that the Coalition had three axes of advance."

In fact, there were only two main American axes of advance in the south. Hamdani's patrols had picked up the fact that the 3rd Infantry Division was definitely racing up the west side of the Euphrates and was likely to come through the Karbala Gap. However, he seems to have misinterpreted the US Marine feint towards Ad-Diwaniyah as a major effort. The 1st Marine Division was in reality about to switch its advance from the northwest to the north and drive through An-Numiniyah across the Tigris to attack Baghdad from the east. Hamdani's misreading of the situation may have resulted from his own pre-conceived notions of Coalition intentions. Talking about a war game in 2002 he stated, "I warned strongly against keeping the Baghdad Division in Al-Kut, if enemy forces ever reached Ad-Diwaniyah. I did not want the Baghdad Division cut off from Baghdad."[75] Now that the Baghdad Division was in Al-Kut, he saw his fear coming true and warned the division commander to "pay closer attention to his west than the south." Unfortunately for the Baghdad Division, the Marines were coming from the south.

One of Hamdani's patrols that escaped American attention reported a critical piece of information: the Americans were establishing a large logistics base to the west of Najaf in the desert.[76] The establishment of a logistics base so far north confirmed in Hamdani's mind that the Americans were going to come through the Karbala Gap. In his view, it made no sense for the Americans to establish a massive logistics base on the west side of the Euphrates if they had any intention of attacking up the east side. Unfortunately for the prospects of a more successful defense, none of his warnings had much effect on those in command in Baghdad. Instead, the Baghdad command became ever more obsessed with imaginary American and Israeli forces coming through Jordan, while it ignored the reality that American forces were already on its doorstep.

By the time the last of Hamdani's patrols reported in, fighting was breaking out all across the Republican Guard II Corps' entire front. Hamdani's forces were under heavy pressure from the Marines who were closing in on the east side of the Tigris, and by renewed attacks by the 3rd Infantry Division that had finished re-arming and re-fueling on the west side of the Euphrates River. As he attempted to reposition force to meet these threats, he was stymied by the seeming complacency of the regime, which apparently failed to recognize how desperate the Iraqi position was becoming. At the end of March, Hamdani finally received permission to move the Baghdad Division from Al-Kut and back to the capital. However, by the time it arrived in the vicinity of Abu Gayreb, it had become a battered wreck of less-than-brigade strength. The division was replaced in Al-Kut by the 34th Regular Army Division, which bore the brunt of the Marine attack on the city and promptly collapsed.[77]

On 30 March, American pressure increased considerably with a series of attacks toward Al-Hillah and Al-Hindiyah. Unsure of what to make of conflicting reports, Hamdani went forward himself to see what was transpiring. His personal reconnaissance led him to believe that "the attacks toward Al-Hindiyah were more dangerous..., because it looked like the Americans were trying to secure their flank for an attack into Karbala."[78]

With pressure mounting on both flanks, Hamdani found himself in an increasingly difficult situation. Returning to his headquarters, he called Qusay to urge a fundamental re-deployment of Iraqi forces to meet the American threat at Al-Hindiyah and to prepare to meet an assault through the Karbala Gap. He asked that the Al-Nida Division be moved south to defend the approaches to the city from the Euphrates, while the rest of the Medina Division would be re-deployed to the west bank of the Euphrates to meet the threat to Karbala. Qusay was non-committal, but the Republican Guard Chief of Staff castigated Hamdani. Hamdani recalled that "I was told that I was not fighting the plan. This was incredible to me—the plan! What plan, I asked him. The Americans had wrecked our plan."[79]

In the end, it was impossible for Qusay and the Chief of Staff to accept Hamdani's warnings of impending doom when they had such a chorus of positive reports flowing in, announcing things such as "the Ba'ath knights, the great Republican Guard soldiers, and the Fedayeen Saddam attacked and forced the enemy to leave Al-Hindiyah...the enemy had great losses in soldiers."[80] In effect, Hamdani had become an Iraqi Cassandra—his predictions entirely discounted in the ever-optimistic land of Saddam's innercircle. The only reinforcements Qusay would part with were elements of a special forces battalion from the Republican Guard I Corps. Hamdani did not receive permission to re-deploy any of his forces to new locations.

Realizing that little help was going to be forthcoming, Hamdani focused on doing the best he could within the restrictions imposed by the regime. By the beginning of April, Coalition attacks were disrupting communications between his headquarters and subordinate units. Hamdani was now forced to undertake time consuming and arduous trips between units that stretched from Karbala to Al-Kut. To make matters worse, when the Marines drove into An-Numiniyah they cut a lateral access road, and he now had to detour through Baghdad to visit each flank of his corps.

On the evening of 1 April, he received reports that American forces, esti-mated to include 150 tanks of the 1st Marine Division, were attacking across the Tigris at An-Numiniyah.[81] The following day he journeyed out to the Tigris where he confirmed the reports, and for the first time realized that the main Marine effort was heading for Al-Kut and not Ad-Diwaniyah. He also now real-ized that the Marine attack on Baghdad would come from the east and not the south as he had originally thought—a direction where he had precious little to stop them. The situation was now critical and about to get worse. On his way back from this trip, Hamdani received more bad news from his Chief of Staff: major American forces were driving toward the Karbala Gap and chewing their way through the Medina Republican Guard's 14th Brigade. Going through Baghdad, Hamdani stopped at the Republican Guard Headquarters to receive whatever updates they had and begged for help. But the Chief of Staff was away from his office, and no one else knew anything. Hamdani stated, "The stop was not helpful."[82]

Upon his arrival at the Karbala battle front, Hamdani met with the Com-mander of the Medina Division who reported that his division was under intense pressure by both American ground and air forces. As for just how intense, Ham-dani got an immediate demonstration. As he listened to the Medina commander, Coalition aircraft savaged "the better part of a battalion in defensive positions right beside us. I think there were something like 39 killed, 100 wounded, and 17 armored vehicles destroyed."[83] During this meeting, both men received orders to meet with the Republican Guard's Chief of Staff. According to Hamdani, when they arrived at the meeting site, "The Medina commander provided a frank and honest assessment. The news he reported was not good. He told the Chief of Staff that the Medina 14th Brigade commander was very brave in battle, but was not having great success against the Americans."[84]

In the middle of this depressing meeting, Hamdani and the Republican Guard Chief of Staff were called to an emergency meeting to be held by Qusay. This was a clear indication that most of the operational decisions had devolved from Saddam to his son at this point in the war. It was to be one of the more important meetings of the war. As Hamdani relates:

> The Minister of Defense had a message from Saddam. The message was an order for immediate execution. The Minister of Defense said that Saddam would not be able to meet dur-

ing the next two days, but that he had just met with Saddam and the plan was explained to him.[85] The minister went on to explain that what had happened over the last two weeks was a "strategic" trick by the Americans. He told us American forces were going to come from the direction of Jordan, through Al-Ramadi, and into northern Baghdad. Emergency procedures were to go into effect at 0500 the next morning.[86] The Al-Nida was supposed to shift to the northwest of Baghdad under the Republican Guard I Corps.[87] Minefields were to be immediately established to the west and northwest of Baghdad. The talk of establishing minefields made me think that they thought we were fighting Iran again or something.[88]

At this point, Hamdani indicated that the plan would leave him with only the Medina and Nebuchadnezzar Divisions with which "to fight the American attacks from the south! I told them that this plan was the opposite of what we were facing."[89] The Minister of Defense replied that he was only the messenger and that there was no further use for discussions since Saddam had spoken. Qusay at least allowed Hamdani to explain his view of the situation:

I said that a minor attack was moving up the Tigris along the line from An-Nasiriyah to Al-Kut. [the Marine's 1st RCT] This attack was actually somewhat of a surprise to me given the tight roads and poor armor terrain in the area. Another minor attack was pushing up the middle ground from As-Samawah to Ad-Diwaniyah. However, the main attack was on the west side of the Euphrates River through Karbala and into the southwest side of Baghdad. The US 4th Infantry Division would soon join in the main thrust. I said that the Americans would own Karbala by that night, and they would move quickly to take the bridge.[90]

Hamdani's operational view on 2 April was surprisingly in line with the latest strategic intelligence provided through the Russian ambassador to Baghdad. According to a memorandum from the Iraqi Minister of Foreign Affairs to Saddam, dated 2 April, Russian intelligence reported through its ambassador that:

1. The American's were moving to cut off Baghdad from the south, east, and north. The heaviest concentration of troops (12,000 troops plus 1,000 vehicles) was in the vicinity of Karbala.

2. The Americans were going to concentrate on bombing in and around Baghdad, cutting the road to Syria and Jordan and creating "chaos and confusion" to force the residents of Baghdad to flee.

3. That the assault on Baghdad would not begin before the arrival of the 4th Infantry Division sometime around 15 April.[91]

It is unclear if Qusay had seen the Russian report, but Hamdani's arguments made him pause. After Hamdani finished his presentation, Qusay turned back to the Minister of Defense and Republican Guard Chief of Staff to ask their opinions. The Minister could only suggest that he did not know whether Hamdani was right or wrong, but plans should still be carried out as President Hussein had ordered. According to Hamdani:

> He said that we should execute the plan as Saddam directed. The Republican Guard Chief of Staff at first did not answer either way. He repeated over and over, "we must fight." The Regular Army Chief of Staff said that he did not agree with my theory and that Saddam was right. He said, "We must all be 100 percent with Saddam." The Republican Guard Chief of Staff then said that I had never executed the plan and that I moved forces without permission. He said that I was to blame for all these casualties.[92]

Qusay remained unsure of what to do, but finally ordered the Al-Nida Division to move in to support the Republican Guard I Corps as they established a defense against the American thrust coming from Jordan. "He also directed a withdrawal from Karbala and that all units move to the east side of the Euphrates."[93] Hamdani, realizing the argument was lost, tried to salvage something and asked for permission to destroy the strategic Al-Qa'id Bridge on the Euphrates (Objective Peach). He received Qusay's permission and then went to talk privately to the Chief of Staff. Hamdani had only been speaking to him for a moment when he received a call informing him that the Al-Qa'id Bridge was already under attack. As he recalls, the officer reporting indicated that columns of enemy armor were moving from Jaraf Al-Sakhr towards the bridge. I gave the report to those present, but they did not believe it."[94]

Only Qusay seemed somewhat alarmed at the news. The other generals ignored it and turned to discussing the shape that the minefields to the west of Baghdad should take. Hamdani commented on the dismal scene: "It was the kind of arguments that I imagine took place in Hitler's bunker in Berlin. Were all these men on drugs?"[95] In a mood of utter disbelief, he left the meeting to fight "two real battles—one on the Tigris and one on the Euphrates"—while the generals, Saddam, and his sons dealt with their imaginary universe.[96]

The question of how such a critical bridge could have been left standing is one of the great mysteries of the war. Hamdani referred to it afterwards as the "Iraqi Remagen Bridge," and it was surely that.[97] Its importance was well understood long before the first American tank arrived, which makes its survival all the more puzzling.

In fact, Hamdani had asked for permission to destroy the bridge as early as 23 March, but was told by Saddam, in a message forwarded by the Republican Guard headquarters, that he was not to destroy the bridge under any circumstances. Nevertheless, Hamdani still had the bridge rigged for demolition.[98] As he related the story later:

> Despite Saddam's orders I moved one company-sized element of the reconnaissance battalion to Karbala to begin screening south of the city along the approaches to the main highway. The reconnaissance battalion was commanded by one of my better young officers, Colonel Hassani. I ordered him in person and in writing to destroy the bridge whenever he felt that Coalition forces were approaching. He was ordered not to wait for additional orders on this point.[99]

A week later, the regime's internal security priorities interceded to undo all of Hamdani's preparations. Early in April, Hamdani had sent his Chief of Staff, Staff Major General Abdullah Mechpass, to the bridge with explicit orders to check on demolition preparations. However, according to Hamdani, "Upon his arrival, he immediately ordered Colonel Hassani to ignore my orders and not to destroy the bridge because it was against the specific direction of Saddam and that I [Hamdani] would be killed by security personnel if the bridge were destroyed."[100] Hamdani later concluded that both officers "acted out of personal loyalty to me, but they were still wrong."[101]

Upon reaching his forward headquarters, Hamdani gave the order for the Medina Division to pull back from Karbala, but to keep one of its battalions on the west bank of the Euphrates to harass and attempt to contain the American penetration. He also began moving elements of the Medina's 10th Brigade to the area. A personal reconnaissance confirmed that the Americans were up on the Euphrates in strength, but information from the front remained ambiguous. There were reports that the bridge had been blown, but those reporting probably did not realize that the demolitions only affected one side of the duel span bridge. At dark Hamdani met up with the Republican Guard Chief of Staff and that organization's director of the staff. Both believed the bridge was destroyed and incredibly explained the presence of American tanks on the far side of the Euphrates by claiming they were being delivered there by helicopters.[102]

Hamdani reported his plans to establish a new defensive line west of Latifiya. However, the Republican Guard Chief of Staff demanded that he use all the combat power in the II Republican Guard Corps to launch an immediate counterattack. Hamdani tried to warn him that the Americans could see at night as well as they could during the day, while his troops would be fighting blind. The Chief of Staff brushed aside Hamdani's arguments and reiterated his demand for an attack.

Over the course of the next few hours, the Iraqis gathered their strength. Armor from the 22nd Brigade moved into position to attack from Al-Iskandariyah, while a portion of the 10th Armored Brigade, reinforced by a special forces battalion was to attack down the road from Al-Yusufiyah. The latter attack was to use the cover provided by a large industrial complex on the southeast side of the bridge to mask its approach. Three truck loads of explosives were to follow up the attack and be blown up on the bridge to ensure that this time it fell into the river. Hamdani was racing against the clock in hopes of launching his attack before 0400, the hour when daylight brought with it American air power out in full force.[103]

But in war nothing is simple. The deployment of a division that had never practiced night movements or even conducted maneuvers together proved frightfully difficult. Hamdani's description of the attack demonstrates the Iraqis were not lacking in courage, only in skill:

> The attack moved forward slowly because we did not have night vision...The Medina Division's commander and I followed the 10th Armored Brigade with our communications groups... At 0200 American jets attacked our force as we moved down the road. We were hit by many missiles. Most of the Medina Division's staff were killed. My corps communication staff was also killed. When we reached the area near the bridge where the special forces battalion had set up a headquarters, we immediately came under heavy fire. Based on the volume of fire, I estimated at least 60 armored vehicles.[104]

At approximately 0430, a team of Iraqi special forces soldiers had managed to creep to within 400 meters of the bridge, but by then the Iraqi attacking force had lost all of its tanks and its ammunition trucks had also been blown up.[105] Hamdani continues:

> At around 0445 the sky started to lighten and the jets returned and started killing us one after another. In the early light I saw more than 60 tanks on the bridge. The firing from the American armored vehicles increased in all directions. Little distinction was made between civilian and military structures and vehicles.[106]

At 0630 on 3 April, Hamdani reported to the Republican Guard Headquarters that the counterattack had failed. He also warned that he desperately needed reinforcements to patch together a line to keep the Americans from marching directly on Baghdad. But only four hours later he received news from local civilians that 150 American tanks were already moving east and northeast and headed straight for Baghdad. The American breakout had begun and Hamdani received no reinforcements with which to stop them.

With his command vehicle and its communications equipment destroyed, Hamdani left the battlefield in a civilian vehicle driven by a junior signal officer. In an attempt to reach his forward headquarters, approximately ten kilometers north of Al-Mahmuiyah, he found himself in a race with American armor:

As we drove we began to see American armor units racing down the roads. I was hoping to make it to my forward headquarters before they did. They were driving and shooting at the same time. There was a lot of firing, and I am sure there were a lot of casualties. As we were about to reach the compound of my forward headquarters, the car I was driving was hit by enemy fire. The tires were all shot out and the lieutenant was killed.[107]

Hamdani managed to link up with the few surviving members of his staff and make it back to his headquarters. As he attempted to gain a handle on the situation and pass along orders to surviving units, he glanced out the window and saw an American M1 Abrams tank in the middle of the courtyard. At that point he told his remaining staff officers to leave and go home. Their war was over:

> We had no more weapons and we had no more morale. Looking out the window was like being in some kind of movie. I could see M1s, M2s [Bradley Fighting Vehicles], and helicopters. I remained hidden away in the building until 7 or 8 April when a civilian in the area told me Baghdad had fallen. I was sleeping in an orchard next to my compound during this time.[108]

The Ba'ath Regime Ends With a Whimper, Not a Bang

The awareness of this catastrophic military defeat only slowly dawned on Saddam and those around him. Those at the center of power still kept a solid hold on unreality. Even if they did grasp the truth, they remained silent or contented to echo Saddam's musings or pass along tidbits of favorable news. The only decisive action many of Saddam's inner circle seemed capable of in the regime's final days were attempts to stem the flow of bad news. For instance, a Ministry of Defense memorandum dated 6 April told subordinate units, "We are doing great" and reminding all staff officers to "avoid exaggerating the enemy's abilities."[109]

Despite such wishful thinking and the willful denial of the truth, Saddam's Ba'athist regime's military was dead or dying by 6 April. Coalition attacks had destroyed almost all of the corps and division headquarters in combat. The few that remained were ineffective due to the furious pace of the American advance. While some isolated units continued to fight, they were no longer connected to a coherent military organization. They were in fact the last twitch of an army in its death throes.

In the final days of the regime, Saddam understood at some level that all was lost, and became focused on his own personal survival. According to debriefs of those closest to him, he moved from safe-house to safe-house every 3 to 6 hours. To the extent possible, his inner circle attempted to update him on the battlefield situation, but continuing the pattern of lies and omissions, much of the information he received was fiction.

According to Tariq Aziz, by 6 April even Saddam had accepted that the end was near. On that day, he called a meeting with the Iraqi leadership at a house in the Mansour District of central Baghdad. During the meeting, Saddam's tone was that of a man "who had lost his will to resist" and "knew the regime was coming to an end."[110] Later that day, Saddam traveled to another safe-house a few miles away and met with his sons Uday and Qusay, the Minister of Defense, the Chief of Staff of the Al-Quds, the Chief of Staff of the Republican Guard, the Chief of Staff of the Fedayeen Saddam, and his ever-present personal secretary. It was now almost midnight, and according to those present, the combination of some truthful battlefield reports and open media (Saddam was known to watch Western satellite news at times during the war) finally affected the leader's decision-making.

Saddam began giving orders to deploy and maneuver formations that had ceased to exist. His attention focused on plans to have the Republican Guard enter Baghdad and join with the Fedayeen Saddam in "preparing" for urban warfare.[111] Late the next day Saddam met again with his closet advisors and accepted "that the army divisions were no longer capable of defending Baghdad, and that he would have a meeting with the Ba'ath Regional Commanders to enlist them in the final defense of the regime." A subsequent meeting on the same day produced an unexecuted concept to divide Baghdad into four quadrants. He placed loyal Ba'ath stalwarts in command of each sector and charged them with defending the city to their deaths.

In Saddam's view, some options still remained. To maintain this fiction, he and his followers had to divorce themselves from the reality outside their safe-houses. At the same time Saddam was holding meetings with his military staff, an American armored brigade already held Baghdad's airport. Worse, as he was discussing with Ba'ath loyalists the plan for the final defense of the city, another brigade of American armor was busily chewing up the manicured lawn in front of his palace in the center of the city.

* * * * * * *

Since the end of the war one question that has come up regularly is whether the regime had made plans to continue the conflict through the insurgency the United States is currently combating. As far as can be determined through interviews conducted for this book, and the tens of thousands of records reviewed so far, there were no national plans to transition to a guerrilla war in the event of military defeat. Nor, as their world crumbled around them, did the regime appear to cobble together such plans. Still buoyed by his earlier conviction that the Americans would never dare enter Baghdad, Saddam held onto his hope that he could stay in power—until the last minute. At the same time, the military and civilian bureaucracy went through their daily routines until the very end, as if their world was not collapsing.

For someone looking at the regime from the outside during its final days, the continued functioning of the regime's bureaucracy appears at times bizarre. However, it is quite clear that even as American tanks were smashing the last armed resistance on the road to Baghdad, the regime, in many respects, continued to function as if it was business as usual, even if it were sometimes a macabre type of business. Some of the orders issued by the regime in its final days underline the surreal atmosphere of the period.

- An order dated 1 April ordered the customs police to return to their positions at the international airport.[112]

- On 2 April, the Ba'ath party asked for inspections of air defense units to be undertaken and these reports to be forwarded to Party Headquarters.

- Another missive ordered all divisions "to stop encouraging people to volunteer for suicide missions."

- In the war's last week, two edicts were signed by Saddam ordering local party officials to clamp down on the black market.[113]

- As Coalition tanks rumbled into Baghdad, the Military Intelligence Directorate confirmed Saddam's order that Arab Fedayeen volunteers receive the same salaries and benefits as Iraq's special forces.[114]

- As the American tanks parked on the grounds of Saddam's Baghdad palace, the bureaucracy produced orders that (1) honored "fighters" of the 1991 Gulf War, (2) increased transportation allowances for all Iraqi armed forces, and (3) informed the Telephone Operator Battalion about "the new numbers of the planning ministry in their replacement location."[115]

Finally, on the regime's last day, the Military Intelligence Directorate produced a memorandum to commanders in the southern areas of Iraq which complained about "the slow process in handling several cases for runaway soldiers." The memo reminded commanders that it was their responsibility to "take actions to speed up the process of handing over these arrested soldiers and returning them back to their army units and to prepare a report for these runaway cases...on a daily basis."[116] The intention was clearly to maintain a list of those whom the regime would punish as soon as the Americans had given up and gone home.

Notes

[1] Captured document (2002), "Soldiers of the SRG."

[2] "Al-Jazirah Correspondent Confirms No US Forces in Baghdad," Doha Al-Jazirah Satellite Channel Television, 7 April 2003.

[3] Address by President Saddam Hussein in the 12th Anniversary of Um Al-Maarik, 17 January 2003 (www.iraqcrisis.co.uk/resources.php), downloaded 1 October 2003. Hulegu was the thirteenth-century Mongol leader who sacked Baghdad. Saddam's reference to the modern day operation in the Jenin refugee camp in Palestinian-controlled territory is another example of his particular histography. Most credible reporting on the Israeli military operation into Jenin places the dead at 52 Palestinian fighters and 24 members of the Israeli Defense Forces (11 April 2002).

[4] The study is limited in its description of the operational/tactical views of regular army forces in the North, general purpose Iraqi forces in the west, and Fedayeen Saddam forces in general. Additional research continues on these and other areas.

[5] "Perspectives II Republican Guard Corps."

[6] Examples of purging within the ranks of Iraq's senior officer corps during the Iran-Iraq War are documented in Said Aburish's *Saddam Hussein: The Politics of Revenge* (Bloomsbury Publishing, London: 2000). pp. 208, 23-239, 245-246, 263, and 312. According to Phebe Marr, 6 of 20 Regular Army division commanders were executed on charges of conspiracy after March 1991. The Modern History of Iraq (Westview Press. Boulder; 2004), p.264.

[7] The documents, interviews, and other source materials that have been reviewed to date confirm General Hamdanis's account.

[8] Here it is worth noting that the history of independent Iraq from 1932, when it gained independence, to 1968, when the Ba'ath assumed control, is a history of one coup after another as senior army officers jockeyed for power. Moreover, there were several coup plots in the 1990s, which heightened the regime's paranoia about its security.

[9] Various Iraqi generals interviewed suggested that they believed that most of the conceptual planning for this order was the work of Saddam, Qusay, and the Chief of Staff of the Republican Guard.

[10] This view was widespread throughout the Iraqi military forces as well as within Saddam's innercircle. General Hamdani, for example, commented in one of his interviews, "I expected a repeat of 1991 with a long air campaign before any [Coalition] ground forces entered Iraq." "Perspectives II Republican Guard Corps."

[11] What the Iraqis missed was the fact that Coalition commanders believed that the large forces they deployed in Kuwait for the coming ground offensive—the 3rd Infantry Division, the 1st Marine Division, the 1st UK Armored Division, and the 101st Airborne represented a tempting target that the Iraqis might attack with any WMD in their possesion once the air campaign began. The best means to avoid chemical attack, Coalition military leaders believed, was dispersion, which the small size of Kuwait did not allow. Hence, the decision to begin the ground offensive concurrently with the air campaign as a means of dispersing Coalition forces forward into enemy territory.

[12] Project interview of Majid Hussein Ali Ibrahim Al Dulaymi, Commander, I Republican Guard Corps.

[13] Project interview of Majid Hussein Ali Ibrahim Al Dulaymi, Commander, I Republican Guard Corps.

14 Project interview of Majid Hussein Ali Ibrahim Al Dulaymi, Commander, I Republican Guard Corps.

15 Project interview of Abd Al-Karim Jasim Nafus Al-Majid, Commander, Al Nida Armored Division, 21 November 2003.

16 Project interview of Abd Al-Karim Jasim Nafus Al-Majid, Commander, Al Nida Armored Division, 21 Nov 2003.

17 Classified Intelligence Report, July 2003. The televised broadcast of this speech, with Saddam uncharacteristically wearing glasses, led to some speculation in the Coalition that it was actually a "body-double" and not Saddam.

18 Captured document, (22 March 2003) "Memorandum #56 from Commander, 1st Air Defense Region to Directorate of Air Defense."

19 Captured document, (8 April 2003) "Air Attack Reports on the Air Defenses."

20 Classified intelligence report, April 2003.

21 Project interview of Abd Al-Karim Jasim Nafus Al-Majid, Commander, Al Nida Armored Division, 21 November 2003.

22 Project interview of Abd Al-Karim Jasim Nafus Al-Majid, Commander, Al Nida Armored Division, 21 November 2003.

23 Project interview of Abd Al-Karim Jasim Nafus Al-Majid, Commander, Al Nida Armored Division, 21 November 2003.

24 Project interview of Abd Al-Karim Jasim Nafus Al-Majid, Commander, Al Nida Armored Division, 21 November 2003.

25 Project interview of Abd Al-Karim Jasim Nafus Al-Majid, Commander, Al Nida Armored Division, 21 November 2003.

26 Project interview of Abd Al-Karim Jasim Nafus Al-Majid, Commander, Al Nida Armored Division, 21 November 2003.

27 "Perspectives Iraqi II Republican Guard Corps."

28 Captured document, (2 April 2003) "Written Summaries for the 37th Division 20 March–2 April 2003." The 37th Division was a part of the 7th Directorate of the Directorate for General Military Intelligence. The 7th Directorate also controlled Special Mission Unit 111.

29 Captured document, (2 April 2003) "Written Summaries for the 37th Division 20 March–2 April 2003."

30 Based on a review of this and other documents there were hundreds of monitoring stations manned by small 3 to 5 man teams spread across Iraq. These stations served as listening posts and reported visual, audio, and occasionally signal collections directly to Baghdad.

31 More than 1 million leaflets were dropped on the "monitoring stations" by USAF MC-130 Talons by 21 March, resulting in many of these stations being abandoned.

32 Captured document, (2 April 2003) "Written Summaries for the 37th Division 20 March–2 April 2003."

33 Captured document, (2 April 2003) "Written Summaries for the 37th Division 20 March–2 April 2003." Coalition forces in the general area at the time were lightly armed special operation force patrols.

34 Captured document, (23 March 2003) "Memorandum 4811 from GMID to Secretary–Presidency

of the Republic." This report is confirmed by the log of the 37th Division of the GMID in captured document, (2 April 2003) "Written Summaries for the 37th Division 20 March–2 April 2003."

35 Captured document, (23 March 2003) "Memorandum 4811 from GMID to Secretary–Presidency of the Republic." Given the tone of the report, it is probable that the Sgt Badi was actually the Unit 111 Lieutenant Colonel in charge of the mission.

36 Captured document, (31 March 2003) "Military Movements Directorate Letter and GMID Correspondence ."

37 Captured document, (23 March 2003) "Memorandum 4811 from GMID to Secretary–Presidency of the Republic."

38 Captured document, (2 April 2003) "Written Summaries for the 37th Division 20 March–2 April 2003."

39 Captured document, (2 April 2003) "Written Summaries for the 37th Division 20 March–2 April 2003."

40 Captured document, (2 April 2003) "Written Summaries for the 37th Division 20 March–2 April 2003."

41 Captured document, (27 March 2003) "Memorandum to Director of the IIS, Subject: Hamas."

42 This same operations log records that on 27 March "three busses of Syrian volunteers [had] arrived." However, "one of them collided with a bombed out bridge, leading to...losses in the ranks of the volunteers." Captured document, (2 April 2003) "Written Summaries for the 37th Division 20 March–2 April 2003."

43 Captured document, (2 April 2003) "Written Summaries for the 37th Division 20 March–2 April 2003."

44 Foreign Broadcast Information Service,"Iraqi Defense Minister Ahmad Holds News Conference 27 March," Dubai Al-Arabiyah Television, 1850 GMT, 27 March 2003.

45 Given the general doctrinal framework within which the Iraqis were operating—namely one in which every move was carefully choreographed much like the French concept of "methodical battle" before the Second World War—it is not surprising that most senior Iraqis were incapable of conceiving of the kind of maneuver the 3rd Infantry Division was executing.

46 Captured document, (2 April 2003) "Written Summaries for the 37th Division 20 March–2 April 2003."

47 Captured document, (2 April 2003) "Written Summaries for the 37th Division 20 March–2 April 2003."

48 Captured document, (26 March 2003) "MOD Report on Iraq's Strategic Defense in Preparation for the Latest War."

49 Captured document, (26 March 2003) "MOD Report on Iraq's Strategic Defense in Preparation for the Latest War."

50 Captured document, (26 March 2003) "MOD Report on Iraq's Strategic Defense in Preparation for the Latest War."

51 The II Republican Guard Corps Commander indicates that this same over-estimation in heavy-lift capabilities was repeated by the Republican Guard's Chief of Staff to explain how the US 3rd Infantry Division could have gotten armor across the Euphrates north of Karbala on 2 April. "Perspectives Iraqi II Republican Guard Corps."

52 "Perspectives Assistant Senior Military Advisor."

53 "Perspectives Assistant Senior Military Advisor."

54 "Perspectives Assistant Senior Military Advisor."

55 Classified intelligence report, April 2003.

56 "Perspectives Assistant Senior Military Advisor."

57 "Perspectives Assistant Senior Military Advisor."

58 "Perspectives Assistant Senior Military Advisor."

59 "Perspectives Assistant Senior Military Advisor."

60 "Perspectives Iraqi II Republican Guard Corps."

61 "Perspectives Iraqi II Republican Guard Corps." The area to which Hamdani was referring is referred to in Coalition planning documents as the "Karbala Gap."

62 "Perspectives Iraqi II Republican Guard Corps."

63 "Perspectives Iraqi II Republican Guard Corps." This is consistent with the description of the Al-Quds and Ba'ath Party Militia operations in As-Samawah in an interview with the assistant military advisor to the middle Euphrates Region Commander.

64 One IIS report dated 29 March 2003, passed information received from "Jordanian drivers" that "about 10,000 Israeli soldiers [are] in Jordan waiting for orders to attack Iraq..." Captured document, (29 March 2003) "Iraqi Intelligence Service Report about American Forces."

65 Captured document, (25 March 2003) "Letter from Russian Official to Presidential Secretary Concerning American Intentions in Iraq."

66 Captured document, (27 March 2003) "Telegrams from the Al-Fajir Regiment."

67 "Perspectives Iraqi II Republican Guard Corps."

68 "Perspectives Iraqi II Republican Guard Corps."

69 "Perspectives Iraqi II Republican Guard Corps."

70 "Perspectives Iraqi II Republican Guard Corps." The latter represented the move by the 1st Marine Division up the central Euphrates Valley; the Marines were about to switch directions to the north to cross the Tigris at An-Numaniyah.

71 Captured document, (28 March 2003) "Situation Reports from the Middle Euphrates Region Command to the Presidential Office and General Command of the Armed Forces."

72 Captured document, (28 March 2003) "Situation Reports from the Middle Euphrates Region Command to the Presidential Office and General Command of the Armed Forces."

73 Project interview of LTG Kenan Mansour Khalil Al-Obadi, Senior Military Advisor to RCC Member Mizban Khudr Al-Hadi, 30 November 2003.

74 "Perspectives Iraqi II Republican Guard Corps."

75 "Perspectives Iraqi II Republican Guard Corps."

76 In US Central Command's OPLAN, 1003V this logistics base was called Logistics Support Area Bushmaster and was established by elements of V Corps on 21 March.

77 "Perspectives Iraqi II Republican Guard Corps." (Also project interview of Salih Ibrahim Hammadi Al-Salamani, Commander, Baghdad Republican Guard Division, 10 November 2003).

78 "Perspectives Iraqi II Republican Guard Corps."

79 "Perspectives Iraqi II Republican Guard Corps."

80 Captured document, (31 March 2003) "Situation Reports, Commander 1st Sector Karbala."

81 Two-thirds of the 1st Marine Division—the 5th and 7th RCTs—had driven up Highway 1 to Ad-Diwaniyah before cutting over to An-Numiniyah on the Tigris. The 1st RCT—the other one-third of the division—had driven up Highway 7 to Al-Kut before turning northwest along the Tigris to reunite with the division's main body at An-Numaniyah.

82 "Perspectives Iraqi II Republican Guard Corps."

83 V Corps Summary from April indicates that the corps' close air support force was focused on destroying the supporting artillery of the Medina Division as well as supporting the close-in fight.

84 "Perspectives Iraqi II Republican Guard Corps."

85 Undoubtedly Saddam was worried about an American precision air attack directed against his person.

86 Hamdani said he had not been informed as to exactly what the natures of those emergency procedures were. Captured documents indicate an extensive series of "emergency plans" (some going back to 1993) at the national and Governorate levels that predominately focused on local Ba'ath militias controlling critical building, key bridges, and local populations.

87 Interviews with the Al-Nida Republican Guards Commander indicate that they received the order on 1 April. However, due to the cumulative effects of air attacks and desertion, the division was only able to move 1,000 troops and 50 armored vehicles into this final defensive line (from a pre-war strength of almost 14,000 troops and 550 armored vehicles).

88 "Perspectives Iraqi II Republican Guard Corps."

89 "Perspectives Iraqi II Republican Guard Corps."

90 "Perspectives Iraqi II Republican Guard Corps." The bridge referred to here was called Objective Peach by the Coalition and was located approximately 20 kilometers northwest of Al-Iskandari-yah.

91 Captured document, (2 April 2003) "Letter From Ministry of Foreign Affairs to Office of the President Regarding Russian Intel."

92 "Perspectives Iraqi II Republican Guard Corps."

93 "Perspectives Iraqi II Republican Guard Corps."

94 Unpublished draft memoirs of LTG Raad Hamdani, Commander, II Republican Guard Corps.

95 "Perspectives Iraqi II Republican Guard Corps."

96 "Perspectives Iraqi II Republican Guard Corps."

97 "Perspectives Iraqi II Republican Guard Corps." Hamdani was referring to the Ludendorff railroad bridge at Remagen that soldiers of the US 9th Armored Division captured on 7 March 1945. Its capture and exploitation allowed the Americans to gain a secure bridgehead over the Rhine and eventually led to the surrounding of the Ruhr pocket in which much of the German Army in the west went into captivity.

98 "Perspectives Iraqi II Republican Guard Corps."

99 "Perspectives Iraqi II Republican Guard Corps."

100 "Perspectives Iraqi II Republican Guard Corps."

[101] "Perspectives Iraqi II Republican Guard Corps."

[102] This is a physical impossibility and something well known by most competent Iraqi military officers. The 25,000-pound usable load of a CH-47 falls well short of being able to lift a Bradley fighting vehicle, much less an Abrams tank.

[103] "Perspectives Iraqi II Republican Guard Corps."

[104] "Perspectives Iraqi II Republican Guard Corps."

[105] "Perspectives Iraqi II Republican Guard Corps."

[106] "Perspectives Iraqi II Republican Guard Corps." It is worth noting here that American forces were firing on buildings from which they were taking fire, while many US troops had begun to regard any civilian vehicle driving around in the midst of a massive firefight during the dawn hours as being a suicide bomber's vehicle, bent on attacking them.

[107] "Perspectives Iraqi II Republican Guard Corps."

[108] "Perspectives Iraqi II Republican Guard Corps."

[109] Captured document, (6 April 2003) "Ministry of Defense/Air Force Command Memorandum No. 171, Referring to a Minister of Defense Chaired Conference on 30 March 2003."

[110] Classified Intelligence Report, May 2003.

[111] Classified Intelligence Report, October 2003.

[112] Captured document, (1 April 2003) "Memorandum to Customs Police."

[113] Captured document, (2 April 2003) "Orders from the Arabic Socialist Ba'ath Party to the General Command of the People's Army."

[114] Captured document, (4 April 2003) "General Military Intelligence Directorate to the 8th Adjutant Confirming Saddam Hussein's Order to Treat the Arab Fedayeen Volunteers the Same Way as Special Forces Troops in Terms of their Salaries and Supplies." The total number of Arab volunteers is not clear. However, an 11 March 2003 memo indicates significant bureaucratic efforts by the Ministry of Defense to integrate Arab volunteers into training camps, to get them equipped, and to get them paid. Volunteers noted on this document came from such countries as Bulgaria, Turkey, Syria, Tunisia, Egypt, United Arab Emirates, Libya, and the Palestinian territories. Captured document, (11 March 2003) "Military Command Memos Concerned with the Arabian Volunteers to the Iraqi Special Forces."

[115] Captured document, (6 April 2003) "Correspondence of the Communications Directorate on Order to Honor Fighters in 1st Gulf War, Orders to Increase Allowance for Transportation."

[116] Captured document, (7 April 2003) "GMID Commanding."

Illustrations

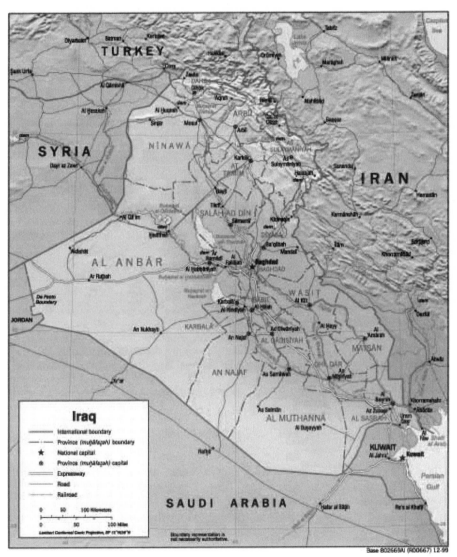

Iraq. Source: Courtesy of Central Intelligence Agency,
CIA Atlas of the Middle East, 1993.[1]

Iraqi's Regional Command Plan Sectors.[2]

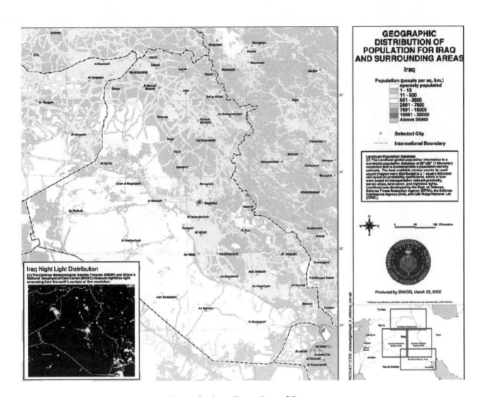

Population Density of Iraq.

Using Iraqi perpectives of the American "Way-of-War," the
obvious terrain to attack through was from the West.[3]

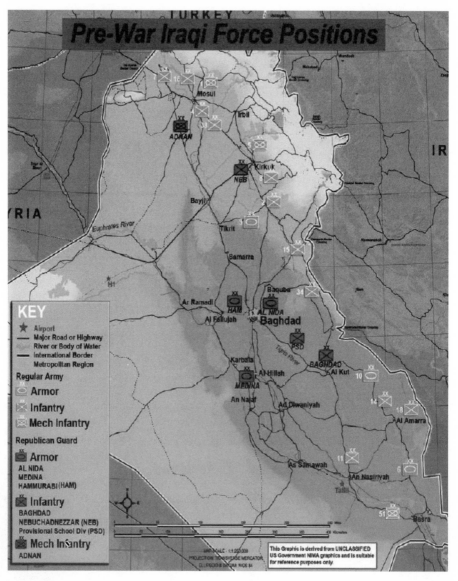

Iraqi forces on the eve of Operation Iraq Freedom February/March 2003.[4]

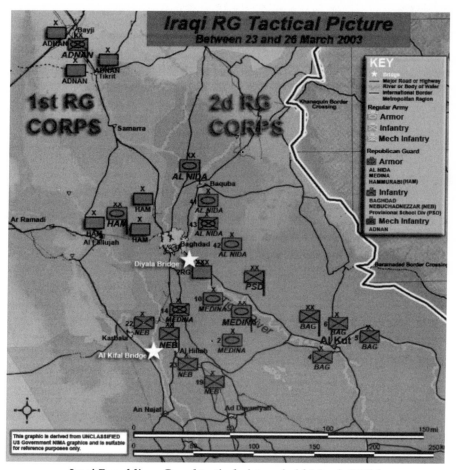

Iraqi Republican Guard tactical picture (mid-March 2003).[5]

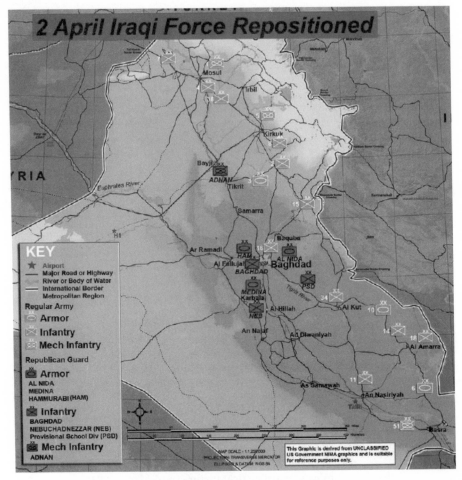

Iraqi Force Repositioned (2 April 2003).[6]

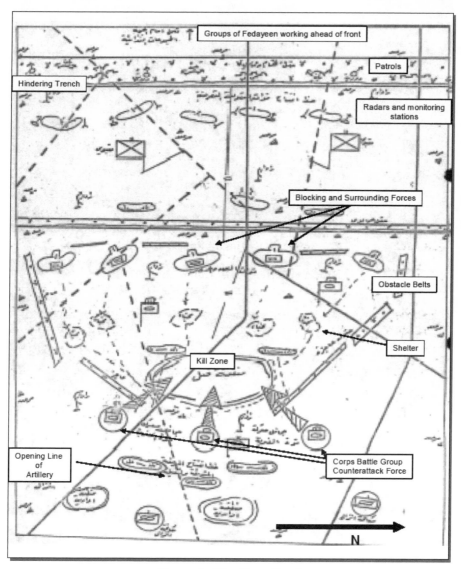

Concept of the Operation.[7]

Extract from *Iraqi Plan For the Defense of Basra*

Dictator-in-Training.[8]

Saddam visits the Soviet Union (mid-1970s).

Saddam meets with tribal leaders (21 September 1996).[9]

Saddam and tribal leaders (undated).[10]

Saddam pinning medal on Tariq Aziz and Taha Yasin Ramadan, members of the
Revolutionary Command Council (Circa 2002).[11]

Special Republican Guard exercise.[12]

Special Republican Guard Mortar Squad during a scripted exercise.[13]

Iraqi-sponsored Palestinian training camp.[14]

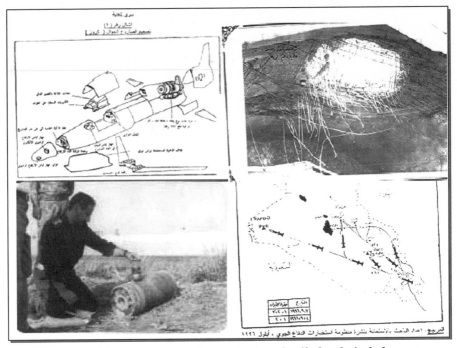

Examples of Iraqi military studies, including detailed technical, damage, and operational assesments of US airpower.[15]

Iraqi Air Force MIG-25 Foxbat being excavated near Al Taqqadum Airfield (July 2003).[16]

Undated photograph of Saddam in formal military attire.[17]

Undated photo of the Minister of Defense Sultan Hashim Ahmed Al Hamed Al Tai.[18]

Izzat Al Duri, Deputy Prime Minister and Commander of the Northern Region.[19]

LTG Raad Al-Hamdani Commander II Republican Guard.[20]

Staff LTG Huwaysh-Fadani Al-Ani Deputy Military Advisor to Central Euphrates Region.[21]

This is part of their (The United States) sick mentality. The US villains have no presence in Baghdad City. They tried to bring in a group of tanks and armored personnel carriers through al-Darah. They were besieged there. Most of them were dealt with. Their villains were slaughtered. We made them drink poison last night and the great forces of leader Saddam Hussein have taught them a lesson that history will never forget (7 April 2003).

Iraqi Information Minister Muhammed Saeed Al-Sahaf.[22]

Patch of the Fedayeen Saddam.[23]

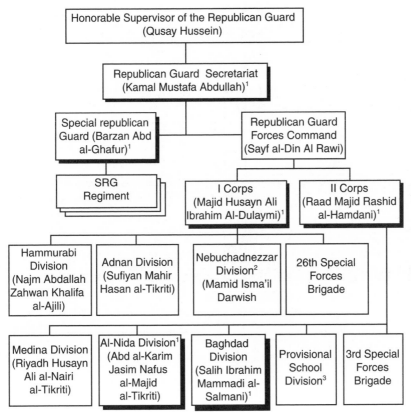

Notes:
1. Interviewed for IPP.
2. This division was transferred from I Corps to II Corps in mid-March 2003.
3. This unit was created from the cadre and students of the advanced infantry
   and armor school and employed near Al Aziziyah.

Overview of the Republican Guards, Regular Army, and Special Forces.[24]

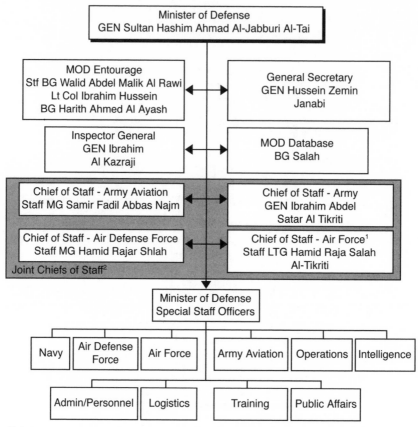

Notes:
1. The Chief of Staff of the Air Force became the Chief of Staff of the Air Defense just prior to OIF.
2. The Iraqi Joint Chiefs of Staff included Army, Air Force, Air Defense, and Army Aviation but not the Iraqi Navy.

Overview of the Ministry of Defense Organizations.[25]

NOTES

1 Courtesy of Central Intelligence Agency, CIA Atlas of the Middle East, 1993.

2 Iraqi Perspectives Project Graphic.

3 Defense Intelligence Agency, 22 March 2002.

4 Iraqi Perspectives Project Graphic.

5 Iraqi Perspectives Project Graphic.

6 Iraqi Perspectives Project Graphic.

7 Captured document, (20 February 2003) Report by the Office of the Chief of Staff of the Army on Iraq Battle Plans."

8 Captured document, "War photos and pictures from Saddam's visit to the Soviet Union in the 1970's."

9 Captured document, (21 September 1996) "Photograph of Saddam Hussein and letters from tribal leaders."

10 Captured document, (date unknown) "Saddam and tribal leaders."

11 Captured document, (date unknown) "Tariq Aziz photographs."

12 Captured document, (date unknown) "Special Republican Guard photos."

13 Captured document, (undated) "Special Republican Guards photographs."

14 Captured document, (undated) "Military style parade at an unlocated Palestinian training camp."

15 Captured documents, (21 December 1991): "Letters from GMID regarding unexploded American missile," (1990) "MOD/AFC study on strategy behind hostile air attack on air bases in 1991," (6 December 1999) "MOD conference report on Cruise Missile technology."

16 Iraqi Perspectives Project Graphic.

17 Captured document, (date unknown) "Undated photograph of Saddam Hussein."

18 Captured document, (July 2002) From an issue of Iraq's military magazine.

19 Captured document, (July 2002) "The Military Magazine issued by Ministry of Defense."

20 Iraqi Perspectives Project Graphic.

21 Iraqi Perspectives Project Graphic.

22 Foreign Broadcast Information Service, (7 April 2003) "Iraqi Information Minister denies presence of U.S. Forces in Baghdad."

23 Iraqi Perspectives Project Graphic.

24 Iraqi Perspectives Project Graphic.

25 Iraqi Perspectives Project Graphic.

ANNEX. THE IRAQI PERSPECTIVES PROJECT: METHODOLOGY AND SOURCES OF INFORMATION

> Archival restraints, personal predications, limitations of time and energy help explain the frequent practice of concentrating on only one side of a conflict; but combat is more than shadow boxing.

> — Peter Paret[1]

Methodology

For those trying to learn military lessons, the best teacher is often defeat in a battle.[2] Historical cases of the winning side making adaptive changes based on careful study of "how we won" are difficult to find.[3] The most notable examples of militaries learning lessons are those recovering from defeat, such as the German Army after World War I or the US Army after Vietnam. The perspective of the losing side provides a powerful agent of change.[4] To buck that historical pattern, any study of "how we won" must include a careful study of the adversary's perspectives on "how he lost." Other nations are already conducting campaign analyses of the 2003 invasion of Iraq. These nations may have a better chance of seeing lessons from the "loser's perspective" than Americans would, given the afterglow of a conventional success.[5]

The distinction between learning lessons and collecting lessons is critical. The relevant metric for successful "learning" as a part of a lessons-learned activity should be the extent to which past experience informs the preparation of US military forces for future possibilities. Americans are often self-critical; some have declared the US military is again preparing for the last war and that it can learn little "fighting such fools."[6] The fact that the United States can only guess as to its next adversary suggests that using Iraq as a "surrogate" for potential conventional foes may be appropriate; the war of 2003 was a battle of wills and not a sterile battle against a "rent-a-foe" in a training exercise. As with any surrogate, understanding the likely similarities and differences is crucial.

In general terms this project has followed the basic outline for critical analysis put forward by the Prussian theorist Carl von Clausewitz in his *On War*: "War is not waged against an abstract enemy, but against a real one who must always be kept in mind."[7] The first step requires the discovery and interpretation of equivocal facts. The second step aims to trace effects back to causes. Finally the third step requires an investigation and evaluation of the means employed.[8] Even with a narrowly defined project purpose, task, and methodology, there are still limitations to the analysis. In the next section, we categorize and discuss four limitations: (1) understanding, (2) accounting for chaos and the nature of war, (3) bounding the project or identifying the "trade space," and (4) recognizing preconceived notions about the adversary.

Understanding

Understanding the limits that impede one's ability to understand or even adequately perceive the "perspective" of another person, organization, or culture (much less to place that understanding in the context of an event) is foundational. Many well-founded theories explain why it is difficult for individuals and organizations to understand others.[9] For the purposes of this project, the three most relevant reasons why this is difficult are (1) the way human beings manage the information they possess, (2) the way they deal with new information, and (3) finally how they attempt to place that information in a meaningful context of past events.

Managing information. The first barrier to understanding is the tendency for individuals to be overconfident in their ability to combine information in complex ways. Such overconfidence has three major elements. The first is, in reality, the majority of people do not know what information they rely on or how they actually use the information they have. In other words, they do not even understand themselves. Such blindness inevitably leads to an overestimation of the sophistication of the thought processes. The second element is a lack of self-awareness of the extent to which individuals lock information into preconceived beliefs and assumptions. Throughout history, military leaders and staffs have consistently attempted to force reality into their vision of the future rather than adapt the vision to the reality. Finally, the third element leading to overconfidence is a lack of self-awareness of the extent to which individuals rely on analogies with past events, "especially recent events that they or their own country have experienced first hand."[10]

Assimilating new information. The second barrier to understanding is the tendency for individuals to assimilate new information into preexisting beliefs. Robert Jervis argues that "ambiguous or even discrepant information is ignored, misperceived, or reinterpreted so that it does minimum damage to what the person already believes."[11] Assimilating new information presented significant challenges to US policy makers and military professionals, given the long, adversarial relationship the United States had with Saddam's regime.

Avoiding the Hindsight Bias. The third major barrier to understanding is what political scientists have termed the "Hindsight Bias." This bias results from the psychological dilemma confronted when trying to reconstruct and understand a series of decisions and judgments when you know how events actually played out. As Roberta Wohlstetter stated:

> It is much easier after the fact to sort the relevant from the irrelevant signals. After the event, or course, a signal is always crystal clear. We can now see what disaster it was signaling since the disaster has occurred, but before the event it is obscure and pregnant with conflicting meanings.[12]

The challenge is, how do you reconstruct the battlefield in such a way that the operational and intelligence communities can benefit? The solution is finding a balance between knowledge of actual events from both sides free from preconceived interpretations. Because this challenge falls into the nature of how human beings think and perceive, knowledge of the bias is the only defense against its effect.[13]

Accounting for the Nature of War

> It is impossible to foresee with any degree of certainty which effects will be brought about by this particular cause, nor is it possible to state with any degree of certainty in retrospect what particular cause has produced this effect.
>
> — Hans J. Morgenthau[14]

Accounting for the nature of war is critical if analysts, commentators, and historians are to avoid over-simplification or—even worse—the creation of a perfectly elegant but perfectly wrong description of what happened. The nature of war, being the domain of chance, does not lend itself to a clear description of cause-and-effect, no matter how determined or detailed the investigation.

The character of the Coalition's campaign (e.g., multidimensional, rapid, precise) only serves to exacerbate the nature of what is a natural state of affairs in warfare—chaos. The use of the term "chaos" applies not only to the general conduct of the Iraqi defense but also to a fundamental, conceptual description of war itself. The non-linear effect of obscure, unrecorded, and often unknowable events makes any detailed analysis subjective and, in some instances, no better than the pre-war intelligence estimates of "what might be."[15]

Throughout the ages, military historians have struggled to bring order to battlefield chaos and match cause-and-effect to outcomes and actions in a campaign. The advantage enjoyed by a historian's *post-facto* view of the world, as opposed to the intelligence officer's *predictive view*, does not confer any special key to the puzzle of chaotic events.[16] The nature of war makes the historian's question "Why did this adversary react this way?" no less challenging than the intelligence officer's question of "How will this adversary react to us?"

The Trade Space

The trade space consists of areas open to exploration at the outset. The trade space for the Iraqi Perspectives Project was initially defined as the same space covered by the US Joint Forces Command Lessons Learned Report on the conduct of major combat operations during OPERATION IRAQI FREEDOM, only from the adversary's point of view. The Iraqi Perspective Project focuses on the military aspects at the operational level of war and does not overlap with other major areas of investigation, which fall into the following categories:

Tactical perspective. First, the Services and other groups are examining the conduct of OPERATION IRAQI FREEDOM from a tactical and weapon system level. These studies will include references, findings, and background at the operational level, but the primary focus remains on building a *tactical perspective*.[17]

Strategic perspective. The second area consists of ongoing studies to examine the strategic issues associated with OPERATION IRAQI FREEDOM. Evaluations of its strategic nature are in the open press and academic journals. Most strategic lessons-learned studies however, are being conducted by the US Department of Defense's Joint Staff. As with tactical studies, elements of operational warfare are a natural component of these strategic views, but for the most part they remain distinct in their focus on strategy. There is an overlap between the strategic areas examined from the Coalition and Iraqi perspectives by the Iraqi Perspectives Project. This overlap results from the nature of the campaign. From the coalition perspective, OPERATION IRAQI FREEDOM was a major campaign conducted in a theater of war. However, from the Iraqi perspective, OPERATION IRAQI FREEDOM was a strategic campaign representing the gravest threat to the regime.

Ongoing issues. The third area of the trade space not covered by this project involves the issues studied by the Iraqi Survey Group and those topics related to ongoing intelligence operations (specifically international terrorism and insurgency) after 9 April 2003. The Iraqi Perspectives Project had unprecedented access to the information, facilities, and people necessary to develop this report. Nonetheless, it was difficult to come to significant conclusions or insights into the basic study questions while issues were still unfolding and remain a focus of the study. For example, when focusing on weapons of mass destruction, the Iraqi Survey Group had over 1,200 qualified professionals working to resolve the fundamental questions surrounding Iraq's weapons of mass destruction programs. The Iraqi Perspectives Project does not have the expertise or resources to address those issues in detail. The conduct of a parallel study effort to the Iraqi Survey Group would be difficult and disruptive to the study's efforts to explain the Iraqi perspective on the conduct of the war.[18] Thus, the Iraqi Perspectives Project did not explicitly address the issue of weapons of mass destruction (WMD). The same logic applied to the Iraqi Survey Group mission holds true to the other organizations collecting information on international terrorism and the ongoing insurgency.

Preconceived Notions About the Adversary

Finally, this study has a view of OPERATION IRAQI FREEDOM that remains influenced by the long relationship the United States had with the former Iraqi regime. We should be wary of the tendency to fit available evidence into previously developed concepts of the problem. In addition to perceptions of Iraq,

Americans remain bound up within their own perceptions of themselves. At first blush, many post-war analyses from the 1991 Gulf War seem applicable to the public analyses of the recent campaign.[19] Given the continuous nature of the US–Coalition conflict with Iraq since 1990, this appears to make sense at first. The problem however, is the analysis of the first Gulf War included very little information available from the "losing side." As one commentator noted "[i]t is rather common for American military analysts substantially to ignore the enemy when they assess a war; this pattern seems to hold for the Gulf War in 1991."[20] It is likely that with America's "easy success in major combat operations," analysts are enthusiastically fitting the new information of the 2003 Gulf War into comfortable, old analytical frameworks—only with more confidence than before.[21]

Major Sources of Information

Most of this study on Iraq's military performance rests on two primary sources of information: (1) interviews, debriefs, and interrogations of a significant cross-section of the senior leaders of the military and the Ba'ath regime; and (2) captured Iraqi documents.[22] Augmenting these primary sources are extensive open-source reporting, academic research, and declassified extracts of US government intelligence material, assessments, and reports.[23] The foundation of this Iraqi performance study rests on Iraqi primary sources—it is their perspective.

People

The Iraqi Perspectives Project Team identified the Iraqis that would, in a perfect world, provide the most historical insight into the study questions. The personnel selection process took into account the centralized but complex chain of command that existed in Iraq. The simplest analysis began with the well-known list of individuals identified as the "Top-55" Black List—the "deck of cards" (see Figure A-1). With the exception of Saddam Hussein, many of these individuals were available (i.e., in custody) to the Iraqi Perspectives Project Team between November and December 2004 (see Table A-1). Of the Iraqis available, we determined that 20 of the 55 were the most likely to provide the strategic and/or operational military insights necessary to satisfy the project's questions. Most of those identified had been directly involved in military or political command and control during OPERATION IRAQI FREEDOM. For example, the Secretary of the Republican Guard or Saddam's personal secretary provided insights into Saddam's decisions or his actions immediately prior to the war.

Saddam was captured after the interview phase and was not available as of this writing for an interview. But the Iraqi Perspectives Project Team has had access to most of the existing debriefs and documentation captured with him.

Figure A-1. The "Top-55" Black List leaders of the former Iraqi regime.

The photos with purple borders are considered significant sources of information for this study.

While this information did not directly support to the study questions, it provided insights into Saddam's personality and habits. Therefore, Saddam's picture was added to Figure A-1.

A significant number of Iraqis were determined to be of potential value but ended up not being placed in the "Top-55". They were selected on the basis of their commands and location on the battlefield. In two other cases, other Iraqis were selected by the study team based on the recommendations of Iraqis previously interviewed.

Not all interviews were of equal value. In addition to the diverse conditions in which the various interviews took place, each Iraqi subject had different motivations for answers.[24] Some Iraqis were clearly anxious to appear cooperative in hopes of gaining favor later. Others attempted to establish a rationale for why they should not be considered a threat. Still other interviewees attempted to hide the fact they were persons of considerable and significant influence over events or were, in fact, personally implicated in the regime's crimes.

For example, Lieutenant-General Raad Hamdani (Commander, II Republican

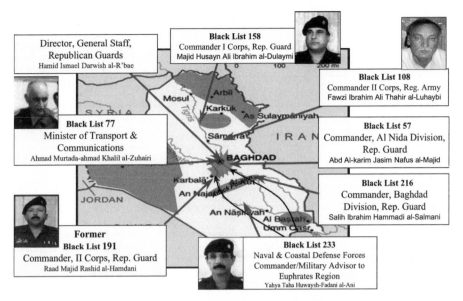

Figure A-2. Sources Below the "Top 55."

Guard Corps) was interviewed on five different occasions, totaling more than 20 hours. According to Hamdani, the primary motivation for discussing his actions during the war was one of a professional soldier trying to establish an honest history of what occurred. He viewed history as a "sacred duty" of all soldiers and an important step in building a new Iraq. In nearly every respect, the team found his answers truthful and honest to the extent that his memory would allow.

On the other hand, General Ali Hassan Al-Majid Tikriti was quite different. Number 5 on the Coalition's Black List, "Chemical Ali" was a member of the Revolutionary Command Council. The Iraqi Survey Group Interrogation Team assessed him as an intelligent individual, highly manipulative of those around him—"a consummate con-man." A US officer with ten years of interrogation/ debriefing experience who was working with the IPP team was able to observe the debriefs of Chemical Ali. The officer noticed that in subtle but effective ways, Chemical Ali managed to manipulate the assigned interrogation team and supporting analysts. Based on the collected interviews and reviews of previous interrogations, it became obvious to the team that Chemical Ali's memory for details was impressive—as long as that memory did not include his own actions or decisions.

For the most part, the Iraqi Perspectives Project Team accepted the judgments of US Government experts on the veracity of the subjects they interviewed; the team made no attempt to reach independent conclusions. Where possible, the team corroborated the statements with other interviews or hard data such as imagery or battlefield reporting.

BG – Brigadier General
Cdr – Commander
CoS – Chief of Staff

GEN – General
LTG – Lieutenant-General
MG –Major General

RCC – Revolutionary
Command Council
RG – Republican Guard

Name	Rank	Black List #	Former Position
Abid Hamid Mahmud Al-Tikriti	GEN	4	Saddam's Personal Secretary
Ali Hassan Al-Majid Tikriti ("Chemical Ali")	GEN	5	RCC/Regional Commander
Kamal Mustafa Abdullah	LTG	10	Secretary of Republican Guard
Barzan Abd Al-Ghafur Sulayman Majid Al-Tikriti	LTG	11	Cdr, Special Republican Guard
Muzahim Sab Hasan Al-Tikriti	LTG	12	Cdr, Air Defense
Ibrahim Ahmad Abd Al-Sattar Muhamad Al-Tikriti	LTG	13	CoS, Armed Forces and Army
Hamid Raja Shalah Al-Tikriti	LTG	17	Cdr, Iraqi Air Force
Abd Al-Tawab Abdullah Mullah Al-Huwaysh	GEN	19	Director, Office of Military Industrialization
Tariq Aziz		25	Deputy Prime Minister/RCC
Sultan Hashim Ahmad Al-Jabburi Al-Tai	GEN	27	Minister of Defense
Hikmat Mizban Ibrahim Al-Azzawi		28	Deputy Prime Minister of Finance
Ayad Futayyih Khalifa Al-Rawi		30	Al-Quds Force Chief of Staff
Zuhayr Talib Abd Al Sattar Al Naqib	LTG	31	Director, Military Intelligence
Mohammad Mahdi Al-Salih		35	Minister of Trade
Samir Abd Al Aziz Al Najim		42	Central Ba'ath Party Chairman
Abd Al-Karim Jasim Mafus Al-Majid	MG	57	Cdr, Al-Nida RG Division
Ahmad Murtada-Ahmad Khalil Al-Zuhairi		77	Minister of Transport and Communication
Fawzi Ibrahim Thahir al Luhaybi	LTG	108	Cdr, Regular Army 2nd Corps
Majid Husayn Ali Ibrahim Al-Dulaymi	LTG	158	Cdr, RG I Corps
Raad Majid Rashid Al-Hamdani	LTG	191	Cdr, RG II Corps
Salih Ibrahim Hammadi Al-Salmani	MG	216	Cdr, Baghdad RG Division
Yahya Taha Huwaysh-Fadani Al-Ani	LTG	233	Cdr, Naval and Coastal Defense Forces
Saif Al Din Nasr Yusif Al Ugaydi	BG		Cdr, Talil Air Base
Kenan Mansour Khalil Al Obadi	LTG		Military Advisor Central Euphrates
Muhammid Sattam Abdullah Al Hamdani	BG		CoS, Al-Nida RG Division
Yunis Mohammed Therir Suliman Chidadi	LTG		Governor, Thiqar Dist (Nasiriyah)

Table A-1. List of primary sources for interviews, debriefs, or written responses to questions.

Documents

The seemingly obvious place to gather insights on Iraq's operational planning would be to examine the Iraqi equivalent of OPLAN 1003V—US Central Command's classified theater-level war plan. In fact there was no equivalent document. Even if such a document had existed, the nature of document exploitation after OPERATION IRAQI FREEDOM would not have guaranteed it would have been available to this study. Document exploitation is challenging under the best of circumstances. For every document seized, someone must determine the content (translation), the context (e.g., at what level was it written, for what purpose), the relative value (e.g., was it a draft, was it seen or acted on by a principle or organization) or even whether it was ever promulgated. The rapid collapse of Saddam's regime resulted in the opening of a relatively well-documented and technologically advanced government bureaucracy to examination. That is the good news; the bad news is the scope and scale of the documentation available for exploitation. The Iraqi Perspectives Project Team's first encounter with the challenge came on a visit to the document exploitation operation in Qatar in November 2003.

Upon entering the main warehouse (Figure A-3), the team confronted a scene reminiscent of the end of the Steven Spielberg movie *Indiana Jones and the Raiders of the Lost Ark*. After recovering the lost Ark of the Covenant from

Figure A-3. Captured-documents warehouse.

the Nazis, the audience watches archivists box it up and slowly wheel it into an anonymous US Government warehouse already filled with similar boxes, presumably only to be lost again.

As a supporting organization to the Iraqi Survey Group, the Combined Media Processing Center has the mission of processing masses of documents, maps, digital, and analog media captured during OPERATION IRAQI FREEDOM. From the standup of the Combined Media Processing Center in the summer of 2003 through the writing of this document, that organization has amassed a document collection of over almost 600,000 files, including thousands of media files. Archivists have triaged the collection for critical data, scanned them into a captured documents database, and made them available to analysts through a classified government network.[25]

The Iraqi Perspectives Project team has taken full advantage of this operation in preparation of this study. In addition to maps, the team has drawn heavily on the captured documents database and used almost 700 document and media files to support this analysis with more than 100 cited. Materials range from a planning map of the Republican Guard headquarters displaying the defensive scheme of Baghdad to the Top Secret transcribed minutes of the meeting between the Russian Ambassador and members of the Iraqi Foreign ministry immediately prior to the outbreak of war.[26]

Research Methodology

Phase I: Background Research

The first phase of the Iraqi Perspectives Project began with a survey of available open-source and classified literature on the subject of Iraq, the regime, and OPERATION IRAQI FREEDOM. The aim was to establish and understand the sources of information and how the team could gain the highest return on time invested. The output of this phase was a database of classified and unclassified references, a bibliography of published works, and a plan of action for primary interviews. (See References for a partial bibliography.)

The team leveraged a considerable collection of open-source material on Iraq's military capabilities ranging from historical reviews on Iraq's military capabilities, in Kenneth Pollack's *Arabs at War: Military Effectiveness 1948-1991* and military assessments after the first Gulf War to more current estimates ranging from the excellent series published by the Center for Strategic and International Studies to the growing volume of post-war analyses.[27] Additionally, there are several works on the nature of the Saddam Hussein regime and its inner workings, including Kanan Makiya's seminal work *Republic of Fear* and a number of academic articles.[28]

Prewar classified material on Iraq's regime is voluminous. The majority of classified sources deal with externally observable capabilities (e.g., force structure, training events, force disposition) and the resulting analysis of how the Iraqis might use them in different scenarios. Some prewar analysis did prove accurate in assessing the internal relationships and potential impact on operational effectiveness, but its utility to the operational planners is hard to judge.

The team also made use of the extensive intelligence produced during the prewar period and, to a lesser extent, analyses of major combat operations after 1 May 2003. These assessments include analyses of Iraqi military capability and orders of battle, background material on Iraqi military doctrine, intelligence summaries from coalition units, commander's assessments and planning documents of the coalition units in the fight, and imagery. These documents represent a valuable secondary source of information to provide context; establish a background; and, in many cases, validate primary sources. The other valuable purpose of these documents, specifically the operations planning documents prior to the major combat operations and the intelligence assessments prior and during major combat operations, is to provide a basis to contrast perspectives.

Phase II: Collection

The second phase involved deploying a portion of the Iraqi Perspectives Project Team to Baghdad to conduct individual interviews with Iraqis. An accomplished Arabic linguist and trained strategic debriefer, as well as complete access granted by US Central Command, the Iraqi Survey Group, the Coalition Provisional Authority, and various US Government agencies, supported this phase.

The primary method during this phase was to conduct interviews, acting as historians collecting oral histories. There were two distinct advantages to this approach. First, since this project represents a historical inquiry, the authors provided a clear distinction between themselves and the intelligence teams that had been talking to the detainees for upwards of six months on a narrow range of questions. While the answers (and sometimes non-answers) to the interrogations have provided background and, in some cases, direct information to the study, they generally failed to provide the context within which the Iraqis made operational decisions.

The second advantage of the historical approach was the tendency of professional soldiers to want to tell their own war story.[29] To be clear some of those interviewed had other motivations. These ranged from a sense of professional duty as a soldier, to an attempt to recover a sense of martial pride after Iraq's catastrophic defeat on the battlefield, to boredom and a desire to talk and not just answer questions. In several cases, the Iraqi Survey Group interrogation teams and analysts noted the increased willingness of several detainees to talk under these "oral history" conditions.

The Iraqi Perspectives Project interviewed the subjects under three distinct

Figure A-4. Iraqi Perspectives Project interview with former Republican Guard officer in Baghdad – November 2003.

circumstances. The first was to utilize the debriefing centers established by coalition military commands. The process involved reviewing the available dossier information on the subject, to include previous interviews, interrogations, and debriefs. The next step required coordinating with the interrogation teams working with the subject to clear both the method of interview and the actual interview questions. This step had the additional advantage of providing insights on the disposition, personality, and perspective of the interviewees.[30] The team conducted these interviews in a relaxed environment, usually with a 1:250,000 scale military map on the table and a translator (see Figure A-4). The interview lengths varied from one to two hours.

The second method of conducting interviews involved meeting Iraqis not in coalition custody but instead at various public locations in Baghdad. It was clear to the Iraqis that the interviews were part of a US Government history project. The advantage of these interviews was that they generally were not constrained by time, conditions were more conducive to a relaxed discussion, and they provided easy access to the Iraqis of interest.

Finally, the third method was through a third party, usually a coalition debriefing team already working with the subject. In these cases, the basic set of questions was modified for the subject and provided to the debriefer. In some cases, the team observed the interviews; in other cases, it received answers to the questions through the debriefing team or after the answers had been published in US government reports.

As with all instances of collecting information from individuals (whether in journalism, oral histories, or human intelligence), there are certain caveats readers should keep in mind. Individuals provide information for reasons of the following: (1) honestly trying to present the truth, (2) exercising their own sense of self-importance, (3) attempting to deceive or influence, (4) attempting to curry favor, or (5) providing out of fear. There are no automatic filters to account for these variations, but there are some simple techniques. Among the techniques to control for variations in motivation, the team used the US Government assessments of a particular source, multiple sources for a given comment or story, and cross-referenced facts with alternative sources (i.e., finding documents that corroborate an interview). In the final analysis, historical analysis comes down to a matter of judgment, based on the data available.

Phase III: Exploitations and Analysis

The third phase of the project involved follow-up and exploitation of the material gathered to date. The interviews were transcribed and correlated to other sources of information (i.e., other interviews; documented interrogations; imagery; and, in some cases, intelligence assessments or battlefield reports from the coalition). In addition, with the contacts and leads developed in Phases I and II, the team was able to focus its remaining research into key areas of the growing Iraqi exploited documents available through the US Government.

The document exploitation conducted in support of the Iraqi Perspectives Project has provided a significant amount of critical information from inside the regime. Examples of these documents exist throughout the body of the study, including such items as Iraqi Ministry of Foreign Affairs transcriptions of conversations with the Russian Ambassador to Iraq prior to and during OPERATION IRAQI FREEDOM (March 2003), Iraqi Republican Guard staff studies of probable coalition military courses of action and recommended reactions (February 2003), plans for surviving precision air attacks (2002), and Iraqi studies of US satellite capabilities (February 2003). The volume of documents and the fact that the number of newly translated documents is growing daily means that while the team screened a large percentage of the database with a priority document filter, this study could utilize only a small fraction of what potentially would be available in less relevant translations.[31]

As with the previously cited cautions on using information gathered from humans, there are concerns relating to documents. Basil Liddell Hart once suggested that "[n]othing can deceive like a document. A purely documentary history is akin to mythology."[32] As this study will illustrate, the cautions on documents may be even more important, especially when following the paper trail within the bureaucracy of such a corrupt regime. Among the reasons one must view documents with caution are the possibility of forgeries, official documents written for less than honest purposes, missing documents, documents out of context, or those left purposely incomplete. The Iraqi Perspectives Project has attempted to place documentary evidence in context with information from multiple human sources and, where possible, cross-reference with secondary sources to include coalition intelligence information.

The Iraqi Perspective

What was the Iraqi view of the operation? The simplicity of this question belies the challenge and complexity of answering it. The challenge is even more daunting when considering the friction and sometime controversy, of describing the intent, plans, and actions of the coalition during OPERATION IRAQI FREEDOM, where one has access to many original documents, first-person interviews, and a common culture. In investigating the Iraqi perspective of OPERATION IRAQI FREEDOM, the Iraqi Perspectives Project made every effort to access original documents and personal interviews. Given the security situation in Iraqi during the major investigation phase of this study, access to Iraqi material remained more limited than access to Coalition material. However, the authors believe that the benefits of this study, and others like it, far outweigh any methodological shortcomings.

Notes

1   Peter Paret, "Military Power," The Journal of Military History, vol. 53, no. 3, (July 1989), pp. 239–256.

2   The distinction between learning lessons and just collecting lessons is critical. The metric for the "learning" part of lesson-learned activities can be summarized as the extent to which past experience informs actions in the preparation for some future possibility.

3   An exception to the rule might be the German OKH, which after the 1939 campaign in Poland instituted numerous changes to organization and doctrine prior to the 1940 campaign in France. See Williamson Murray, "The German Response to Victory in Poland: A Case Study in Professionalism," Armed Forces and Society (Winter 1981).

4   Although this is not always the case (the Italian military being a case in point). See Macgregor Knox, Mussolini Unleashed, 1939-1941: Politics and Strategy in Fascist Italy's Last War, Cambridge University Press, Cambridge, 1982.

5   For example, FBIS documents from DPRK, Russia, China, Ukraine, and many others all indicate an active examination of relevant lessons.

6   Loren Thompson, "Lessons of Iraq: Strategic and Joint Implications," briefing presented at the Defense News Force Projection Conference, 22 September 2003.

7   Carl von Clausewitz, On War, ed. and trans. by Michael Howard and Peter Paret, Princeton University Press, Princeton, NJ, 1976, p. 161.

8   Clausewitz, On War, pp. 156–169.

9   A significant body of work (case studies and theoretical analysis) relating to the issue of thinking about the adversary perspective are found in the broader analyses of surprise and deception. Setting the differences in context aside, these works all explore the implications of considering alternative theories as well as the practical impacts of analytical processes on decision-makers, and are applicable to the Iraqi Perspectives Project. For example, see Roberta Wohlstetter, Pearl Harbor: Warning and Decision (Stanford: University Press, 1962); Graham Allison and Philop Zelikow, Essence of Decision – Explaining the Cuban Missile Crisis, 2nd edition. (New York, Longman Press, 1999); Robert Jervis, Perception and Misperception in International Politics (Princeton, NJ: Princeton University Press, 1976); Richards J. Heur, Jr., "Strategic Deception and Counterdeception – A Cognitive Process Approach," International Studies Quarterly, Vol. 25, No. 2 (June 1981) p. 294-327; Richard K. Betts, "Analysis, War, and Decision: Why Intelligence Failures are Inevitable," World Politics, Vol. 31, No. 1 (October, 1978) p. 61-89; Abraham Ben-Avi, "The Outbreak and Termination of the Pacific War: A Juxtaposition of American Preconceptions," Journal of Peace Research, No. 1, Vol. XV (1978) p. 33-49.

10   Robert Jervis, "Deterrence and Perception," International Security, Winter 1982/1983, vol. 7, no. 3.

11   Jervis, "Deterrence and Perception."

12   Roberta Wohlstetter, Pearl Harbor: Warning and Decision (Stanford, CA, 1962), p. 387.

13   A more detailed discussion of this phenomenon and its effects can be found in the Central Intelligence Agency, Center for the Study of Intelligence report; Psychology of Intelligence Analysis, chapter 13, "Hindsight Biases in Evaluation of Intelligence Reporting," (Washington DC, 1999).

14   Hans J. Morgenthau, "The Limitations of Science and the Problem of Social Planning," Ethics, vol. 54, no. 3, April 1944.

[15] A good description of the challenges and limitations in attempting to "unravel" the chaotic nature of the battlefield can be found in Roger Beaumonts's, War, Chaos, and History (Novato, CA, 1994), especially chapters 2, 3, and 5).

[16] Continuing debates and newly published books on such topics such as generalship in the US Civil War, the causes of World War I, or even the impact of air power in Vietnam, point to the inherent limits of analysis (specifically cause-and-effect) relating to warfare.

[17] For example: The US Army's On Point (Washington DC, 2004) and CENTAF's data filled reference "Operation Iraqi Freedom - By The Numbers" (classified Secret version released by CENTAF Assessment and Analysis Division on 22 April 2003).

[18] For a detailed description of the Iraqi Survey Group mission and methodology, see Scope Note, vol. I, "Comprehensive Report of the Special Advisor to the DCI on Iraq's WMD" (Central Intelligence Agency, 30 September 2004), pg. 1-5.

[19] For example: Rick Atkinson, Crusade: The Untold Story of the Persian Gulf War (Boston, 1993), Summers, Harry Glenn, On Strategy II: A Critical Analysis of the Gulf War (New York, 1992), or Freeman and Karsh, The Gulf Conflict, 1990-1991: Diplomacy and War in the New World Order (Princeton, 1993), and the US Army, Certain Victory: The US Army in the Gulf War (Washington DC, 1993).

[20] John Mueller, "The Perfect Enemy: Assessing the Gulf War," Security Studies vol. 5, no. 1, Autumn 1995.

[21] For example, compare the debate surrounding judging military performance after the first Gulf War in Steven Biddle, "Victory Misunderstood: What the Gulf War Can Tell US About the Future of Conflict," International Security, vol. 21, no. 2, Fall 1996; Daryl Press, "Lessons from Ground Combat in the Gulf: The Impact of Training and Technology," International Security, vol. 22, no. 2, Autumn, 1997; Thomas Mahnken and Barry D. Watts, "What the Gulf War Can [and Cannot] Tell Us about the Future of Warfare," International Security, vol. 22, no. 2, Autumn 1997) with the emerging popular consensus after OPERATION IRAQI FREEDOM as seen in Dr Steven Biddle's Testimony, Committee on House Armed Services, October 21, 2003 "OPERATION IRAQI FREEDOM Outside Perspectives;" Walter Boyne, OPERATION IRAQI FREEDOM, What Went Right, What Went Wrong, and Why (New York, NY, 2003), Andrew Krepinevich, "OIF: A First Blush Assessment," CSBA Publication, 2003; Frederick Kagen, "War and Aftermath," Policy Review, no. 120, Aug/Sep 2003, plus a rapidly growing list of contemporary history books and personal memoirs.

[22] For the purpose of the project, primary source material is considered to be either interviews with the former regime official or documents believed to have been a part of the former regime. Secondary material is someone's (other than the team's) analysis of material relating to the former regime.

[23] All classified material referred to or quoted has been cleared for use in this unclassified manuscript by the appropriate US Government agencies.

[24] See the section "Research Methodology."

[25] A "document" can range from a single-page note between the Iraqi Intelligence Service and the Iraqi President's Office to several hundred-page documents on a wide range of military plans and studies. The US Government maintains a centralized database for foreign military, technical, and open-source documents and their translations.

[26] The exploitation challenge in regard to maps is perhaps more challenging than documents. In December 2003, the Iraqi Perspectives Project was the first group of analysts to begin examining the maps collected at the Combined Media Processing Center facility. The challenge is that no apparent discipline existed on the part of the Iraqi map maintainers to document the date, time, and purpose of the map; nor were the maps marked at capture with similar information.

The dilemma is determining the relative value of maps in terms of those used for the war, those used for planning and exercises, or those dating to a previous war.

27 For example, among the many CSIS Studies (including drafts) authored by Anthony Cordesman: "Iraqi Armed Forces on the Edge of War," (revised 7 February 2003); "The Lessons of the Iraq War" (21 July 2003); "Iraqi Intelligence and Security Forces and Capabilities for Popular Warfare" (16 January 2003); and "The Iraq War: Iraq's Warfighting Strategy" (11 March 2003).

28 Kanan Makiya; Republic of Fear, The Politics of Modern Iraq (Berkeley CA) Updated 1998. Journal articles include Ahmed Hashim, "Saddam Husayn and Civil-Military Relations in Iraq: The Quest for Legitimacy and Power," Middle East Journal, vol. 57, no. 1, Winter 2003.

29 This desire to tell their "soldier's story" included officers who may not be deemed "professional" by Western standards but like to think of themselves as such.

30 The Iraqi Perspective Project developed a basic list of 45 questions and then tailored the list to cover strategic, operational, and tactical categories. The list of questions was developed in such a way that the questions were not leading or did not describe a coalition understanding of the events. While the team used this list as a guideline, most interviews were tailored to the subject and circumstances.

31 As of the end of August 2005, the Iraqi Perspectives Project had screened (software keyword search) most of the almost 600,000 Iraqi documents posted to the Department of Defense captured document database.

32 Cited in Harold C. Deutsch, "The Matter of Records," The Journal of Military History, vol. 59, no. 1 (January, 1995).

REFERENCES

Captured Iraqi Documents

The following documents are content summaries, partial translations, or full translations of the original Arabic.

Captured media file, (27 May 1987) "Saddam and Inner Circle Discuss USS Stark Incident."

Captured document, (date unclear - from late 1980's) "Handbook on Ideology and Requirements of Being an Iraqi Soldier."

Captured document, (undated – believed to be pre-1990) "Discussion Between Saddam and His Advisors about the Election in Iraq and Transportation after the War."

Captured media file, (19 April 1990) "Video Containing a Recorded Meeting That Took Place Among President Saddam Hussein, the Iraqi Cabinet, President Yasser Arafat, and the Palestinian Delegation."

Captured media file, (pre-August 1990) "Saddam Hussein and Official Discuss the Case of Kuwait and the American Position."

Captured media file, (Sept/Oct 1990) "Saddam and Members of the RCC Discuss American Reactions to Invasion of Kuwait."

Captured document, (30 September 1990) "The Minutes of the Reception Held Between Saddam Hussein and As'ad Byud Al-Tamimi, Chief of the Islamic Jihad Movement (Bait Al-Maqis)."

Captured document, (22 March 1991) "Notes Between [field] Agents and General Military Intelligence Directorate (GMID) about the Riot Incidents in 1991."

Captured media file, (1 May 1991) "Saddam Meeting with High Ranking Officials Evaluating Iraqi Military Performance in the 1991 War."

Captured media file, (5 May 1991) "Saddam Hussein's Meeting with High Ranking Iraqi Officials, Evaluating the Iraqi Military Performance on the Battlefield during the first Gulf War 1991."

Captured media file, (29 February 1992) "Saddam Meeting with Military Commanders Discussing 1991 Uprisings."

Captured media file, (15 March 1992) "Meeting of High Ranking Military Officials Supervised by Minister of Defense Regarding Lessons of the 1991 War."

Captured media file, (15 May 1992) "Seminar held by Al Bakir University for Military Studies on the Strategic Role of the Um Al Ma'arik Battle."

Captured document, (1992) "Interrogation Records of a Father and Son For Insulting the Saddam Regime, the Daughter Informed the IIS."

Captured document, (30 August 1993) "Chief of the Seventh Section and Chief of the First Section Correspondence Regarding Desire for a Study About the Role of Air Forces in the Gulf War 1991."

Captured document, (13 October 1993) "Iraqi Intelligence Service Memo to Iraqi Head of State Regarding American Position in Somalia."

Captured media file, (approximately 1993) "Iraqi Command Meeting Regarding the Coalition Attack on Iraq and the 1991 Uprising."

Captured document, (approximately 1993) "9th Session on the Role of the Republican Guard."

Captured media file, (approximately 1993) "Saddam Discussing Issues Related to the War in 1991."

Captured media file, (date unclear - late 1994) "Saddam Meeting with High Ranking Officials Regarding the New Clinton Administration and its Attitudes Towards Iraq."

Captured media file, (15 April 1995) "Saddam Hussein, Council of Ministers, and Ba'ath Party Members Discussing UN sanctions against Iraq."

Captured document, (14 June 1995) "RCC Decision About Fedayeen Saddam Rights and Privileges Forwarded to MIC."

Captured media file, (10 August, 1995) "Saddam Hussein Meeting with Leaders of the Republican Guard Regarding Readiness of the Guard."

Captured media file, (8 October 1995) "Saddam Hussein Meeting with Qusay and Leaders of the H-J Operation Regarding Republican Guard Movements."

Captured document, (2 November 1995) "Military Directorate Correspondence Reports About Fedayeen Saddam Troops and their Organizational Structure."

Captured media file, (5 November 1995) "Saddam and Senior Leaders Discuss the Republican Guard."

Captured media file, (20 November 1995) "Military Scientific Conference by Air Force and Armored Forces Command on Um Al Ma'arik Battle."

Captured document, (22 November 1995) "Military Directorate Correspondence Regarding Secret Visit from Vietnam Army Chief of Staff."

Captured media file, (approximately 1995) "Saddam and Senior Advisors Discuss International Reaction to UN Inspection Report."

Captured document, (2 July 1996) "IIS Memorandum 945/712: Secret Instructions When International Inspection Teams Check Sites."

Captured document, (21 August 1996) "Reference File of the Laws of the Fedayeen Saddam."

Captured document, (13 July 1997) "Letter from Secretary of the Presidential Office to SSO Director and Others Ordering Security Employees Not to Address Secretary."

Captured document, (1 January 1998) "The Leader and the Masses: A Book About Saddam."

Captured document, (15 January 1998) "Memos Issued by the Head of the Fedayeen Saddam Passing Down Regulations for Executions."

Captured document, (April 1998) "Um Al-Ma'arik Magazine Article Regarding Masons Coalition with Zionists."

Captured document, (4 May 1998) "SSO Report on the Masons and the Secrets Behind Their Hatred of Iraq."

Captured document, (25 May 1999) "Fedayeen Saddam Instructions."

Captured document, (8 July 1999) "Saddam Meeting with Ba'ath Party Comrades."

Captured document, (11 July, 1999) "Plans and Analysis Reports by the Fedayeen Saddam Secretariat."

Captured document, (22 October 1999) "Correspondence from Ministry of Foreign Affairs to Iraqi Embassy in Tripoli Regarding Jehovah's Witnesses and Other Groups."

Captured document, (1999) "Presidential Order to Monitor All Internet News Concerning Iraq."

Captured media file, (1999) "Saddam Hussein's Meeting with a Group of Ba'ath Party Members to discuss Ba'ath Party Theories and Issues."

Captured document, (approximately 1999) "1999 IIS Plan for Training Fedayeen Saddam Using IEDs."

Captured document, (after 1999) "Saddam Discusses Western Politics and America's Involvement in Somalia."

Captured document, (3 February, 2000) "Correspondence Between Yugo Import and MOD Regarding Visiting Yugoslav Delegation."

Captured document, (14 March 2000) "Memo from Office of the Fedayeen Saddam Chief of Staff about Special Operations Against Car Thieves."

Captured document, (26 April 2000) "SSO Study on Masonic Movement and Its Conspiracies Against Iraq."

Captured document, (12 July 2000) "Saddam Speech to the Iraqi People Regarding Preparations for the Coming Battle."

Captured document, (7 October 2000) "Correspondence from Presidential Office to Secretary General of the Fedayeen Saddam Regarding Foreign Arab Volunteers."

Captured document, (16 November 2000) "Military Orders for Fedayeen to Blow up a Building."

Captured document, (23 December 2000) "Fedayeen Saddam UAV and Special Boat Plans."

Captured document, (12 May 2001) "Open Letter to the President of USA."

Captured document, (1 July 2001) "Correspondence Between Fedayeen Saddam and Iraq National Olympic Committee Regarding a Letter from a Widow."

Captured document, (9 September 2001) "Republican Guard Plan Report Entitled 'Operation Holy Conquest: Evacuation and Dispersal'."

Captured document, (12 December 2001) "Meeting Minutes Between Saddam Hussein and Leader of Serbian Radical Party."

Captured document, (2001) "A Report on a Cartoon Character Called 'Pokemon' from Directorate of General Security."

Captured document, (5 February 2002) "Memo from the Assistant of Intelligence Service for Operations, 4th Directorate, to Director of the IIS Regarding French-Iraqi Relations."

Captured document, (15 March 2002) "Report on the Study 'Next Stop Iraq' by American Kenneth Pollack."

Captured document, (20 March 2002) "Security Plan for Karbala Force of Fedayeen Saddam from Fedayeen Secretariat."

Captured document, (9 May 2002) "Correspondence Issued by Secretariat of Fedayeen Saddam Regarding Cutting Off Hands of the Fedayeen Saddam Members Who Were Smuggling Weapons to the Saudi Side During 2001."

Captured document, (28 June 2002) "Report on Study by Richard Betts."

Captured document, (25 August, 2002) "Soldiers of the Republican Guards Headquarters of Offensive Mission as Noted in Republican Guards Training Guidance."

Captured document, (29 August 2002) "Correspondence Issued from Al-Ta'mim Branch Command under the Arab Socialist Ba'ath Party to Emergency Regiment Command Secretary."

Captured document, (5 September 2002) "Military Training Manual Based on Lessons from the Al-Khafji Battle."

Captured document, (11 October 2002) "Memos Within Fedayeen Saddam General Secretariat Regarding Disciplinary Actions and Punishment Orders."

Captured document, (8 November 2002) "Letter Addressed to Saddam and Signed by the Minister of Defense Referring to the Summer 2002 Military Exercise 'Golden Falcon'."

Captured document, (1 Dec 2002) "Memo from Ali Libi Hajil to All Party Commands."

Captured document, (15 December 2002) "Correspondences and Circulations of Ba'ath Party, Fallujah Branch Including Emergency Plans."

Captured document, (15 December 2002) "UN Inspection Visit."

Captured document, (date undetermined, but after 26 December 2002) "Ba'ath Implementation of Local Defense Plans."

Captured document, (27 Dec 2002) "Memo To All Party Commands Regarding Outsiders Planting Sanctioned Materials in Iraq."

Captured document, (December 2002) "Ba'ath Military Branch Memorandum - Emergency Plan B."

Captured document, (December 2002) "Memo From Iraqi Secretary of State Office to Commanders in Charge of All Parties Organizations Regarding Emergency Plans."

Captured document, (11 January 2003) "Ba'ath Party Memo Number 460."

Captured document, (16 January 2003) "Training Exercise 'Heroes Attack' Plan for Kadhima Command, Al-Muthana Force of the Fedayeen Saddam."

Captured document, (Jan – Mar 2003) "Meeting Minutes: Hussein Military Branch Command, Sinhareeb Division."

Captured document, (20 February 2003) "Report by the Office of the Chief of Staff of the Army on Iraq Battle Plan."

Captured document, (23 February 2003) "Special Unit in Fedayeen Organization Formation Orders from Military Intelligence Director."

Captured document, (25 February 2003) "Military Industrialization Commission Annual Report for 2002-2003 Investments, Projects, and Plans."

Captured document, (date unclear - probably first week of March 2003) "Russian Report on American Troop Dispositions in the Gulf."

Captured document, (8 March 2003) "Correspondence Between Air Force Command and the Office of the Commander Regarding Orders for Psychological Operations Units."

Captured document, (8 March 2003) "Top Secret Letter of Army Chief of Staff #2195 Dated 23 February 2003."

Captured document, (9 March 2003) "Movement Order No. 3 for 2003, al-Hussein Brigade General Staff Headquarters."

Captured document, (9 March 2003) "Plan by al-Quds for Defending District Issued by Karbala Division Commander."

Captured document, (9 March 2003) "Saddam's Speech to IIS Directors Before the War."

Captured document, (11 March 2003) "Information Letter from the Iraq Military Intelligence Directorate about Anthrax; Leaflets; American Forces Impersonation, and Oil Barrel Trenches."

Captured document, (11 March 2003) "Military Command Memos Concerned with the Arabian Volunteers to the Iraqi Special Forces."

Captured document, (15 March 2003) "Letter from Qusay to Saddam Regarding the Preparation of Fedayeen Forces to Strike Deep within Kuwait if American Forces Converge on Baghdad."

Captured document, (16 March 2003) "Memorandum From Army Chief of Staff: Subject – Moving Munitions."

Captured document, (17 March 2003) "Report on Emergency Plan Training of al-Muthanna Governate."

Captured document, (19 March 2003) "Correspondence Among High Level Officials Regarding the Amount of Money Needed for Emergency Plans for the Various Governates."

Captured document, (21 March 2003) "Memorandum From Commander, Combat School of the 1st Corps to BUI Arsenal."

Captured document, (22 March 2003) "Memorandum #56 from Commander, 1st Air Defense Region to Directorate of Air Defense."

Captured document, (23 March 2003) "Memorandum 4811 from GMID to Secretary - Presidency of the Republic."

Captured document, (25 March 2003) "Letter from Russian Official to Presidential Secretary Concerning American Intentions in Iraq."

Captured document, (25 March 2003) "Correspondence from Fedayeen Saddam to Uday Regarding Fedayeen Saddam Suicide Mission Team."

Captured document, (26 March 2003) "MOD Report on Iraq's Strategic Defense in Preparation for the Latest War."

Captured document, (27 March 2003) "Memorandum to Director of the IIS, Subject: Hamas."

Captured document, (27 March 2003) "Telegrams from the Al-Fajir Regiment."

Captured document, (28 March 2003) "Situation Reports from the Middle Euphrates Region Command to the Presidential Office and General Command of the Armed Forces."

Captured document, (29 March 2003) "IIS Report about American Forces."

Captured document, (31 March 2003) "Military Movements Directorate Letter and GMID Correspondence."

Captured document, (31 March 2003) "Situation Reports, Commander 1st Sector Karbala."

Captured document, (1 April 2003) "Memorandum to Customs Police."

Captured document, (2 April 2003) "Letter From Ministry of Foreign Affairs to Office of the President Regarding Russian Intel."

Captured document, (2 April 2003) "Orders from the Arabic Socialist Ba'ath Party to the General Command of the People's Army."

Captured document, (2 April 2003) "Written Summaries for the 37th Division 20 March – 2 April 2003."

Captured document, (4 April 2003) "General Military Intelligence Directorate to the 8th Adjutant Confirming Saddam Hussein's Order to Treat the Arab Fedayeen Volunteers the Same Way as Special Forces Troops in Terms of their Salaries and Supplies."

Captured document, (6 April 2003) "Correspondence of the Communications Directorate - Order to Honor Fighters in 1st Gulf War, Orders to Increase Allowance for Transportation."

Captured document, (6 April 2003) "Ministry of Defense / Air Force Command Memorandum No.171, Referring to a Minister of Defense Chaired Conference on 30 March 2003."

Captured document, (7 April 2003) "GMID Commanding Office Correspondence."

Captured document, (8 April 2003) "Air Attack Reports on the Air Defenses."

Captured document, (2003) "Emergency Plan for Al Basrah Governate."

Captured document, "Iraqi Strategic Defense Plan of the Four Regional Commands."

US Government Documents

Central Intelligence Agency, "Hindsight Biases in Evaluation of Intelligence Reporting," Psychology of Intelligence Analysis, Chapter 13, (Washington DC, 1999).

Central Intelligence Agency, Comprehensive Report of the Special Advisor to the DCI on Iraq's WMD, Vol. I, (Central Intelligence Agency, Langley, VA, 30 September, 2004).

Central Intelligence Agency, The Iraqi Senior Officer Corps: Shaped by Pride Prejudice, Patrimony, and Fear, 18 March 2003.

Foreign Broadcast Information Service (FBIS), "Saddam Addresses Air Defense Officers," Baghdad, Republic of Iraq Radio Main Service, 13 May 2000.

FBIS, "Saddam Discusses Possible 'Enemy' Landing Operations With Military Commanders," Republic of Iraq Television, 1 February 2003.

FBIS, "Iraq RCC Decree Forms Four 'Commands of Regions' in Case of War," Baghdad Iraqi Satellite Channel Television, 15 March 2003.

FBIS, "Iraqi Army General Command Issues Statement on Military Operations 23, 24 Mar," Baghdad Iraqi Satellite Channel Television, 24 March 2003.

FBIS, "Iraqi Defense Minister Ahmad Holds News Conference 27 March," Dubai Al-Arabiyah Television, 27 March 2003.

FBIS, "Iraq's Al-Sahhaf Holds News Conference on Military Situation," Doha Al-Jazirah Satellite Channel Television, 31 March 2003.

FBIS, "Al-Jazirah Correspondent Confirms No US Forces in Baghdad," Doha Al-Jazirah Satellite Channel Television, 7 April 2003.

FBIS, Transcripts and News Items from DPRK, Russia, China, Ukraine.

House Committee on Armed Services Hearing, Testimony from Steven Biddle, "Operation Iraqi Freedom Outside Perspectives," 21 October 2003.

Multiple Classified Intelligence Reports Dated Between December 2002 and August 2004 (Declassified Excerpts Only).

Powell, Colin, US Secretary of State, "Statement in the Security Council on Iraq," United Nations Security Council, 5 February 2003.

The White House, Office of the Press Secretary, White House Announcement of Tomahawk Strike (Text of a Letter from the President to the Speaker of the House of Representatives and the President Pro Tempore of the Senate), June 28, 1993.

United States Senate Permanent Subcommittee on Investigations, Committee on Homeland Security and Governmental Affairs, Report on Oil Allocations Granted to the Russian Presidential Council, Report on Oil Allocations Granted to Vladimir Zhirinovsky, and Report on Oil Allocations Granted to Charles Pasqua & George Galloway, May 17, 2005.

US Central Command CONPLAN 1003-V (Declassified Excerpts Only).

Iraqi Perspectives Project Interviews

Abd Al-Karim Jasim Nafus Al-Majid, Commander, Al Nida Armored Division, 21 Nov 2003.

Abid Hamid Mahmud Al-Khattab, Saddam's Personal Secretary, 15 Nov, 2003.

Al Nida Division Chief of Staff, 28 Nov 2003.

Ali Hasan al-Majid (Chemical Ali), 10 Nov 2003.

Barzan Abd Al-Ghafur Sulayman Al-Tikriti, Commander, Special Republican Guard, 16 Nov 2003.

Hamid Isma'aeli Dawish R'baei, Director, RG Staff, 18 Nov 2003.

Hamid Raja Shalah Al Hadithi Al Tikriti, Commander, Iraqi Air Force, 12 Nov 2003.

Kamal Mustafa Abdullah Sultan Al-Tikriti, Secretary of the Republican Guard and Special Republican Guard, 14 Nov 2003.

LTG Kenan Mansour Khalil al-Obadi, Senior Military Advisor to RCC Member Mizban Khudr Al-Hadi, 30 Nov 2003.

LTG Raad Hamdani, Commander II Republican Guard Corps, 10 Nov 2003

Majid Hussein Ali Ibrahim Al Dulaymi, Commander, I Republican Guard Corps.

Salih Ibrahim Hammadi Al Salamani, Commander, Baghdad Republican Guard Division, 10 Nov 2003.

Staff BG Muhammad Sattam Abdullah Al Hamdani, former Chief of Staff Al Nida Division, 19 Nov 2003.

Sultan Hashim Ahmed Al Hamed Al-Tai, Minister of Defense, 13 Nov 2003.

Zuhayr Talib Abd al Satar Al Naquib, Director of Military Intelligence, 16 Nov 2003.

Other (Books, Academic Articles, Media Reports, Online Articles, etc.)

Aburish, Said K., Frontline - The Survival of Saddam: Secrets of his Life and Leadership. Interview, November 2001. Transcript downloaded 15 March 2003. (HTTP://WWW.Pbs.Org/Wgbh/Pages/Frontline/Shows/Saddam/Interviews/Arburish.Html)

Aburish, Said, Saddam Hussein: The Politics of Revenge (London: Bloomsbury Publishing, 2000).

Al-Jabbar, Faceh Abd, "Why the Uprisings," Middle East Report, May-June 1992.

Allison, Graham and Philop Zelikow, Essence of Decision – Explaining the Cuban Missile Crisis, 2nd Edition. (New York: Longman Press, 1999).

Al-Marashi, Ibrahim, "Iraq's Security and Intelligence Network: A Guide and Analysis," Middle East Review of International Affairs, September 2002.

Altaaey, Colonel Jamal, Iraqi Prisoner of War, Camp Bucca, Joint Forces Command Lessons Learned Team Interview, 10 July 2003.

Atkinson, Rick, Crusade: The Untold Story of the Persian Gulf War (Boston: Houghton Mifflin, 1993).

Beaumont, Roger, War, Chaos, and History (Novato, CA: Praeger, 1994).

Beeston, Richard, "Saddam Stuck to His Fantasy of 'Victory' as Evil Regime Collapsed," New York Post Online Edition, 18 March, 2004. Found online at www.nypost.com/news/worldnew/21186.htm. Downloaded 20 April 2004.

Beeston, Richard, "Secret Files Show Saddam Deluded to the Very End," The London Times, 18 March, 2004.

Betts, Richard K., "Analysis, War, and Decision: Why Intelligence Failures are Inevitable," World Politics, Vol. 31, No. 1 (October, 1978).

Biddle, Steven, "Victory Misunderstood: What the Gulf War Can Tell US About the Future of Conflict," International Security, Vol. 21, No. 2, Fall 1996.

Boyne, Walter, Operation Iraqi Freedom, What Went Right, What Went Wrong, and Why, (New York: Forge Books, 2003).

Branigin, William, "A Brief, Bitter War for Iraq's Military Officers," Washington Post, 27 April, 2003.

Clausewitz, Carl von, On War, ed. and trans. by Michael Howard and Peter Paret (Princeton, NJ, 1976).

Coll, Steve, "Hussein Was Sure of Own Survival," Washington Post, 3 November, 2003.

Cordesman, Anthony, Iraqi Armed Forces on the Edge of War, (7 Feb 2003), The Lessons of the Iraq War (21 Jul 2003), Iraqi Intelligence and Security Forces and Capabilities for Popular Warfare (16 Jan, 2003), and The Iraq War: Iraq's Warfighting Strategy (11 Mar, 2003), Center for Strategic and International Studies Reports.

Coughlin, Con, Saddam: King of Terror, (New York: Harper Collins, 2002).

Deutsch, Harold C., "The Matter of Records," The Journal of Military History, Vol. 59, No.1, January 1995.

Eisenstadt, Michael and Kenneth Pollack, "Armies of Snow, Armies of Sand: The Impact of Soviet Military Doctrine on Arab Militaries," Middle East Journal, Vol. 55, No. 4, Autumn 2001.

Fleishman, Jeffrey, "Ex-Ba'athists Offer U.S. Advice, Await Call to Arms," Los Angeles Times, 27 April, 2004.

Fontenot, Gregory COL (Ret.) and LTC E.J. Degen, and LTC David Tohn, On Point: The US Army in Operation Iraqi Freedom, (Fort Leavenworth, KS: 2004).

Freeman and Karsh, The Gulf Conflict, 1990-1991: Diplomacy and War in the New World Order (Princeton, 1993).

Gerstein, Remy, "Documents Show Urgent Iraqi Push to Recruit and Control Troops," New York Times, 18 April, 2003.

Haldane, Sir Aylmer L., The Insurrection in Mesopotamia, 1920 (Edinburgh and London: William Blackwood and Sons, 1922).

Hamdani, Lieutenant General Raad, Commander II Republican Guard Corps, Unpublished Draft Memoirs, Iraqi Perspectives Project Collection.

Hashim, Ahmed, "Saddam Husayn and Civil-Military Relations in Iraq: The Quest for Legitimacy and Power," Middle East Journal, Vol. 57, No. 1, Winter 2003.

Herodotus, The Histories, trans. by G.C. Macaulay, revised by Donald Lateiner. (New York: Barnes and Noble Books, 2004) p. 290.

Heur Jr., Richards J., "Strategic Deception and Counterdeception – A Cognitive Process Approach," International Studies Quarterly, Vol. 25, No. 2 (June 1981).

Hooker, Gregory, Shaping the Plan for Operation Iraqi Freedom: The Role of Military Assessments, (Washington Institute for Near East Policy, 2005).

Hussein, Saddam, Public Speeches downloaded from http://www.info-imagination.org/ps/iraq/iraq.saddam.html, 17 January 2003.

Hussein, Saddam, Speech Printed in the Iraqi newspaper Al-Jumhouriyya, 4 February, 2003. Reported in MEMRI - Special Dispatch Series - No. 467 The Iraq Crisis (1): Iraq Prepares for War, 11 February, 2003 (http://memri.org/bin/articles).

International Crisis Group, Iraq Backgrounder: What Lies Beneath, ICG Middle East Report, No. 6, Amman/Brussels, 1 October 2002.

Jervis, Robert, "Deterrence and Perception," International Security, Vol. 7, No. 3, Winter 1982/1983.

Jervis, Robert, Perception and Misperception in International Politics, (Princeton, NJ: Princeton University Press, 1976).

Kagen, Frederick, "War and Aftermath," Policy Review, No. 120, Aug/Sep 2003.

Knox, MacGregor, Mussolini Unleashed, 1939-1941: Politics and Strategy in Fascist Italy's Last War (Cambridge: Cambridge University Press, 1982).

Krepinevich, Andrew, OIF: A First Blush Assessment, Center for Strategic and Budgetary Assessments, 2003.

Mahnken, Thomas and Barry D. Watts, "What the Gulf War Can [and Cannot] Tell Us about the Future of Warfare," International Security, Vol. 22, No. 2, Autumn 1997.

Makiya, Kanan, Cruelty and Silence: War, Tyranny, Uprising and the Arab World, (New York: W.W. Norton & Company, 1993).

Makiya, Kanan, Republic of Fear, (Berkeley: University of California Press, 1990).

Marr, Phebe, The Modern History of Iraq (Boulder: Westview Press, 2004).

Middle East Media Research Institute (MEMRI), "First Interview with Saddam Hussein in 12 Years" (5 November, 2002), "Iraq News Wire No. 14," (6 March 2003), "Iraq Wire No. 7," (12 August, 2002). Found online at http://www.memri.org/bin/articles.cgi?Page=countries&Area=iraq&ID=INW702#I. Downloaded 17 October, 2003.

Morgenthau, Hans J., "The Limitations of Science and the Problem of Social Planning," Ethics, Vol. 54, No. 3, April 1944.

Mueller, John, "The Perfect Enemy: Assessing the Gulf War," Security Studies, Vol. 5, No. 1, Autumn 1995.

Murray, Williamson, "The German Response to Victory in Poland: A Case Study in Professionalism," Armed Forces and Society, Winter 1981.

Natsios, Andrew S., Iraq's Mass Graves, (United States Agency for International Development, 22 July 2004, http://www.state.gov/s/wci/rm/36198.htm).

Paret, Peter, "Military Power," The Journal of Military History, July 1989, Vol. 53, No. 3.

Pollack, Kenneth M., Arabs at War: Military Effectiveness, 1948-1991 (Lincoln: University of Nebraska Press, 2002).

Project Notes from Iraqi Survey Group, (September – December 2003).

Sama Abdul Majid, Saddam's personal interpreter cited in "Saddam May Be Using Vietnam Tactics," USA Today, 13 November, 2003.

Scales, Robert H., Certain Victory: The U.S. Army in the Gulf War (Washington DC, 1993).

Summers, Harry Glenn, On Strategy II: A Critical Analysis of the Gulf War (New York: Dell Publishing, 1992).

Taylor, William J., and James Blackwell, "The Ground War in the Gulf," Survival, 33(3) May-June 1991.

Thompson, Loren. "Lessons of Iraq: Strategic and Joint Implications," Defense News Force Projection Conference, 22 Sep 2003.

US Air Force, Central Command (CENTAF), Operation Iraqi Freedom - By The Numbers, CENTAF Assessment and Analysis Division, 22 April 2003.

Voice of America Report, 16 May 2003. Found online at www.globalsecurity. org/wmd/library/news /iraq/2003/05/iraq-030516-3e198477.htm. Downloaded 16 April 2004.

Wohlstetter, Roberta, Pearl Harbor: Warning and Decision (Stanford, CA: Stanford University Press, 1962).

Woods, Kevin, "Perspectives on OIF from the Former Commander of the Iraqi Navy and Assistant Senior Military Advisor to the Central Euphrates Region," v2.02, Unpublished Project Monograph, 17 March 2004.

Woods, Kevin, "Perspectives on OIF from the Former Commander of the Iraqi II Republican Guard Corps," v3.3, Unpublished Project Monograph, 28 May 2004.

Zucchino, David, "Iraq's Swift Defeat Blamed on Leaders," Los Angeles Times, 11 August, 2003.